The **Evolving Maritime Balance of Power** in the **Asia-Pacific**

Maritime Doctrines and Nuclear Weapons at Sea

The **Evolving Maritime Balance of Power** in the **Asia-Pacific**

Maritime Doctrines and Nuclear Weapons at Sea

Editors

Lawrence W Prabhakar
Joshua H Ho
Sam Bateman

World Scientific

Institute of Defence and Strategic Studies

Published by

Institute of Defence and Strategic Studies
Nanyang Technological University, Block S4, Level B4
Nanyang Avenue, Singapore 639798

and

World Scientific Publishing Co. Pte. Ltd.
5 Toh Tuck Link, Singapore 596224
USA office: 27 Warren Street, Suite 401-402, Hackensack, NJ 07601
UK office: 57 Shelton Street, Covent Garden, London WC2H 9HE

Library of Congress Cataloging-in-Publication Data
The evolving maritime balance of power in the Asia-Pacific : maritime
    doctrines and nuclear weapons at sea / edited by Lawrence W. Prabhakar,
  Joshua H. Ho, Sam Bateman.
     p. cm.
  Includes bibliographical references and index.
  ISBN 981-256-828-X
  1. Sea-power--Pacific Area. 2. Nuclear weapons--Pacific Area.
  3. Pacific Area--Strategic aspects. I. Prabhakar, Lawrence W. II. Ho, Joshua.
  III. Bateman, W. S. G. (Walter Samuel Grono).

  VA620.E86 2006
  359'.0309164--dc22

                                            2006045701

British Library Cataloguing-in-Publication Data
A catalogue record for this book is available from the British Library.

Typeset by Stallion Press
Email: enquiries@stallionpress.com

Printed in Singapore by World Scientific Printers (S) Pte Ltd

Contents

Acknowledgements

The authors would like to acknowledge the support and encouragement provided for the conference and this volume by Barry Desker, Director, Institute of Defence and Strategic Studies, Nanyang Technological University. The comments and advice from Professor Amitav Acharya are also gratefully acknowledged. The contributions of the authors, without which this volume would not have been possible, are much appreciated. The authors also wish to thank those who attended the conference and contributed so richly to enhancing our understanding of the regional maritime doctrines as well as ballistic missile developments. The authors would also like to place on record sincere appreciation and thanks to Dr. Arvind Kumar, Associate Fellow, International Strategic and Security Studies Programme, National Institute of Advanced Studies, Indian Institute of Science Campus, Bangalore, India for his invaluable inputs, suggestions and comments. Rupali Sarkhel, IDSS graduate student for her excellent academic support. Regina Ariokasamy, Caroline Ng, Peter Ee and the administrative staff of IDSS have also rendered excellent administrative support without which the conference would not have been possible. The authors would also like to thank Adrian Kuah who worked out the conference report. Finally, the excellent support given by Cheong Chean Chian and Lee Hooi Yean of World Scientific Publishing is gratefully acknowledged.

Foreword

The Asia-Pacific has emerged as the hub of global geo-political, geo-economic and geo-strategic significance in the post-Cold War period. It has even displaced the Euro-Atlantic region, which had been dominant during the Cold War. The emergence of the Asia-Pacific is reflected in the region's high economic growth and large volume of maritime trade. For example, intra-Asia-Pacific Economic Cooperation (APEC) trade exceeds intra-European Union (EU) trade. In terms of volume of trade as well as the location of the future engines of economic growth, the APEC region could be regarded as the powerhouse of the present global economic order.

Besides strong economic growth, the Asia-Pacific has also been a vibrant region of regional institution building. This is evidenced by regional groupings such as the Association of South East Asian Nations (ASEAN), the ASEAN Regional Forum, the Asia-Pacific Economic Cooperation and various other regional bilateral and multilateral security institutions. The recent East Asia Summit is yet another indicator of growing regionalism. The positive effects of globalisation and strong economic growth have also resulted in the emergence of the Asia-Pacific as a hub of technological innovation. While the past 50 years have been characterised by the rapid growth of Japan and the newly industrialising economies of South Korea, Taiwan, Hong Kong and the ASEAN countries, the rise of China and the resurgence of India will be the hallmark of the next 50 years. For the United States, the only superpower today, a key question will be how the US responds to the emergence of these rising powers.

However, we should not under-estimate the risks arising from regional rivalries and competition.

The maritime identity of the Asia-Pacific region opens the region to traditional power based rivalries based on unresolved territorial and maritime boundary issues. There is also increasing attention to the legal and political significance of the 1982 UN Convention of the Law of the Sea, and its implementation by archipelagic states.

Traditional power based rivalries are also evident in the modernisation and transformation processes of the region's naval and air forces and the increasing significance of nuclear weapons in the region. The defence transformation process has spawned new maritime doctrines and reinvigorated the role of naval forces in the region.

The volume is a product of the conference that was organised by IDSS on the theme "Maritime Balance of Power in the Asia-Pacific" in March 2005. The conference focused on the following themes: (1) the evolving paradigms of maritime transformation in strategy & technology in the Asia-Pacific; (2) the emergent new maritime doctrines and evolving force postures in the naval orders of battle of the United States, Japan, China and India; (3) the role and operations of nuclear navies in the Asia-Pacific, and (4) the implications and impact of nuclear weapons, ballistic missiles and sea-based missile defence responses in the region.

The volume is also an outcome of the Institute's Maritime Security Programme, one aspect of which is to study the changing maritime balance of power in the Asia-Pacific region. IDSS would like to thank Dr. Lawrence Prabhakar, who was a visiting research fellow with the programme, for conceptualising the theme of the volume. The excellent contribution of the authors of the chapter and that of the three co-editors is gratefully acknowledged. The programme remains committed to providing an avenue for cutting-edge research and publication on major issues and trends in maritime security in the Asia-Pacific.

Barry Desker
Director
Institute of Defence and Strategic Studies
Singapore

Biographies of Contributors

Sam Bateman is a Senior Fellow and Adviser to the Maritime Security Programme at the Institute of Defence and Strategic Studies (IDSS). On retirement from the Royal Australian Navy in 1993 and until 2000, he was the Director of the Centre for Maritime Policy at the University of Wollongong where he retains status as a Professorial Research Fellow. His naval service included four ship commands, five years in Papua New Guinea and several postings in the force development and strategic policy areas of the Department of Defence in Canberra. Current research interests include regional maritime security, strategic and political implications of the Law of the Sea, and maritime cooperation and confidence-building. Sam Bateman completed his PhD at the University of New South Wales in 2001. He has written extensively on defence and maritime issues in Australia, the Asia-Pacific and Indian Ocean, and edited or co-edited several books on maritime security, and the law of the sea. During 2002 he was a Visiting Fellow at the East–West Center in Honolulu. He is a Co-Chair of the Council for Security Cooperation in the Asia Pacific (CSCAP) Study Group on Capacity Building for Maritime Security.

Donald Berlin is a Professor in the College of Security Studies, Asia-Pacific Center for Security Studies in Honolulu. He focuses on strategic issues in the Indian Ocean region. Among his recent publications are articles on arms and security rivalry in the Indian Ocean in Orbis, Harvard International Review, the Journal of Indian Ocean Studies, Contemporary South Asia, Force, Asia Times, and Asia Annual 2003. He also recently organised and led a major international conference on "India and the Emerging Geopolitics of the Indian Ocean Region" and presented papers on various Indian Ocean issues at the initial conference of the Indian Ocean Research Group at the University of Punjab in India, at the UN–ROK Joint Conference on Disarmament and Non-proliferation Issues on Jeju Island, South Korea, at the military staff colleges of India, Sri Lanka, Bangladesh and Nepal, and at institutes in Singapore and Malaysia. Since joining the Center as one of its first senior professors in

1998, Dr. Berlin has lectured on Force Modernisation, Arms Control and Diplomacy, Globalisation, and the Proliferation of Weapons of Mass Destruction. In addition, he teaches an elective on "Security and Politics in the Indian Ocean Region".

Dr. Berlin served with the Defense Intelligence Agency in Washington, DC from 1976–1998. Before leaving DIA, he was responsible for producing all Defense Intelligence mid- and long-range assessments of the global threat to US national security. Dr. Berlin also supported international peacekeeping efforts in Bosnia when he served as DIA Element Leader, National Intelligence Support Team, Naples, Italy. Dr. Berlin was commissioned a second lieutenant in the USAF in 1968 and served in a variety of assignments including duty in the Philippines with 13th Air Force Intelligence. Later, as a USAFR intelligence officer, he commanded the Exercise and Gaming Support Flight, War Gaming and Simulation Center, National Defense University, and subsequently was a faculty member and Professor at the Joint Military Intelligence College, Washington, DC. Dr. Berlin holds PhD and Master of Arts degrees in International Studies from the University of South Carolina and a Master of Arts in National Security and Strategic Studies from the United States Naval War College.

Katsuhisa Furukawa is a Senior Fellow of Research Institute of Science and Technology for Society of Japan Science and Technology Agency in Tokyo since 1 October 2004 where he is in charge of new projects on homeland security and non-proliferation. Prior to coming to IASC, he was a Senior Research Associate with the Center for Non-proliferation Studies (CNS) of the Monterey Institute of International Studies and an Executive Director of US–Japan Track II Project on Arms Control, Non-proliferation, and Verification, since 1 November 2001. Prior to this position, Mr. Furukawa was a Research Associate with the Council of Foreign Relations, working on projects related to democracy and economic development as well as East Asian Security, especially on Japan and North Korea.

Mr. Furukawa has worked in the United States for the American Enterprise Institute, the NHK Japan Broadcasting Corporation, as an Adjunct Associate Producer, and the Center for Strategic and International Security's Pacific Forum, as a Visiting Fellow, with Mr. Torkel Patterson, who is currently the Deputy Assistant Secretary of State for South Asia. In Japan, Mr. Furukawa worked together Dr. Kenichi Ohmae, then-President of Asian brunch of Mackinsey and Company, as Chief of Policy Planning Staff at the Reform of Heisei, an NGO that specialised in promoting programs on political and economic reform in Japan, where he was charged with overseeing activities on a variety of issues and was responsible for liaison with government and business leaders as well as labour union chairmen.

He holds a BA in Economics from Keio University, in Tokyo, and a Master of Public Administration from the John F. Kennedy School of Government of the Harvard University. Mr. Furukawa has published numerous articles, participated in the creation of several documentary films, and lectures occasionally, on a wide range of issues, especially, Japan's national power.

Eric Grove was born in Lancashire in 1948, is a graduate of Aberdeen (MA in History 1970) and London Universities (postgraduate MA War Studies 1971). He became a civilian lecturer at the Royal Naval College, Dartmouth in 1971 and stayed for 13 years, leaving as Deputy Head of Strategic Studies. He then worked as a self employed strategic analyst and defence consultant, among other things acting as principal consultant to the Foundation for International Security's Common Security programme, starting the Russia–UK–US naval talks, helping design the Sea Power gallery at the National Maritime Museum and teaching strategic studies and international relations at The Royal Naval College Greenwich and the University of Cambridge. Since 1993 he has been at the University of Hull where he now directs the Centre for Security Studies as Reader in the Department of Politics and International Studies. His duties include teaching at undergraduate and postgraduate level and supervising PhD students (of which 15 have successfully passed so far). His books include *Vanguard to Trident* (the standard work on post-1945 British Naval policy), *The Future of Sea Power, Sea Battles in Close-Up: World War Two, Fleet to Fleet Encounters,* and *The Price of Disobedience* (a reassessment of the Battle of the River Plate). He was the co-author of the 1995 edition of the official publication BR1806, *The Fundamentals of British Maritime Doctrine.* A new history, *The Royal Navy Since 1815* was published in January 2005. His publications were the basis of a PhD in Security Studies awarded by the University of Hull in 1996. Dr Grove has recently begun to appear frequently on television and radio as a contributor to programmes on modern naval history and other defence subjects. He spent a year teaching at the US Naval Academy in 1980–81 and six months in 1997 as a visiting research fellow at the University of Wollongong's Centre for Maritime Policy. He has taken part in the discussions of the Maritime Cooperation Working Group of CSCAP and is a Vice President of the Society for Nautical Research and Fellow of the Royal Historical Society.

Hideaki Kaneda, JMSDF (Japan Maritime Self Defense Force), (retd.) is a Special Research Advisor for The Okazaki Institute and Mitsubishi Research Institute, and a member of Policy Proposal Committee for Japan Forum for Strategic Study. He was a Senior Fellow of Asia Center and J.F. Kennedy School of Government of the Harvard University for last two years. He became a Guest Professor of Faculty of Policy Management of Keio University from September 2002.

He is the author of published books and articles about security, including "Proposal for Maritime Coalition in East Asia and West Pacific Region", *IMDEX*, Germany, November 2000, "Changing situation of China's and Japan's national security", *World and Japan*, Tokyo, September 2001, "Role of JMSDF in peace time", *Securitarian*, Tokyo, August 2001 and "BMD for Japan", *Kaya-Shobo*, Tokyo, March 2003.

Admiral Kaneda is a graduate of the National Defense Academy in 1968, the Maritime War College in 1983, and the US Naval War College in 1988. He served in the JMSDF from 1968 to 1999, primarily in Naval Surface Warfare at sea, while in Naval and Joint Plans and Policy Making on shore.

His career highlights include tours on Commanding Officer of *JDS Akigumo*, Chief of Plans and Policy Section of MSO (Maritime Staff Office), Commander of Escort Division 61, Head of Plans and Policy Division of MSO, Chief of Staff of Commandant Maizuru District, Commander of Escort Flotilla 4, Director of Joint Staff Office (J-5, Plans and Policy), and Commander Fleet Escort Force as the last assignment. He retired from JMSDF in July 1999.

Joshua Ho is a Senior Fellow at the Institute of Defence and Strategic Studies, Singapore. He obtained a BA and MA in Engineering from Cambridge University, UK on an SAF (Overseas) Scholarship, and also holds a MSc (Management) (Distinction) from the Naval Postgraduate School, California, where he was awarded the Graduate School of Business and Public Policy Faculty awards for Excellence in Management, given to the top student in the faculty, and Outstanding International Student. Joshua is a serving Naval Officer with 18 years of service and currently holds the rank of Lieutenant Colonel. He was trained as a Principal Warfare Officer and completed his command and staff training at the Royal Australian Navy Staff College and the Singapore Command and Staff College. He has served in various shipboard and staff appointments including the Command of a Missile Gun Boat and stints in the Naval Operations, Plans, and Personnel Departments as well as an attachment to the Future Systems Directorate, MINDEF. He has held concurrent appointments of Honorary Aide de Camp to the President, Secretary to the Naval Staff Meeting, and Secretary to the Policy and Strategy Meeting, MINDEF.

Joshua Ho's research interests include military transformation and maritime security. He is a co-editor for the volume, *The Best of Times, The Worst of Times: Maritime Security in the Asia-Pacific* (Singapore: World Scientific, 2005), and has written commentaries on military transformation and maritime security, some of which have been published in the *Straits Times*, Singapore's leading broadsheet newspaper, as well as *Today*, Singapore's leading free daily. He has also published in well known local and overseas journals like *Defence Studies, Asian Survey, Australian Army Journal, Journal of the Australian Naval Institute* and *Pointer*, and presented papers at conferences organised by the Center for Strategic & International Studies, Washington DC, the Observer Research Foundation, New Delhi, National Institute for Defence Studies, Tokyo, NUPI (Norwegian Institute of International Affairs), Oslo, Maritime Institute of Malaysia, Kuala Lumpur, The National Institute of South China Sea Studies, Hainan, People's Republic of China, as well as by local conference organisers Defence Directory and Defence IQ, a local subsidiary of IQPC. He has also lectured at the Singapore Command and Staff Course as well as the Home Team Command and Staff Course, and his article on the topic of "Effects Based Operations" has been published in a Swedish National Defence College book volume on the same topic.

Arvind Kumar is currently working with National Institute of Advanced Studies (NIAS), Bangalore. He joined this institute as a Research Faculty in 1996 and has been conducting policy and academic research on nuclear, missile, strategic, foreign policy issues and matters related to International and Asian security. His area of expertise is also in the field of IR theory, deterrence and regional security system. Prior to joining NIAS, he was working with the Institute for Defence Studies & Analyses (IDSA), New Delhi. He was conducting research on the matters related to South Asian Security affairs and was making news review on South Asia. His most prominent publication in IDSA journal *Strategic Analysis* was on US nuclear policy and Hank Brown amendment and its implications.

He was also a teaching Faculty at Delhi University during 1993–94. He was a Visiting Fellow at the Henry L. Stimson Center, Washington, DC during April–May 2000. His research study on "Missile Defence and Strategic Modernisation in Southern Asia" which he carried out at the Stimson highlights an Indian perspective on the whole debate. This research paper has been published by the Stimson Center in an edited volume and released in July 2002. He has also delivered a number of talks both in India and abroad. His prominent talks among them are "The Rationale behind India Going Nuclear" at the School of Advanced International Studies, Johns Hopkins University Washington, DC in the year 2000, Ballistic Missile Stability in Southern Asia at the US State Department in the year 2002 and "The Glenn Amendment Sanctions and its Impact on India" at Fudan University, Shanghai, China immediately after India went nuclear.

He was also a Visiting Fellow at the Cooperative Monitoring Center of Sandia National Laboratories, New Mexico, USA and the Centre for International Security and Cooperation (CISAC) in the Institute for International Studies at Stanford University, USA in the year 2002. He worked on "Ballistic Missile Stability in Southern Asia" at Sandia National Laboratories and "the Implications of US' Nuclear Posture Review for South Asia" at Stanford. He also delivered a number of talks on his studies conducted at Sandia both at the governmental (Department of State, Department of Energy, Sandia National Laboratories and Pentagon in the USA) and non-governmental organisations (Center for Non-Proliferation Studies, Monterey and Washington, The Henry L. Stimson Center, Brookings Institution, Woodrow Wilson Center for International Scholars and others). He also disseminates his views on pertinent important themes through the websites including Southern Asia Internet Forum dialogues maintained by Stimson Center and he was a guest commentator for www.stratfor.com, which is the Internet source for global intelligence.

Lawrence Prabhakar is Associate Professor of Political Science at Madras Christian College, Chennai (Madras). He graduated with MA and MPhil Degrees in Political Science from the Madras Christian College. He specialises in Nuclear Missile issues in Southern Asia and on Maritime Security issues in the Indian Ocean–South East Asia. His most recent academic stint has been as Visiting Research Fellow in the Institute of Defence & Strategic Studies (IDSS) Nanyang Technological University, Singapore. Dr. Prabhakar was working on the project Competitive and Cooperative Maritime Strategies of US, Japan, China and India: Implications for South East Asia. His work on this project would soon be published as a volume entitled *The Evolving Maritime Dynamics in the Asia-Pacific* by the Institute of Defence and Strategic Studies, Singapore.

Dr. Prabhakar is a Consultant to the Directorate of Net Assessment Office of the Chiefs of Integrated Defence Staff, Chiefs of Staff Committee, Ministry of Defence, Govt. of India; with two projects: (i) "The Role of the Dragon: Strategic Role and Posture of China in the India–Pakistan Conflict Spectrum" in the Simulation-cum-Scenario Development Exercise: India–Pakistan Conflict Spectrum Under the Nuclear Backdrop Under the Nuclear Backdrop at the Army War College, Mhow, February 2003; (ii) "Extra-regional Naval Presence and Posture: Implications for the Indian Navy" in the Project Regional Maritime Balance in Indian Ocean 2020; (iii) Escalation Dynamics Based on Nuclear Doctrines and Force Postures in Southern Asia (March 2004) Commissioned by the Directorate of Net Assessment, Office of the Chiefs of Integrated Defense Staff, Ministry of Defence, Govt. of India, New Delhi.

Dr. Prabhakar is a Visiting Faculty to the Defence Services Staff College, Wellington, India and to the College of Naval Warfare, Karanja Mumbai, Army War College, Mhow, Indore, India.

His earlier research fellowships have been Visiting Fellow, The Henry Stimson Center, Washington DC, USA, where he worked on "The Draft Indian Nuclear Doctrine: Perspectives of Regional and Global Nuclear Powers" May–August 2001. In this stint, he also worked on "Indian Security Perspectives of the PLA Navy in South Asia" for the Center for Naval Analysis, Alexandria, Virginia, USA. A sample of his most recent publications in various volumes include India and the Ballistic Missile Defenses in the four-volume *The Scribner's-Gale Encyclopaedia of India*, co-edited by Stanley Wolpert and Raju Thomas, published by Scribners-Gale-Thomson, New York (2005); *The Challenge of Minimal Nuclear Deterrence* (2002); *The Maritime Strategic Perspectives of the PLA Navy in South Asia-Indian Ocean Region* (2003); *Asymmetric Warfare and the New War: Implications for Policy and Strategy* (2002); *India's Case for a Limited Missile Defense* (2002).

Lynn D. Pullen is a Senior Advisor, Naval Strategy and Policy, in the Center for Security Strategies and Operations (CSSO), within Anteon's Systems Engineering Group. Coming to the CSSO in 1994, she has conducted a wide array of research and analysis on international affairs, national security, defence, and naval issues, generally, with a special focus on the East Asian and Pacific region.

Ms. Pullen completed service in the US Navy as a Captain in 1994, and has extensive experience in joint intelligence and international political-military affairs, with particular emphasis on Asia and the Pacific Rim. Prior to her retirement from the Navy, she was the Head, East Asia-Pacific Politico-Military Affairs Branch in the Office of the Chief of Naval Operations, advising senior US Navy personnel on issues of Navy, Joint Staff, and Defense Department interest regarding US relationships with Asian-Pacific nations. She represented the US Navy at conferences and seminars on Asia-Pacific policy issues, and organised and actively participated in US Navy staff talks with the senior leadership of the Australian, Korean, and Japanese navies.

As a Federal Executive Fellow at RAND in 1990–1991, Ms. Pullen was the co-author of a major study on strategic alternatives for the Pacific Rim prepared for the Under Secretary of Defense for Policy. In addition to extensive research on the value of security assistance programs in the Pacific, she also prepared a RAND Note, published as "Legal and Related Constraints on US Basing in the Western Pacific". She has served as a Foreign Liaison Officer with the Defense Intelligence Agency, and on the Intelligence Directorate Staff of the Commander, US Pacific Command, and performing research and analysis on Pacific Rim intelligence issues of concern to the J-2 USPACOM.

Ms. Pullen holds a BA in French from Humboldt State University and an MS in Strategic Intelligence from the Defense Intelligence College in Washington, DC.

Vijay Sakhuja is Research Fellow at the Observer Research Foundation, New Delhi, India. A former Indian navy officer, he took early retirement from the navy. He has held several appointments including Commanding Officer. He was Research Fellow at the Institute for Defence Studies and Analyses, New Delhi, and United Service Institution of India, New Delhi. He received his Doctorate from the Jawaharlal Nehru University, New Delhi. Earlier, he completed his MPhil studies from the same university. He has authored a book titled *Confidence Building From the Sea: An Indian Initiative* and is the recipient of Vice Admiral S.L. Sethi National Maritime Media Award, 2002.

Dr. Vijay Sakhuja has written extensively on maritime security issues and presented papers at international and national conferences. At the Observer Research Foundation, Dr. Vijay Sakhuja's project is titled "Emerging Maritime Security Environment in the Indian Ocean and Challenges for India". He is also undertaking studies relating to risk analysis of global maritime supply chain particularly in the domain of container trade.

Scott C. Truver is Group Vice President, National Security Programs, and directs the Center for Security Strategies and Operations (CSSO) in Anteon's Systems Engineering Group. In addition to his leadership and business-development responsibilities, he supervises and carries out research and analytical efforts relating to international relations and US national security, defence, naval, and maritime issues and concerns. He holds a Top Secret clearance.

The CSSO comprises of approximately 450 people and has annual revenues of some $70 million.

Since 1972, Dr. Truver has participated in numerous studies for government and private industry in the United States and abroad; he has also written extensively for US and foreign publications. He joined TECHMATICS in March 1991, and in May 1998 Anteon Corporation acquired TECHMATICS. From February 1984 to March 1991 he served as Director, National Security Studies, at Information Spectrum, Inc. From May 1977 to February 1984, he was the Senior Marine Affairs Analyst at the Santa Fe Corporation. He was a Research Associate and Research Fellow (Rockefeller Foundation Grant) at the Center for the Study of Marine Policy, University of Delaware, from September 1974 to May 1977, and held a University Fellowship in Political Science at the University of Delaware, 1972–1973.

Dr. Truver is the author, co-author or editor of numerous papers and reports, several hundred articles, and four books — *The Strait of Gibraltar and the Mediterranean Sea* (1980), *Weapons that Wait* (2nd ed., 1991), *America's Coast Guard: Safeguarding U.S. Maritime Safety and Security in the 21st Century* (2000), and *Riders of the Storm* (2000). He assisted in the production of the Navy-Marine Corps strategy papers, ". . . From the Sea" (1992), ". . . Forward From the Sea" (1994), "2020 Vision: A Navy for the 21st Century" (draft, July 1996), "Operating Forward. . . From the Sea" (1997), the "Maritime Concept" (2000), and "Sea Power 21" (2002); the Navy Secretary's "Posture Statement" (1999–2001 editions); the CNO's "Naval Mine Warfare Plan" (1992, 1994, 1996–1998, and 2000 editions); the CNO's "Force 2001 and Vision. . . Presence. . . Power" program guides (1993–2005 editions); "Changing the Calculus: Guide to U.S. Navy Anti-Submarine Warfare. . . Threats, Concepts and Programs" (2005), the Commandant, US Marine Corps' "Concepts & Programs" (2003–2005 editions); "UNDERSEA WARFARE Magazine" (1998–present); "U.S. Aircraft Carriers" (1991), "America's Nuclear-Powered Submarines" (1992), "Naval Surface Forces" (1993), "Naval Aviation: Forward Air Power. . . From the Sea" (1997), "International Programs: Enhancing Global Security" (1997); a history of sealift operations in the 1991 Gulf War for the Military Sealift Command; the 2004 annual report, "Science and Technology for the 21st-Century Warfighter", for the Chief of Naval Research; and the Coast Guard Commandant's "Coast Guard 2020" (1998) vision publication, "Coast Guard Publication One" (2002), and "Maritime Strategy for Homeland Security" (2002), among other Navy and Coast Guard studies and reports. He supported the interagency task force drafting the "National Strategy for Maritime Security (2005). He was the principal author of the 2001 report of the Deputy Under Secretary of Defense, Installations and Environment, "Defense Installations: Framework for Readiness in the 21st Century". Additionally, he served on Future Aircraft Carrier studies conducted by the Center for Naval Analyses and the Naval Studies Board of the National Academy of Sciences, including the Naval Studies Board's "Navy 21" and "Mine Countermeasures Technology" studies, among other strategic planning and communications efforts, threat assessments, competition analyses, and congressionally mandated reports.

For the Instituto de Cuestiones Internacionale, Madrid, Spain, he prepared a study of the environmental aspects of modern coal-fired marine propulsion plants. During his work with the Center for the Study of Marine Policy, he supported research into the environmental policy implications of offshore industrial-port islands, for the National Academy of Sciences; environmental and operational issues related to vessel-traffic safety systems, for the US Coast Guard; and alternative fisheries enforcement regimes, for the National Science Foundation.

Dr. Truver holds a Doctor of Philosophy degree in Marine Policy Studies (1978) — the first PhD in this field ever awarded by an institution of higher education — and a Master of Arts degree in Political Science/International Relations (1974) from the University of Delaware. He also holds a Bachelor of Arts degree in Political Science from Susquehanna University (1972), and is a 1968 graduate of Forrest Sherman High School, Naples, Italy.

You Ji is a senior lecturer in School of Political Science, the University of New South Wales. He is now a visiting research fellow in East Asian Institute, National University of Singapore. You Ji has published widely on China's political, economic, military, and foreign affairs. He is author of three books: *In Quest of High Tech Power: Modernization of China's Military in the 1990s, China's Enterprise Reform: Changing State/Society Relations after Mao,* and *The Armed Forces of China;* and numerous articles. The most recent ones include: "The Rise of China and Its Implications on the ASEAN–EU–America Triangle Relations", *Panorama: Insights into Southeast Asian and European Affairs,* No. 2, 2004. "Nationalism, Defense Culture and The PLA", in Wang Shaoguang and Leong Liew (eds.), *The Chinese Nationalism,* 2004; "Learning and Catching Up: China's RMA Initiative", in Emily Goldman and Tom Mahnken (eds.), *The Information Revolution in Asia,* 2004; "China's Multilateral Diplomacy and the DPRK Nuclear Crisis", in Young-jn Choi (ed.) *North Korea, Multilateralism and the Future of the Peninsula,* 2004; "China's Aircraft Carrier Ambition: Seeking Truth from Rumors", *Naval War College Review,* Vol. 41, No. 4, Fall, 2004.

I. *Introduction*

Chapter 1

Cooperation or Competition in Maritime Asia-Pacific?

Joshua Ho

With the end of the Cold War, the speed and magnitude of change resulting from a globalising world have become defining features of the international system as witnessed by the rise of new powers in Asia. This rise has caused a major flux in the regional system as China and India emerge as new major global players. Similar to the advent of a united Germany in the 19th century and a powerful United States in the 20th century, their emergence could transform the regional geopolitical landscape and the combination of high economic growth, expanding military capabilities, and large populations will be at the root of the expected rapid rise in economic, political, and military power for both China and India.

With the arrival of new powers, traditional regional powers may need to re-evaluate their strategies in the light of the new environment. Japan's aging population and shrinking workforces, for example, could crimp its longer run economic recovery, and challenge it to evaluate its regional status and role. Tokyo will have to choose between "balancing" against and "bandwagoning" with China. The United States will also have to re-examine its policies towards the regional powers vis-à-vis whether they are to take a cooperative or a competitive stance.

The new powers will likely start to exert their influence in the maritime domain because of the importance of the sea to countries in the region. Countries in the region depend on the sea as an avenue for trade and also for energy transportation. The dependence on the sea for trade and for the energy and resource transportation will increase in the future as the regional economies mature. Indeed, we are already witnessing signs of an increased use of the sea in the region arising from increased trade flows into and within Asia, the increased demand in Asia for energy and raw material resources and the increased strength of merchant fleets and navies in the region.

In this changing world, how the surge in power is accommodated by the incumbent powers like the United States and Japan, and how the new regional powers like China and India manage the power politics that emerge will be key determinants of regional stability. The edited volume aims to establish if a cooperative or competitive regime is developing as a result of the rise of the new regional powers, China and India, vis-à-vis the incumbent powers of the United States and Japan. China, India, the United States and Japan are the naval "elephants" of the Asia-Pacific that are competing for strategic influence.[1] The study is done by looking at the maritime strategies and the doctrines of China, the United States, India, and Japan to discern if these are competitive or cooperative. An examination of the ballistic missile and missile defence developments in the four countries also sheds further light on whether a cooperative or a competitive relationship is likely to develop in the future.

The volume is divided into four basic parts. Part I addresses the general issues, trends and paradigms that countries in maritime Asia-Pacific are facing currently. Part II then does a detailed analysis of the maritime doctrines and capabilities of China, India, Japan, and the United States respectively. Part III follows this by examining the nuclear doctrine, nuclear missile, and missile defence capabilities of the four Asia-Pacific nations of China, India, Japan, and the United States. The volume then concludes with what the emergent maritime future of the Asia-Pacific looks like. What follows is a summary of the chapters from each of the contributors, after which conclusions are drawn on whether a competitive or cooperative maritime regime is emerging and the possible steps that can be taken to promote stability in maritime Asia-Pacific.

Issues, Trends and Paradigms in Maritime Asia-Pacific

In the chapter, "Sea Power in the Asia-Pacific Region", Eric Grove mentions that "Earth" is a very bad name for our planet. Two thirds of it is covered by sea and although the world's inhabitants live on that relatively small part of the surface that is above water, most live close to the ocean, with some 70% of the world's population living within 100 miles of a coastline. The historic importance of water transport, as until the last century and a half, the only effective long distance medium, has had indelible effects on patterns of trade and population distribution. Moreover, sea transport still has vital advantages over other modes for the carriage of all but those items with the highest value to weight ratios. It is cheaper to transport a tonne of coal 5,000 miles in a bulk carrier than 500 kilometres by rail. Shipping dominates world trade, some 90% by volume going by sea. The sea thus remains *the* key element in the Asia-Pacific. It is the basic form of freight transport, a key source of food and an increasingly important source of oil and gas. Conflict over its use has led to violence in the past and may lead to more in the future. It is vital, therefore that everything be done to mitigate rivalries and stress common interests. The Maritime Cooperation Working Group of CSCAP has put much effort into trying to suggest modalities for cooperation to prevent conflict and mitigate it when it occurs. The laudable co-operative efforts to counter piracy and terrorism in the region show what can be done. The seas unite this region; its maritime forces should do the same.

In the chapter, "Maritime Strategic Trends in the Asia-Pacific: Issues and Challenges", Lawrence Prabhakar states that the Asia-Pacific has emerged as the maritime strategic hub in the 21st century. The quantum of sea-borne trade of resources and merchandise trade had bestowed the region its strengths and vulnerabilities. The maritime geography of the Asia-Pacific presents the interface of the continental landmass of Asia and the Pacific Ocean and the region is abounded by the maritime flanks of the Persian Gulf and Indian Ocean constituting its intertwined maritime geographical boundaries. The maritime geographical complex of the Asia-Pacific is bounded by archipelagos, islands of Southeast Asia; hemmed by the extensive littoral of the Asian landmass and the continental powers of the United States, Russia and China.

The international relations of the Asia-Pacific in the post-Cold War era is also essentially an emergent multipolar Balance of Power system with a continued hegemonic dominance of the United States.[1] The rise of new powers has been in competitive patterns of power with growing strategic capabilities with nuclear and missile arsenals even as economic interdependence has ushered in cooperative relations.[2] The Asia-Pacific is known for its dichotomy of growing economies and spiralling arms races that is persistent. Military power remains a robust variable even as the region emerges to displace the Euro-Atlantic region in terms of the largest trading area and a region of territorial and sovereignty contestations.

The balance of power in the Asia-Pacific is maritime centric as the contiguity of sea spaces have emphasised the significance of civilian shipping and navies. Sea Lanes of Communication (SLOCs) constitutes the arterial networks of resources and energy flows with the deployment of the regional and extra-regional navies in the region. The Asia-Pacific is a region known for its long spans of latitudinal maritime expanse that has rendered the importance of maritime access and forward presence a vital factor in maritime balance of power.

National Maritime Doctrines and Capabilities in Maritime Asia-Pacific

In the chapter, "China's Naval Strategy and Transformation", You Ji mentions that 25 years have passed since the Peoples' Liberation Army Navy (PLAN) put forward its blue water maritime strategy, which is a three-phase 50 year grand plan. According to the projection of People's Liberation Army (PLA) researchers, the PLA Navy should have acquired sea-control within its coastal waters by 2000, and achieved a sea-denial capability within the first island chain in the West Pacific by the 2010–2020 timeframe. However, a review of each phase to examine the extent to which the PLAN has achieved its objectives reveals that the Chinese may have failed to attain the goal of the first phase on time, as the overall growth of naval capabilities remained flat between 1990 and 1999. However, since 2000 the progress of PLAN transformation has been visibly accelerated, and there is no doubt that it has increased its operational readiness. The number of new major surface combatants and submarines that have entered service between 2000 and 2004 was more than double that of the entire decade of the 1990s. After a delay of half a decade, it appears that the goal of the first phase of development has been met. The PLAN has now entered the fast track of modernisation and if the current trend of growth continues, China can attain its Second and Third Phase objectives, that is, the exercising of maritime influence beyond the second island chain by the year 2020, and becoming a naval power capable of making its presence felt globally by 2050.

In the chapter, "Indian Navy: Keeping Pace with Emerging Challenges", Commander (Retired) Dr. Vijay Sakhuja says that after India's independence in 1947, the Royal Indian Navy was divided into two different entities, the Indian navy and the Pakistan navy. The Indian navy continued to be commanded by British Royal Navy officers due to the absence of experienced senior Indian naval officers. As the ruling elite in India was conscious of the fact that the absence of sea power had led to the colonisation of India, it was generally agreed that a strong navy was essential for India. The Indian navy of the 1950s was perhaps the most powerful in Asia, given the defeat of the Japanese navy during the World War II, and its near total disarmed status and that the Chinese navy was preoccupied with Taiwan. Despite this, Indian naval growth did not progress as projected at the time of independence as continental threats dominated the minds of the government and ruling establishments in India as evidenced by the subsequent wars with China and Pakistan in the 1960s and 1970s over boundary disputes and perennial tension between New Delhi and Islamabad. Today, however, the Indian navy is the largest in South Asia and the third largest in the Asia-Pacific region after the PLAN and the Japanese Maritime Self Defence Force. The Indian navy has grown in numbers and the quality of weapons and sensors has also improved. The Indian navy has also conducted advanced exercises with several advanced navies involving multiple platforms. The chapter then goes on to examine the geostrategic imperatives that are shaping the growth of the Indian navy. It highlights the Indian navy's strategy and force structure, as well as examines the roles and missions of the Indian navy.

In the chapter, "Japan's National Maritime Doctrines and Capabilities", Vice-Admiral (Retired) Hideaki Kaneda mentions that there are four basic characteristics of the Asia-Pacific region that serves as the backdrop and impacts on the maritime security doctrines and capabilities of Japan. The first characteristic is that the basic structure of strategic environment in the North East Asian region can be characterised by the remnants of the Cold War overshadowing the Korean Peninsula and Taiwan Strait, while South East Asia features extensive geopolitical diversification. The second characteristic is the change in the security framework, as the "apparent threats" of the Cold War era is replaced by more complex and diversified "potential threats" and "risk factors" of the post Cold War era, commonly spread throughout the region. As a result, the regional countries appear to be adopting risk aversion measures by multilateral cooperation and coordination. The third characteristic is that the emergence of asymmetric "new threats" is about to bring significant changes in the geopolitical strategic environment of the region, along with various factors of historic regional tensions. Furthermore, the wars occurring outside the region with new types of threats have extensively affected the situation characteristic to the region. The fourth and last characteristic is that the region finds a strong move towards the pursuit of a new maritime order. As the UN Convention on the Law of the Sea entered into force, regional countries on the coast have increased their reliance on, and expectation from, the oceans. Intensified competition over maritime resource acquisition and territorial disputes are likely to bring more factors of potential conflicts. Among those countries building stronger naval forces, China's trajectory, especially, causes anxieties in regional countries. The possibilities of maritime terrorist attacks and piracy are other factors that may cause instability in the region.

Lynn Pullen and Scott Truver, in their chapter "Security in the Asia-Pacific Rim: Evolving US Strategies, Doctrines, and Forces for Maritime Cooperation and Regional Collective Action" mentions that the US concept of maritime security has undergone broad and far-reaching changes especially after the September 11 terrorist attacks on the United States. The process of the change has included changes in how it employs its sea services — the Navy, Marine Corps, and Coast Guard — how the sea services work together or separately, and how they are equipped. The process of change is still ongoing, with some predicting ultimately a merger of the Navy and the Coast Guard. Also continuing is an evolution in the way in which the United States regards the Pacific Rim. After decades of focus on Europe and the Soviet Union, realisation of the importance of the Asia-Pacific region has spread from the uppermost echelons of government throughout the country. The critical economic links between the Pacific Rim states and the United States, and the transnational threats that have characterised the 21st Century thus far, are combining to force adjustments in maritime strategies and doctrines, the forces that support them, and the level of cooperation and collaboration which America seeks with its Asia-Pacific neighbours.

Nuclear Weapons and Missile Defences in Maritime Asia-Pacific

In the chapter, "China's Nuclear Doctrine, Its Strategic Naval Power and Anti-Missile Defence Initiatives", You Ji mentions that the end of the Cold War resulted in a complex global nuclear situation that posed an increased challenge to China's strategic security. Around its territories a number of new nuclear powers have emerged: North Korea, India, Pakistan and Japan, which may be on the edge of nuclearisation. Most importantly, the US *Nuclear Posture*

Review promulgated in 2002 specifically identified the PRC as a potential target for a pre-emptive nuclear strike. In response China has stepped up its nuclear weapons programs. In the last few years new generation nuclear missiles have been introduced to the Strategic Missile Force (SMF) of the PLA. China has also achieved breakthroughs in the associated technologies such as satellite-based control and guidance systems for its intercontinental missiles. It seems that China has moved one step closer to real combat operation. In PLA terminology, this means its nuclear units have set up full protocols to strike their designated targets, immediately after they receive orders from the Central Military Commission of the Party (CMC). In addition, the PLAN has acquired nine new prototype nuclear attack submarines, the 093 Class, which are capable of firing nuclear tipped long-range cruise missiles. The 094 Class strategic nuclear submarines are also undergoing sea trials which have reached the final stages of development. With three multiple war heads in each of the 16 intercontinental ballistic missiles on board, China may soon truly have a triad capability. This sharpening of the nuclear sword is reflected by the Chinese efforts in transforming its nuclear deterrence from a "hiding force" to a "fighting force". Another factor driving China's slow but steady nuclear modernisation is external, namely, the development of the US missile defence system, either in the form of the National Missile Defence (NMD) or in the form of the Theatre Missile Defence (TMD). They are fearful that that missile defence systems may provide a new mechanism for the US to forge closer military ties and develop alliances with regional countries as a way of deterring China. This is especially true if Taiwan is incorporated into the system.

In the chapter, "Nuclear Weapons and Missile Defences: The Maritime Dimension in the Asia Pacific", Arvind Kumar says that the global development, more particularly in the last decade and half especially after the demise of the Soviet Union and end of the Cold War, has focused broadly in the context of emerging power centres in each and every region. The debate between unilateralism versus multilateralism has gained salience and the emergence of the great power concept has dominated the debate. It is generally believed that the global centre of gravity of political, economic, military activities and capabilities is shifting to Asia and to some extent a new strategic balance is emerging among existing powers in the Asian region. Under this existing milieu, South East Asia with its maritime dimension has lots to offer in terms of development in a holistic sense. The extra regional power, the US will continue to make its presence felt and enlarge its tentacles. The role of regional powers including China, India and Japan will keep growing as a result of their strategic security interests. Various studies have indicated that the US will remain the largest economy in the world and the three largest economies in purchasing power parity terms are China, India and Japan.

The presence of American, French, Russian and other navies in the Asia-Pacific region has also changed the scenario completely. It also seems that there is a rapid proliferation of non-conventional threats in the Malacca Straits and adjoining waters. The proliferation of threats like piracy, drug trafficking and human smuggling is of major concern. Many of these nations in Asia and more particularly in South East Asia are critically dependent on regional sea-lanes for trade. These sea-lanes are also the energy lifelines of many East Asian States and are very important for global trade. The Malacca and Singapore Straits are very significant and important. Hence, the maintenance of security of these Straits is a very significant and important role.

In the chapter, "Transforming Old Idealism into New Realism: A New Dimension in Japan's National Security Strategy and Its Implications for the Security Cooperation in the Asia-Pacific Region", Katsuhisa Furukawa mentions that in the current years, global security faces two major challenges: how to deal with the emerging new global threats as represented by terrorism, proliferation of the weapons of mass destruction (WMD), or newly emerging infectious diseases; and how to build constructive security relationships between major land powers whose future still remain uncertain (most notably, China, India, and Russia) and other major powers, namely, the United States, European Union, and their allies and friendly countries.[1] These challenges are most evident in Asia where the geopolitical landscape has been in transition and remain unstable. Indeed, Asia is the very nexus of these global security threats and geopolitical uncertainty. At the core of this nexus are key security problems which have global implications, including the threats of North Korea's nuclear weapons program, Islamic fundamentalist movements in South East Asia, nuclear weapons proliferation by Pakistan, and uncertain future of the land powers, namely, Russia, China, and India, all of which possess nuclear weapons.

On the other hand, while there have been several modest developments in multilateralism in Asia, as represented by East Asia Summit or ASEAN plus Three, the development of institutional tools available for addressing these problems still remains immature in this region. Regional efforts need to intensify in order to build effective regional mechanisms to deal with these threats and uncertainties. Countries in this region sporadically rely upon a combination of their independent capabilities, bilateral and multilateral security relationship with other countries, especially, the United States and the

United Nations (UN) as a primary tool to assure their safety. In the post-Cold War era, Asia presents one of the most pressing needs for stability and predictability that are essential for constructing a benign global security environment.

In the chapter, "Nuclear Weapons and Missile Defence in the Asia-Pacific: A Perspective on the Maritime Dimension", Donald L. Berlin mentions that the Asia-Pacific region will likely be characterised by a gradual increase in the number of nuclear weapons states and in the size and quality of those states' weapons inventories. Moreover, more of Asia's nuclear weapons eventually will have a maritime dimension, either because they will be sea-based or because the battlespace in which they could be employed will be in the maritime domain to a significant extent. These developments will have a significant effect on the maritime balance of power in the Asia-Pacific. This is also true of missile defence, but it is too early to have any clear sense of the implications of such defences for the Asia-Pacific balance of power.

Currently, the Asia-Pacific nations equipped with nuclear weapons are the United States, China, Russia, India, Pakistan, North Korea and, to construe "Asia" broadly, Israel. Asia-Pacific states that could decide to develop and deploy nuclear weapons in the future include Japan, the Republic of Korea, Taiwan and Iran, among others. While the latter states could decide to forego the nuclear option, this is unlikely over the long term. Moreover, while some nuclear weapons states in other regions of the world have given up their nuclear arms, this is improbable in the Asia-Pacific security environment in the foreseeable future. The Asia-Pacific nuclear weapons environment will be also characterised by vertical, as well as horizontal, proliferation. In other words, not only will the region include more nations possessing nuclear weapons but the quality of these forces, particularly the relevant delivery systems, will also increase with time. The advent of more Asian nations equipped with nuclear weapons is an aspect of the general "rise of Asia" that is one of the most significant global phenomena of the 20th and 21st centuries. This trend, of course, will have a profound effect on the maritime balance of power in the Asia-Pacific.

In "The Emergent Maritime Future of the Asia-Pacific", Sam Bateman argues that the maritime scene in the Asia-Pacific region is extremely volatile at present due to the increase in the number of competitive maritime activities. For example, seaborne trade is booming, exploration for offshore oil and gas is running at levels unprecedented in the past, levels of naval activity are high, and naval budgets are continuing to grow at a fast rate. This increase in the number of competitive maritime activities has resulted in an atmosphere of maritime insecurity and uncertainty, rather than one of security and certainty. Lingering bilateral tensions are re-surfacing more frequently, especially in the context of disputed claims to sovereignty over islands or offshore areas. The first few months of 2005, for example, have seen tension between South Korea and Japan over their claims to sovereignty over the Takeshima/Dokdo islands, China's protests over the allocation by Japan of oil and gas exploration rights in an area of the East China Sea claimed by China, and a dispute between Indonesia and Malaysia over hydrocarbon rights in the Sulawesi Sea. Energy and the need to secure sources of supply are increasingly important factors driving maritime developments in the region. This is evident in the strong interests of North East Asian countries in the security of SLOCs across the Indian Ocean and through the "choke points" of South East Asia, and in the competition for offshore oil and gas resources. Managing this volatile maritime scene will be rather like "keeping the lid on the pressure cooker", and is a major challenge for the region. The emergent maritime future of the region vitally depends on how well this challenge is met.

Cooperation or Competition in Maritime Asia-Pacific?

So are we witnessing more cooperation, or more competition in maritime Asia-Pacific? Indeed, the issue of cooperation or conflict between states has been a consistent theme in international relations ever since its inception as an academic discipline. From the previous analyses, it appears that with growing economic power, regional countries also desire to have greater strategic space. The desire of the regional countries for greater strategic space is exhibited by the increased development of their respective naval and nuclear deterrence capabilities.

India for example wishes to have control of its immediate maritime domain and in the seas of South Asia from the Arabian Gulf to the South China Sea and intends to do this through a blue water naval capability centred on two aircraft carrier groups. China on the other hand is concerned with its security of access to energy supplies in the Middle East as well as an unimpeded access to trade. Currently China is able to project her naval forces to the first island chain but harbours blue water intentions so as to be able to project to the second island chain and beyond. In the interim though, the Chinese have secured a string of bases in the Indian Ocean to guarantee it access to the Gulf should the situation warrant it. As part of their desire to have greater strategic flexibility, both countries are also building up their submarine based nuclear ballistic missile capability to preserve a second strike option which will enhance the robustness of their nuclear deterrence.

Japan on the other hand has less ambitious objectives and harbours no blue water intentions. Japan's main concern is over North Korea's nuclear intentions, especially after the launch of the Taepodong missile over its air space, which landed east of Japan. This concern has led Japan to acquire theatre missile defence capabilities both at sea with the SM-3 equipped Aegis cruisers and on land with the Patriot PAC-3s. Japan is also examining a limited power projection capability as a pre-emptive option to deny North Korea's use of its nuclear weapons. Finally, the power projection capability will also allow Japan to retake lost islands as a result of an invasion. However, despite Japanese moves to be more self-reliant in its defence, Japan is still heavily dependent on the US nuclear umbrella to maintain the strategic status quo.

US strategy in the Asia-Pacific can be summed up as being committed to uphold democracy as a criterion for stability and to secure the international trading system from rogue states and countries inimical to the global system. To this end, the US is committed to Taiwan and continues to pressure North Korea to dismantle its nuclear weapons and to a lesser extent for China to adopt a more transparent and accountable system. At the same time it is continuing to assist friendly nations in building up their capacities through bilateral and multilateral exercises, like the Cooperation Afloat Readiness and Training (CARAT) series of exercises, and the Cobra Gold series of exercises. The US is also committed to shoring up the capabilities of friendly nations through military training and aid mainly to help them become stable states and to deal with the transnational terrorist agenda and to a lesser extent to forestall against any hegemonic ambitions by China.

Hence, from the analysis of the strategies of the four big "elephants" in the Asia-Pacific, it would appear that that the accretion of *hard* power in one dimension, the economic dimension, has also led to competition in the strategic dimension, which is also another element of *hard* power according to Joseph Nye.[2] However, this increase in strategic competition may not lead to instability in the region. Geoffrey Till has mentioned that every inter-state relation is characterised by both cooperation and conflict as they sit on the same continuum and that the level of cooperation of conflict in one dimension may not apply in another dimension, hence implying that even in an environment of increasing strategic and economic competition, the outcome is not pre-ordained.[3] As such it may therefore be necessary for regional countries to accentuate the use of *soft* power by increasing cultural and academic exchanges and fostering and promoting other activities that attract rather than repel. In the process, they will accrue *soft* power at the same rate that they are increasing *hard* power. The balance in the accrual of both *hard* and *soft* power may yet prove to be an important aspect in enhancing stability as the regional "elephants" pursue their inter-state relations and enter into an age of increased economic and strategic competition.

Notes

1. Sam Bateman, "Regional Sea Power — The Elephants are Dancing", *Asia-Pacific Defence Reporter,* May 2005, pp. 6–10.
2. Joseph Nye, *Soft Power* (New York: Public Affairs, 2004), pp. 5–15.
3. Geoffrey Till, *Seapower: A Guide for the Twenty-First Century* (London and Portland: Frank Cass, 2004), pp. 1–2.

II. *Issues, Trends and Paradigms in Maritime Asia-Pacific*

Chapter 2

Sea Power in the Asia-Pacific Region

Eric Grove

"Earth" is a very bad name for our planet. Two thirds of it is covered by sea and although the world's inhabitants live on that relatively small part of the surface that is above water, most live close to the ocean, with some 70% of the world's population living within 100 miles of a coastline.[1] The historic importance of water transport, as until the last century and a half, the only effective long distance medium, has had indelible effects on patterns of trade and population distribution. Moreover, sea transport still has vital advantages over other modes for the carriage of all but those items with the highest value to weight ratios. It is cheaper to transport a tonne of coal 5,000 miles in a bulk carrier than 500 kilometres by rail. Shipping dominates world trade, some 90% by volume going by sea.[2] Although Paul Kennedy's neo-Mackinderite analysis of the declining utility of sea power dominated discourse on the subject until recently mature consideration leads one to question it, especially after victory in the Cold War can be added to World Wars I and II as "three in a row" for maritime against continental coalitions. Thanks to Professor Sumida we know that Mahan must not be bowdlerised and misinterpreted as he so often was from 1890 onwards.[3] His ideas were richer and more diverse than implied by the first section of "The Influence of Sea Power upon History", a section it turns out, that was forced on him by his publishers. Mahan soon

17

recognised that naval power did not necessarily depend on a large merchant fleet. Moreover he argued for a naval consortium of like minded states, as we have today based around the USN, rather than an American naval monopoly. One must be careful now to use the term "neo-Mahanian" paradigm referring to those classical and oversimplified tenets that have been understood to stem from Mahan's writings by generations of navalists.

The mercantilist identity of state, merchant ship and warship that lay at the heart of "neo-Mahanianism" was one of the first victims of globalisation. As a recent American source has put it:

> "Maritime commerce today means multinational corporations, multiple countries, owners, crews, cargoes, and insurers. Over 90,000 merchant ships ply the world's oceans, flying 197 separate flags, a number greater than the total number of countries recognised by the United Nations. Their decks are laden with millions of containers each filled with diverse cargoes. A merchant ship at sea today represents the ultimate 'multinational'. Finding out 'who's in charge' can often take months of legal enquiry".[4]

The above source quotes a notional tanker owned in Hong Kong SAR, insured in London, reinsured in Germany, managed in Singapore and flying the Panamanian flag. Chartered by an Iranian oil company its cargo is traded between US, Japanese and South Korean interests during its voyage, all under the legal title of a mortgagee, an offshore bank based in the Cayman Islands. The officers are Norwegian, the seamen Filipinos and Bangladeshis. It is a matter of debate whether this spreads interests so thin that it is impossible to decide whose are being threatened should something untoward happen or spreads the impact to involve many countries significantly.[5] Certainly, it makes the issue of naval protection somewhat problematic.

The major merchant flags are no longer the major naval flags. There is some, but limited overlap. The most significant navies are perhaps those of the USA, UK, France, Russia, Japan, India, both Chinese political entities, the PRC and ROC, the Netherlands, Spain, Germany, Italy, Canada, Australia and Brazil. The largest merchant registers, over 10 million gross tonnes are Bahamas, Cyprus, Greece, Liberia, Malta, Panama, the PRC, Japan, Singapore, the United States and Russia.[6] Of course, this does not reflect beneficial ownership; indeed, over half the world's shipping fly flags of a different nationality from that of the owner. The Liberian flag is in many ways an American offshore register; it is even administered from the USA. Some countries, example, the UK, argue that beneficial ownership rather than flag entitles a ship to naval protection under the self defence provision of the UN Charter. Others, such as the Americans and French will in certain circumstances defend any ship under attack.[7] The situation, however, remains confused and the only certainty is the breakdown of the neo-Mahanian paradigm in its simplest form.

Yet there are connections between the economic use of the sea and naval capabilities. The world's major trading nations are the USA, Germany, Japan, France, the Netherlands, the UK, Italy, Canada, Russia the Netherlands, Belgium, the PRC and South Korea. All (even little Belgium in terms of the reach for its mine countermeasures forces) are significant naval powers. When one comes to sea use therefore Mahan, or his followers, may still be alive after all.

They seem to be particularly alive in the Asia-Pacific. Only in this region is there a congruence of significant naval powers and large national mercantile marines. In part this is because of the rather selective application of free trade principles in the region, not least by the United States who imposes strict cabotage regulations forcing traffic between Alaska, Hawaii and the ports of the Western CONUS into ships flying more than one star together with the stripes.

Yet even here there are key factors mitigating the neo-Mahanian model. Japan, historically one of the greatest naval powers and a nation crucially dependant on seaborne energy imports is limited in her naval capabilities by the pacifist political culture inherited from World War II. Although she is beginning to view her "Maritime Self Defence Force" in slightly more "normal" terms it will be some long time before she will be willing to act, and as important be accepted and trusted by her neighbours as acting, as a normal naval power.

China is also limited, this time by a culture that has historically downplayed maritime endeavour.[8] The Communist regime for a long time was as "continentalist" as any preceding Imperial predecessor. Its "peoples War" rhetoric was decidedly unhelpful to the development of naval forces whose essence has always been high technology. The PLAN, despite creditable and significant recent attempts to increase its capabilities, is still more a littoral force projection force than anything else. The carrier Varyag still rusts at Dalian as new destroyers appear beside it. This may not matter so much in the short to medium term as its main areas of potential interest are around Taiwan and in the South China Sea but China remains far from being a great naval power and she will have great problems in mobilising her mushrooming resources to make herself one.

The dependence of sea trade of the Newly Industrialised Countries (NICs) of the region makes naval capabilities to maintain the free movement of shipping, if only in the near vicinity, very advisable. Not for nothing have Taiwan, South Korea and Singapore all invested heavily in naval forces in recent years and all deploy impressive fleets in capability, if not in reach. The ROC Navy is especially impressive, at present still more or less the equal of its Communist rival in overall capability if not in sheer size.

A major problem with many the navies of the western part of the region is technology. There are two dimensions to this; electronic and mechanical. Naval forces pioneered both information warfare and the related "revolution in military affairs" long before either term was invented. Led by the British in the 1950s the major navies developed computerised combat data systems and electronic links to network them. An unseen revolution took place in naval warfare, a revolution as important as that from sail to steam that consigned to second class status those that could not keep up. Only the USA and its Mahanite consortium of British Commonwealth and NATO navies have kept up; even Japan has not fully adjusted to the information revolution and the PRC remains far behind. The NICs have made some progress with data links and computerised command systems and the ROC's advantage over the PRC has much to do with this. This area remains a key one, however and the lead of the United States is increasing to a point where there are even question marks over its closest allies retaining full interoperability.

At first sight it might be considered strange that mechanical technological problems could be a problem to countries that contain the world's leading shipbuilders but warships require special skills, especially submarines. The only country of the Pacific littoral able to build submarines without significant out-side help has been Japan. The PRC depended on the Russians originally for technology transfer and later for actual imports; her first generation SSNs and SSBNs were indigenous but very troubled as a result and Russians are assisting with the next generation. The Germans have assisted the Indians, who also use Russian expertise and hulls, the Indonesians and the ROK while the Swedes are the submarine patrons of Australia and Singapore. A Franco-Spanish con-sortium does the same job for Malaysia. PRC pressure prevented the Dutch, Germans, French or Australians from supplying the ROC, and the latter has had real problems in its ambitious US backed submarine programme. That such a developed country as the ROC is so dependant on foreign sourcing is significant.

Even surface warships require rare design skills and technologies. Japan relies on US and British equipment to a remarkable extent, the PRC uses the French and the Russians, although domestic technology is being used to an increasing extent, for example, in the active phased arrays of the

052C destroyers. Australia's and New Zealand's latest frigates are German in design and their older units American and British respectively. Malaysia builds in Britain and Germany and buys second hand from Italy — although most of the latest OPVs are being assembled at home. Indonesia builds in the Netherlands and takes the old DDR's fleet from off Germany's hands. Singapore buys second hand Swedish submarines and enhances French frigate and German corvette designs. Thailand gets surface ships from the PRC and the USA and buys a carrier from Spain. The ROC buys second hand destroyers from the USA, new frigates from France and builds frigates to American designs.

The only fully independent naval powers in the Pacific region are Russia and the USA. The power of the former is limited by the inability of the Russian economy to support the super power nostalgia of the Russian Navy. The US navy (USN) remains supreme; its Japan-based battle group a not inconsiderable navy in itself. Supported financially by Japan it is in a sense the "sanitised" offensive arm of the "Japanese Navy", one whose presence and capabilities are generally more welcome than they would be if the ships wore the Rising Sun ensign.

The Russian Pacific Fleet is but a shadow of its former self. It is primarily an extended defence of home waters although its commanders hanker after a more normal naval role when resources allow, which may not be for some time yet. The USN is thus left to occupy the theatre it conquered in the greatest maritime war in history from 1941 to 1945. If maritime power played an enabling and supportive role against Germany it was the basic means of victory against the maritime Empire of Japan. Japan's superb three-dimensional fleet was repulsed at Midway, worn down around the Solomons and then decisively defeated in the Philippine Sea and around the Philippines themselves in 1944 and finished off at sea and in harbour in 1945. American amphibious forces advanced to the gates of the home islands themselves. American submarines assisted by aircraft dropped bombs and mines sank almost all of Japan's merchant fleet and stopped traffic between Japan and mainland Asia. Finally nuclear bombers flying from a Marianas air base captured by naval forces the previous year, using fuel brought in by sea and even, one of them, a bomb delivered to Tinian by a USN cruiser, delivered the coups de grace.

This maritime war reflected the maritime theatre, a particularly watery place even by planet Oceania standards. One of the principal participants was a sea-dependant island state connected to its Empire by shipping, the other a continental super power with a maritime self image and the economic, industrial and technological means to build a fleet that was unsure of its capacity to beat the Royal Navy in a fleet action in 1935, into a maritime capability at which the British could only wonder when they arrived as junior partners in 1945.[9]

The US Navy from the Pacific War onwards has always been happier at power projection rather than defence of shipping even in its post Cold War iterations of strategy. Over the last decade and a half, the power projection mission is the only one that is seriously considered. The main aim of the USN is the assertion of dominance in a multidimensional maritime battlespace that covers a littoral region, "the area from the open ocean to the shore which must be controlled to support operations ashore, and the area inland from the shore that can be supported and defended directly from the sea".[10] Littoral power projection operations are driving the procurement of the new surface combatants that will be orientated primarily for land attack. Even the submarine force is being forced to jump on littoral bandwagon with a new emphasis on operations directly against the shore.

This "power projection" paradigm is being followed by all the world's major navies. The concept of "power projection" has been significantly redefined in the latest official iterations of British defence policy. It has been narrowed down to the deployment of "stand off military capabilities that are able to deliver significant force to deter or coerce". The amphibious landing of troops is part of the surrounding military tasks, that is, humanitarian assistance and disaster relief, evacuation, peacekeeping, peace enforcement, focused intervention ("the ability to disrupt or destroy the threat with the rapid and localised use of force") and deliberate intervention ("with as much combat power as is necessary to defeat or destroy an adversary").[11]

In this context it is natural that the leading "core maritime role" for the modern Royal navy is "maritime force projection" in its two dimensions of "littoral manoeuvre" and "maritime strike". This reflects the expected strategic environment which requires "a clear focus on projecting force further afield and even more quickly than has previously been the case. This places a premium on the deployability and sustainability of our forces, sometimes in circumstances where access, basing and overflight cannot be guaranteed".[12] In this situation, maritime forces must be the natural forces of choice. Their capacity to use most of the surface of this misnamed planet and to gain access to the majority of the world's population means they are basic to an ability to exert military power anywhere in uncertain world — as and when required and with minimum host nation support. Moreover, their capacity to operate in an environment and in a way in which it is difficult for asymmetric threats such as small explosive boats and ballistic missiles to be effective makes them even more useful against current threats.

The definition of the littoral has been stretched a little of late. In Operation "Enduring Freedom", Afghanistan, a land locked country, was converted into the littoral with carrier-based aircraft carrying out most of the bombing sorties and sea basing providing a vital component of land operations. The use of a US aircraft carrier as an early deployed special operations base demonstrated that such activities could be carried out even if host nation support was unavailable (making the eventual provision of that support more likely). The availability of secure floating bases allowed operations ashore a vital measure of greater security.[13]

Power projection assets are becoming the centrepieces of most of the world's navies. In addition to the two projected large 65,000 ton carriers, Britain has two new LPDs and four new LSD(A)s of the Bay class (the latter austere LPDs), a considerable enhancement of expeditionary capability. Other navies are building impressive power projection assets also — France two flat topped 21,500 ton support and command ships of the Mistral class plus a second, larger, aircraft carrier based on the CVF design. The Netherlands is building another Rotterdam type LPD with better helicopter facilities and is examining a helicopter carrying role for its new auxiliaries. Spain, who already has two of the Rotterdam type, is building a larger flat topped strategic projection ship that could act either as an assault asset or as a second carrier. Italy is building a 26,500 ton STOV/L carrier Cavour. More locally Taiwan has modernised its amphibious forces with two recently acquired LSDs and LSTs, Singapore has its four new LPDs, and by 2010 Japan will have two 13,500 ton carriers and three LPDs. Australia plans to build three impressive amphibious assets. By 2012, India should have two new carriers.

The future surface combatants planned by Europe's major navies will have land attack as a major role. The potential of the modern surface combatant against the shore is demonstrated by the planned capabilities of the US Navy's DDX with its 155 mm guns able to fire guided Long Range Land Attack Projectiles (LRLAPs) at ten rounds a minute out to 100 miles. It will be interesting to see how far surface combatants in this region will follow this trend.

With firepower of this range and accuracy the accent is on network enabled capability. As stated above, there is nothing new in this for navies. Since the Second World War the integration and use of electronically generated data has been the essence of naval warfare. Data links and computerised data management have been around for years. What *is* new is the extent of the information now available and the speed of its delivery. The American joint fires system allows timely, precision engagement of targets many miles inland; cooperative engagement capability allows a complete fire control quality radar picture to be obtained across a whole force. These and other networks pose interoperability challenges to coalition allies. In order to fight with the US resources must be spent on making sure one can join the network, even at the expense of platform numbers. Interestingly the latest British White Paper provides a rationale for reduction in surface combatant numbers by arguing that in the most demanding operations, the coalition framework will mean that "naval escorts are less likely to be at a premium".[14]

As stated above the modern surface combatant, in Western navies at least, is now less of an "escort" and more of a general purpose weapons and C2 platform. This brings us to the question of the place of sea control in contemporary maritime strategy. In current Royal Navy terminology sea control is part of "theatre entry" and the core of "flexible global reach". So far so good, but the assured access available in recent operations and the investment priority in power projection have tended to downgrade at least some sea denial threats. New AAW assets are impressive but ASW is being neglected. Reportedly performance in recent anti-submarine warfare exercises has been mixed, to say the least, and care must be taken to stop hard gained expertise withering away to be learnt all over again. The navies of this region may well continue to emphasise the sea control task at the higher end of their capabilities.

Submariners of the dominant global coalition are facing something of a crisis in the modern strategic world. Networking has special challenges for subsurface craft and if one dominates the maritime environment there is little need to submerge. Submarines do still have special advantages as covert intelligence gatherers, as recent operations in the Mediterranean have vindicated. It is interesting, however that the Norwegians, who have taken a leading role in such operations are no longer as interested in air independent propulsion (AIP) as the existing boats can snort with relative security in this less demanding environment. One wonders whether or not this has lessons for the wider context; or, perhaps, things are more traditional in this part of the world. Certainly AIP seems alive and well in some Asian contexts.

Nuclear power is more important than ever as a way of getting a covert cruise missile or Special Forces platform a long way in a short time but the very high costs of ownership lead to questions being posed by naval planners about the expense of SSNs in the longer term. Both Britain and France are still building new and improved classes and neither navy will wish to give up such a fundamental capability that easily. India will soon be back in the SSN business and, as we have seen, the PRC is at last modernising its capabilities.

Another underwater threat that is always with us is the mine, as was shown yet again in the recent Iraq operations. Littoral operations by definition emphasise mine warfare and mine countermeasures (MCM). A major problem here is that the classic MCM vessel is a small, relatively slow asset built essentially for operations in home waters; its strategic mobility is poor. There is a real requirement among the power projection states for MCM capacity that is both more strategically deployable and which can be used more "in stride". It is in MCM that uninhabited underwater vehicles (UUVs) probably have their greatest long term potential. A problem however is that current MCM vessels, given the materials from which they are built, have long lives; they are also expensive. One cannot replace them overnight, even if one wanted to. Here is a place for innovative thinking.

It is often argued that this recent move to the littoral is something novel. In fact the current fixation with this environment has a long pedigree. One can detect a kind of "oscillation" as, due to both strategic and technological factors, navies moved out to sea in the 18th century and then back to the littoral in the 19th. It is instructive to read statements of the mid-19th century that look remarkably modern in their littoral emphasis. Armour was first introduced primarily to assist ships in the engagement of forts. Then, however times changed. In the 1880s, the coast attack armour plated ships of the ironclad age became sea going "battleships". It is no coincidence that this exactly coincided with the renaissance of "sea power" thinking with Colomb and Mahan. The latter disliked amphibious operations as diversions from the main duties of the fleet. By the First World War littoral capabilities had atrophied to a significant extent, as the Dardanelles showed. Naval warfare was all about command of the sea and its possible denial.

Littoral power projection, side by side with the battle for sea control, reappeared once again in World War II both in terms of amphibious landings and carrier air power. The dynamics of the Cold War continued to place some premium on these latter capabilities. Nevertheless the confrontation of Soviet and Western navies on the high seas created a new "blue water" emphasis to which the Mahanian instincts of the US and Royal Navies responded, although, paradoxically perhaps, much of the fighting was planned to take place in the littoral. Only the end of the Cold War nipped this process in the bud and began the return to the current littoral priority.

The British maritime strategist Sir Julian Corbett always emphasised the "maritime" relevance of naval forces, that is, their influence on that part of the world which mankind inhabits, the land. This potential is huge, given the key salience of the oceans as a means of communication and access. As European states move back into a global frame it is natural that they should look to their maritime forces as the foundation of their capabilities to "reach out and touch" enemies. At present those enemies cannot do much in return at sea, but one can almost be sure that this situation will not persist for ever.

For the foreseeable planning horizon, therefore, it is understandable that naval policy in most countries will follow primarily the power projection path. This is, indeed, offering navies one of the most secure futures they have ever faced. By the second decade of this century, for example, the capacity of the Royal Navy to reach out and touch enemies with effectiveness and precision will have been truly transformed. It will be able to make an even more significant contribution to a coalition task force than the current fleet does today.

This emphasis on power projection increases the disconnect between the higher levels of contemporary naval doctrine and the more traditional aspects of "sea power", notably merchant shipping. To be sure, merchant shipping remains vital to the world economy in general and to that of the Asia-Pacific in particular. Although it is more than a decade ago that Admiral Sir James Eberle noted that international financial flows rather than trade flows dominate the international economy, the significance of international trade to the general economic well-being of states and peoples has never been greater.[15]

Exports and imports form a very significant part of the economies of a large number of nations, especially, in this region. Exports comprise over 20% of the GDP of the PRC excluding Hong Kong and Taiwan, almost 150% of the GDP of the Hong Kong SAR and almost 50% of the GDP of the ROC. They are about 40% the GDP of Thailand, a third the GDP of the ROK, the Philippines, Vietnam and New Zealand a quarter the GDP of Indonesia and a fifth the GDP of Australia.[16]

Although Japan's exports are a surprisingly low proportion of her of GDP the absolute value of that trade is enormous and she is one of the world's major trading nations. Moreover the production of Japan's industry is crucially dependant on imports of energy, over 80% of her net energy consumption being imported. The ROK has a similar, indeed slightly larger level of energy import dependence and the islands of Taiwan, Singapore, and the Hong Kong SAR, are entirely import dependant.[17] Those imports must come by sea.

Even countries that are less dependent on international trade as a proportion of GDP such as the USA still have a considerable interest in the free flow of shipping in order to import certain vital commodities at acceptable prices and to maintain a healthy export market. The USA remains the world's largest trading nation. Disruption of shipping could have a massive effect. As Stan Weeks has put it in relation to shipping in the Asia-Pacific:

> "Clearly the US has a growing economic interest in the security of SLOCs in this region, particularly in view of the impact of their disruption on US trading partners".[18]

The energy trades are a special feature of dependence on shipping. Crude oil imports remain massive in the region. Liquid natural gas carried in large refrigerated specialist carriers is also very important. The next most important category of bulk cargo is coal and coke, used for steel making as well as an energy source.[19] Other bulk cargoes that traverse the Pacific in quantity are iron ore, grain, bauxite, phosphates, manganese, copper, nickel, zinc, chrome, sulphur sugar, and chemicals.

High value cargoes are now very largely carried in containers. Over a decade ago 16 million containers were being handled in East and SE Asian ports compared with 14 million in European ports and 12 million in the US.[20] The ports of the Asia-Pacific are among the world's busiest. Of the top ten ports in the world in throughput of metric tons, six are in the Asia-Pacific: Singapore (No. 2), Shanghai (No. 3), Hong Kong (No. 4), Nagoya (No. 5), Yokohama (No. 7) and Pusan (No. 8). Long Beach, America's busiest port (and No. 9 in world rankings) also faces the Pacific.[21]

As shown above, ships that carry these massive trade flows have never been more internationalised. This trend is likely to continue because of increased capital mobility across borders, further reduced state subsidies and tighter profit margins, pressure to reduce costs and ensure tax avoidance and expanding global trade and trade relationships.[22]

Trade, and therefore shipping, is vital to the Asian economies. If anything seriously interfered with the free flow of this shipping, the results could be serious, but just how serious has become a matter of interesting debate. At the Eleventh International Conference of the Sea Lines Of Communication (SLOC) Study Group held in Tokyo in November 1997, American analyst Daniel Coulter threw down a challenge to the conventional wisdom. He argued that the economic value of keeping open specific sea lanes was dubious and that the definition of SLOCs was "confused and imprecise".[23] He argued that modern shipping was much more independent of land than its predecessors and that "sea lanes today are no longer dictated purely by the land bound end points of their trades".[24]

Coulter looked at the South East Asian example quoting the "shibboleth" that the South China Sea was one of the most "strategic" stretches of water in the world as it provides a pathway for the millions of tonnes of oil destined for Japan, South Korea, and China. Quoting a National Defence University study he argued that if all four straits, the Malacca, Sunda, Lombok and Makassar were blocked and the South China Sea itself, the extra steaming costs would account for only US$8 billion a year based on 1993 trade flows, about half the losses suffered by the USA to a major hurricane. If all Arab crude had to divert around Australia some US$1.5 million would be added to Japan's energy bill; if only the South China Sea was closed the cost would only be US$200 million annually. Such figures are minor fractions of Japan's total energy bill of between US$50 and 100 billion, major fluctuations much larger than the costs of diversion being caused by routine oil pricing and exchange fluctuations. The costs to China, South Korea and USA would be less still.

Coulter concluded thus:

> "In assessing the criticality of SLOC, the responsiveness of the shipping community to a disruption determines whether the trade is merely delayed due to longer transit times or denied access to the markets. With the exception of the Hormuz, SLOCs generally fall into the former category. The methodical analysis of both trade and shipping through the SE Asian SLOCs and the Suez Canal suggests that as long as there is sufficient shipping capacity to accommodate the increased demand for tonnage in a diversion scenario, the impact of extra steaming costs is negligible on the economies outside the closure area. No instances could be found where economies would be denied access to the trade due to prohibitive transportation costs. This is further buttressed by the real world closures of the Suez Canal in 1956–7 and 1967–75. In both instances, pressures for outside intervention based on economic rationales did not occur. Why? The reason is simple: the shipping markets responded by providing the appropriate tonnage necessary to carry that trade at minimal cost, both financial and political, to the global economy".[25]

Coulter was trying to make the point that one should not overstate the global and wider regional impact of shipping disruptions. He admitted that "no one disputes that those nearest the SLOCs would certainly be affected".[26] Indeed he used this to argue that those South East Asian countries that straddle the major SLOCs thus had a major interest in maintaining the free flow of shipping as to do otherwise "would be akin to cutting their own throat".[27]

Yet there are many countries in the Asia-Pacific who would be deeply affected if someone less dependant on the free flow of shipping took measures to interdict it either in choke points or on the open sea. Coulter is right to point to the problematic nature of the concept of "SLOCs" and some of the rhetoric surrounding them but his thesis should not be misinterpreted to downgrade the key importance of shipping arriving and departing in the ports of the region, and this could be attacked at many points, not least off the ports themselves.

Ships can be diverted, indeed one of the basic means of defending them from attack is to do so, as seen in both World Wars. But diversion has its limits and there are costs that could be significant. Coulter points to the potential winners in the case of increased costs, notably ship owners, but there would be losers too. Certain exporters might well lose markets if marginal costs showed only minor increases. This might not affect the global economy too much, but its local effects could be catastrophic.[28] Equally the local effects of loss of imports might be highly significant indeed.

Key factors in the Asia-Pacific region are the relatively ill developed networks of land transport available. With the exception of the PRC and Japan, railway systems in East and South East Asia are underdeveloped and inadequate in haulage capacity. Even Australia is limited in its land transport links and has more the character of an archipelago. There is less buffering effect from alternative transport modes than would be available in Europe and North America. The sea is therefore the basic means of transport in the Asia-Pacific in a way that is more the case than in other regions; interfering with shipping is therefore of particular salience.

There are those, however, who argue that it is difficult to inflict serious damage on shipping. The events in the Gulf in the 1980s are sometimes held to have demonstrated these problems. Much damage was inflicted, up to a billion US dollars' worth, and some ships were sunk or damaged beyond repair in the 483 attacks that were carried out, but the price of oil was largely unaffected. Maybe, but much of this occurred at a time when the price of oil was being kept low by the USA as a decisive Cold War tactic. The capabilities brought to bear in the Gulf were limited in power; the merchantmen were increasingly effectively defended by warships and in the end a really serious threat to Iran's vital sea communications posed by the USN did indeed help bring her to the Conference table. Maritime pressure had worked with the US threatening Iran's very economic survival. The same could happen in certain circumstances in the Asia-Pacific.

Merchant shipping might well suffer attack either because of its direct involvement in local conflict or because it happens to have to pass through an area of conflict on its route. Nations may well use the threat to shipping as an effective means of bringing pressure to bear upon a nation with which it is in dispute. This can take various forms, attack by missile or torpedo from a variety of maritime platforms, or perhaps more cost-effectively, mining. The threat of ballistic missile bombardment may also be used in a coercive way to deter the free passage of shipping as it has been done by the PRC against the ROC. The best way of avoiding such threats is to use other routes that are often available. But sometimes there may be no alternative and naval protection of some kind may well be required. This could be problematical to organise given the mismatch of flags between warships and modern merchantmen but the tendency has been to interpret association between the two in the liberal manner dictated by the economically liberal maritime environment.

The threat may not be a fully official one. Criminal activity remains a problem, particularly in this region. According to a published USCINCPAC document put onto the internet on 1 October 2004, "the world's most piracy infested channel is... the Strait of Malacca between Malaysia and Indonesia".[29] There is much scope for co-operative measures to help deal with this problem, as has been done with some success in the past. In 1991 there were 32 attacks in the Straits of Malacca; these were reduced to seven and then to five or less in succeeding years by co-operative measures taken by Indonesia, Malaysia and Singapore. One should not over-state the piracy problem as the global listings often cover relatively minor crimes carried out in harbour, but the tendency for acts against ships underway to proliferate and escalate makes constabulary countermeasures an essential feature of the Asia-Pacific maritime scene. Not for nothing is Malaysia emphasising offshore patrol vessels in its current procurement programme.

There is a tendency to equate the "pirate threat" with maritime terrorism. Like Brian Jenkins at the last IMB conference, I am sceptical of too much association of the two.[30] However if this topical threat encourages further regional cooperation, as it has done, the effects on maritime order must be positive, as, indeed, they have been.[31] It will be interesting to see how far piracy in the region makes a resurgence after the tragic Tsunami, whose one positive effect was to stamp out the problem in the Straits in its immediate aftermath.[32]

Although shipping is the most important economic use of the sea there are two others that are of considerable regional importance. The first is fishing. More than half the world's fish are caught or bred in Asian waters and about half the world's fish are consumed in the region. Six of the top ten fishing countries are Asian; the PRC, ROC, ROK, India, Japan and Thailand. Over 40% of the world's fishing vessels are registered in these states. The PRC has the world's largest catch. The world's largest fish buyer is Japan, responsible for a third of global imports and the largest fish seller is Thailand. In Asia, fish provides about 30% of daily animal protein, more than anywhere else and fishing as an activity sustains more jobs than in any other region.[33] Demand is beginning to outreach supply. All South East Asian stocks are fully exploited, if not over-fished and the value of well established fisheries has declined.

Given both increasing competition and the enclosure of the world's oceans with the general adoption of national fishing jurisdiction out to 200 miles, a measure which brought 90% of the world's fish within the control of the coastal state, there is much scope for conflict. Japanese boats fish in Russian waters, PRC in ROK, ROK in Japanese and Thais in waters belonging to Myanmar, Malaysia, Cambodia, Indonesia and Vietnam.[34] Armed clashes are not uncommon and there is a major enforcement task for regional navies and coast guards, especially as states reach agreement on common approaches on the exploitation and management of diminishing stocks.

The other major economic use of the sea is as a source of hydrocarbons for fuel. Indonesia, Malaysia, Brunei Vietnam, Thailand and the PRC have long had a major energy stakes in the seabed. All have major reserves, as does Myanmar. The increased expected demand for energy should see China soon importing energy to the same extent the USA does today as well as other countries becoming net oil and gas importers. This will put more of a premium on undersea sources of supply and will increase the possibilities for potential rivalry in any disputed areas, such as the South China Sea.

The sea thus remains *the* key element in the Asia-Pacific. It is the basic form of freight transport, a key source of food and an increasingly important source of oil and gas. Conflict over its use has led to violence in the past and may lead to more in the future. It is vital, therefore that everything be done to mitigate rivalries and stress common interests. The Maritime Cooperation Working Group of CSCAP has put much effort into trying to suggest modalities for cooperation to prevent conflict and mitigate it when it occurs. The laudable co-operative efforts to counter piracy and terrorism in the region show what can be done. The seas unite this region; its maritime forces should do the same.

Notes

1. BR 1806, *The Fundamentals of British Maritime Doctrine* (London: HMSO, 1995).
2. US Office of Naval Intelligence, *Worldwide Maritime Challenges 1997*, p. 24.
3. J. T. Sumida, *Inventing Grand Strategy and Teaching Command; The Classic Works of Alfred Thayer Mahan Reconsidered* (Baltimore and London: Johns Hopkins Press, 1997).

4. *Worldwide Maritime Challenges 1997*, p. 8.
5. Ibid. This view versus the well disseminated thoughts of Admiral Sir James Eberle (RN retired.) as articulated, for example, at the Sealink Conference at Annapolis in 1986.
6. *Janes Fighting Ships, 1997–98.*
7. This occurred in the closing days of the Iran–Iraq War.
8. For a good historical survey of China's uncertain "quest for sea power", see B. Swanson, *Eighth Voyage of the Dragon* (Annapolis: Naval Institute Press, 1982).
9. For American doubts on their capacity against the British, see the Plan Red game scenarios worked on until 1935 at the Naval War College at Newport and held in the College's archive.
10. BR 1806, p. 221.
11. Ibid., p. 5.
12. *Delivering Security in a Changing World (Cm 6041-1)* (London: UK Defence White Paper, December 2003), p. 7.
13. Norman Friedman, *Terrorism, Afghanistan and America's New Way of War* (Annapolis: Naval Institute Press, 2003).
14. Ibid., p. 7.
15. Sir James made the points on financial flows in an address at the Sealink Conference at Annapolis in 1986.
16. *Asia 1998 Yearbook* (Hong Kong: Far Eastern Economic Review, 1997), pp. 12–13.
17. Ibid., pp. 14–15. For the order of major trading nations, see *Worldwide Maritime Challenges, 1997*, p. 24.
18. S. B. Weeks, "Sea Lines of Communication — Security and Access", *Paper for the NEACD Workshop on Maritime Trade and Transportation*, Arden House, New York, 4 April 1997, p. 4.
19. I predicted that coal would be an increasingly important cargo. See E. J. Grove, *The Future of Sea Power* (Annapolis: Naval Institute Press, 1990), p. 177.
20. Ibid., pp. 12–13.
21. *Worldwide Maritime Challenges 1997*, p. 25.
22. Ibid., p. 9.
23. D. Y. Coulter, "The Economics of SLOC Protection: An Overvalued Mission", *Paper presented to Sea Lines of Communications Conference*, Tokyo, November 1997, p. 1.
24. Ibid., p. 2.
25. Ibid., p. 7.
26. Ibid., p. 3.
27. Ibid., p. 4.
28. LCDR Dick Sherwood, RAN, made this point in discussion in Tokyo and in private conversations with the author.

29. *Primer: Piracy in Asia*, US CINCPAC Virtual Information Center, 1 October 2004, p. 2.

30. Ibid., p. 48.

31. Ibid., pp. 50–51.

32. T. Selva and M. Lourdes, "IMB: Piracy will carry on when commerce resumes", *The Star (Malaysia)*, 17 January 2005.

33. Trish Saywell, "Fishing for Trouble", *Far East Economic Review*, 13 March 1997, p. 51.

34. Ibid., p. 52.

Chapter 3

Maritime Strategic Trends in the Asia-Pacific: Issues and Challenges

W. Lawrence S. Prabhakar

The Asia-Pacific has emerged as the maritime strategic hub in the 21st century. The quantum of sea-borne trade of resources and merchandise trade had bestowed the region its strengths and vulnerabilities. The maritime geography of the Asia-Pacific presents the interface of the continental landmass of Asia and the Pacific Ocean and the region is abounded by the maritime flanks of the Persian Gulf and Indian Ocean constituting its intertwined maritime geographical boundaries. The maritime geographical complex of the Asia-Pacific is bounded by archipelagos, and islands of Southeast Asia; hemmed by the extensive littoral of the Asian landmass and the continental powers of the US, Russia and China.

The international relations of the Asia-Pacific in the post-Cold War era is essentially an emergent multipolar Balance of Power system with a continued hegemonic dominance of the US.[1] The rise of new powers has been in competitive patterns of power with growing strategic capabilities with nuclear and missile arsenals even as economic interdependence has ushered in cooperative relations.[2] The Asia-Pacific is known for its dichotomy of growing economies and spiralling arms races that is persistent. Military power remains a robust variable even as the region emerges to displace the Euro-Atlantic region in terms of the largest trading area and a region of territorial and sovereignty contestations.

The Balance of Power in the Asia-Pacific is maritime centric as the contiguity of sea spaces have emphasised the significance of civilian shipping and navies. Sea Lanes of Communication (SLOCs) constitutes the arterial networks of resources and energy flows with the deployment of the regional and extra-regional navies in the region.

The Asia-Pacific is a region known for its long spans of latitudinal maritime expanse that has rendered the importance of maritime access and forward presence a vital factor in the maritime balance of power. The analysis of the Asia-Pacific maritime strategic trends would focus on:

(1) The nature and salience of naval transformation that has affected traditional naval doctrines and force postures.
(2) The transformation of the concept of Forward Naval Presence of extra-regional powers and the regional naval/maritime responses.
(3) The pertinent issues of security of sea-lanes of communication, challenges of maritime terrorism; energy flows and its security and the containment of the proliferation of weapons of mass destruction.
(4) The evolving naval doctrines and technological templates in the region.
(5) The operational dynamics evident in the competitive and cooperative maritime strategies in the region.

Maritime Strategic Trends in the Asia-Pacific

The Asia-Pacific is known to be the region that is pivoted on geopolitics and geo-strategic factors that conditions the region. While the logic of geo-economics sustains the cooperative relations among the states in the Asia-Pacific, there is strong discernible evidence of geo-political and geo-strategic factors that works as the dynamic of balancing in the region. It presents the coexistence of the territorial state and the globalising state.

The strategic environment of Asia is characterised by the presence of three great continental powers: China, India, and Russia. There is also an arc of maritime powers Japan, South Korea, Taiwan, the ASEAN countries, Australia and New Zealand, and the small island nations of the South Pacific.

The region's maritime expanse is being characterised by the *tyranny of maritime distance* for the US, Japan Russia, China, Australia and India that has necessitated them for the deployment of merchant shipping and navies to maintain their maritime presence.

The region has emerged as hub of increasing economic development, integration as well as a region of transitional and asymmetric challenges that have been on land and in sea. The increasing prospect of maritime transnational and asymmetric challenges of terrorism, piracy and the vulnerabilities of supply chains has complicated the security of Sea Lanes of Communication.

Naval transformation has been one area that has gained salience since the end of the Cold War that has come along with the concurrent developments in globalisation. The emergent missions and roles of navies in relative peacetime contexts have substantially modified the traditional paradigm of Naval Power and Maritime Strategy. The emergent benign roles of cooperative maritime security are evident in joint exercises, interoperable missions; the constabulary roles in humanitarian missions have been substantially complementing the prevalent coercive and compellence missions of navies.

The Asia-Pacific region is a globalised maritime environment with its accents on global maritime trade and pacific cooperation. There has been a growing significance of transnational maritime issues that has the portents of threats and challenges evident in maritime terrorism and piracy and the cooperative accents in maritime regime building.

The salience of these complementing trends is quite evident in the evolving maritime dynamics of the Asia-Pacific. The evolving dynamics of maritime security has been vivid in the dichotomous nature and scope of competitive and cooperative dimensions of maritime power.

Naval Transformation and its Impact on Maritime Security

Maritime Strategy in specific focus to naval strategy has an "externalised" essence of National Strategy with the scope of enormous momentum and transformation. The scope of transformation is evident in strategy, tactics, operations and the dynamic nature of technology. The impact of transformation is quite profound on the nature and dynamics of national security strategy of maritime and continental powers.

Maritime Strategy and Security is thus evident in:

(1) The seamless and transnational nature of ocean environment that enables naval deployments in missions of showing the flag, naval diplomacy, littoral power projection cooperative maritime security, and in various modes of strategic articulation.

(2) Maritime space envisions for a three-dimensional means of power projection in the *maritime-air-space* terrains that provides for a networked operational and technological environment in maritime operations.
(3) The stealth and speed in deployments of naval platforms provides subtle overtones in diplomacy and leveraging impact in force projection. The possibilities of pre-emptive attacks on naval platforms are remote given the rapid and flexible redeployments and manoeuvres.
(4) Nuclear weapons at sea provide the most significant and substantial mode of assured deterrence with a viable second-strike capability. Deployments of nuclear-powered submarines with nuclear-tipped ballistic and cruise missiles have formidable roles in posturing and nuclear signalling.
(5) The preference of sea-based ballistic missile defences on high performance naval platforms would be the emergent strategic and technological templates in the years to come. The deployment of Navy Theatre Wide missile defence systems would be in contiguous sea space of several littoral countries.

Naval strategy and the civilian maritime paradigm have been in the throes of transformation due to the impacts of three cardinal forces:

(1) The transformed geopolitical and geostrategic canvas of the post-cold war, globalisation dynamics.
(2) The transformation of alliances and counter alliances that spurn the dynamics of maritime access and basing; cooperative naval and maritime security.
(3) The transformation of technology and strategy evident in the cumulative impact of the Revolution in Military Affairs (RMA) and more specifically a Revolution in Naval Affairs (RNA).

Forward Presence and Naval Transformation in the Asia-Pacific

The concept of the Forward Presence has been a primary mission of naval forces engaged in Sea Control operations. Naval Forward Presence has been the most visible commitment of a nation's forces to secure its security and economic interests in distant regions. Traditionally, the salience of Forward Presence had provided for coercive and benign naval operations. It has fostered naval diplomacy in the form of joint naval exercises, joint naval patrols and sharing of maritime intelligence and surveillance, humanitarian missions that have been coalition efforts. Significantly, naval presence had also reinforced expeditionary operations in coercive missions and has enhanced deterrence and compellence in times of crisis.[3]

The salience of forward presence in the Indian Ocean Region and South China Sea in the post-Cold War and post 11 September 2001 periods have emerged in different contours and they have implications that affect the traditional salience of the concept.

The Cold war and the immediate post-Cold War era had an established pattern of naval forward presence that was structured around the concept of physical access and basing based on onshore facilities.

The post 11 September 2001 period have witnessed the emergence of the new trend of strong littoral opposition to extra-regional forward presence that has emanated from traditional sources of opposition and transnational challenges like maritime terrorism.

Four causal factors affect the salience of the traditional forward presence of naval forces and land bases that host extra-regional powers in the Indian Ocean Region–South China Sea. It is characterised by the emergence of anti-access/area-denial strategies.

(1) The first causal factor is the *anti-access political opposition* emanating from adverse popular perceptions to extra-regional forces access in littoral and regional deployments in the allied territories. Anti-access political sentiments are frictions that have emanated from a hostile populace in the host nation that have complicated basing and access process of extra-regional powers, for example, the US in Okinawa and in South Korea, despite the host national governments ready acceptance of the forward presence.

(2) The second causal factor has been the emergence of *strong littoral defence responses* from regional powers in the form of naval forces modernisation as an area-denial measure. New technological capabilities evident in the proliferation of the supersonic anti-ship cruise missile systems and land attack cruise missile systems deployed on improved diesel-electric submarines have opened vulnerabilities in the forward presence of the extra-regional powers.

(3) The third factor has been the emergence of the regional ballistic missiles and weapons of mass destruction arsenals that are considered as *area-denial measures* that target the land bases and access of the extra-regional forward presence.

(4) The fourth factor could be the irregular asymmetric threats that are defined as non-conventional threats based on brinkmanship, that is,

maritime terrorist threats that are catastrophic with WMD effects, emanating from state and non-state actors or in collusion intended to *erode* the salience of forward presence.

Naval forward presence has been sustained by the US, UK, France, Russia, Japan and Australia.

United States

The US is the predominant naval power in the region that has durable bilateral strategic relationships with Japan and Korea bound by treaty obligations. It has nurtured several bilateral arrangements with Australia, Singapore, Thailand and Philippines (both declared as US non-NATO allies). The continued role and presence of the US in the region is widely regarded as a factor of stability. In Asia, the US perceives the prevalence of several regional threats. This has been responded by the US and its regional allies with the agency of bilateral alliances and joint responses.

The US Navy display of its capabilities during the 2003 Iraq conflict was a demonstration of its enabling capabilities. Its naval logistical support and deep strike capability through its air power and Tomahawk Land Attack Missiles provided decisiveness in its strike capabilities. US Naval power has been the foundation of US military power and it played an important role in global operations launched after 11 September 2001 Operation "Enduring Freedom" with its first strikes against Afghanistan. The carrier air wings were the mainstay of aerial operations against the Taliban and Al-Qaeda targets even as neighbouring states proved reluctant to let US air forces use land bases. The US Navy has demonstrated the vitality of carrier air power and air expeditionary force projection.

The US submarine force has been in full deployment optimising its cruise missile strike potential. The US is converting some of its nuclear ballistic missile submarines for land attack cruise missile platforms with new options to deploy the Trident D-5 ballistic missile submarines for insertion of Special Operations Forces for littoral operations and modifying those with better intelligence, surveillance and reconnaissance assets for its new missions in the region.

The US Navy is evolving new sea basing capabilities to support marine operations ashore with modified *Wasp* class multipurpose amphibious assault ship (LHD-8) baseline design that could support its new generation F-35 *Joint Strike Fighters* and V-22 *Osprey* tilt-rotor aircraft operations. Its Naval Support Facility at Diego Garcia in the Indian Ocean and its forward access facilities in Oman, UAE, Bahrain, access facilities in Trincomalee in Sri Lanka,

Changi Naval Base in Singapore, facilities in Northern Australia offer the US "lily pads" for a rapid surge in the region from its rearward bases in Guam and Hawaii.

The US Forward Presence is fostered by inducing defence transformation in its allied regional force capabilities with technology transfers. The US forces in the region have emerged to augment the capabilities of its allies; that is, Japan, South Korea, and Australia with whom it has statutory defence agreements. Singapore and Thailand enjoy special relationships with the US in the region. Indonesia and Malaysia enjoy cordial relations. US naval forces posture would be focused for rapid response and surge capabilities in times of crisis and intervention.[4]

The stakes of the US commitments to the allies by its deployment of enhanced long-range precision air strike assets and the deployment of dedicated naval and air assets provide rapid reinforcements in power projection and littoral strike capabilities against adversaries.

The US has a transforming offshore presence that would be in the form of effective expeditionary forces with the advantages of Sea lift, transfer and reinforced with air–naval dominance and lethal strike capabilities. This transformation is in tune with the Quadrennial Defence Review (QDR) 2005 as a follow on of the earlier QDR 2001 force posture and the implementation of the US Navy Sea Power 21 force posture.[5]

United Kingdom

The UK's commitments in the region have been in the Indian Ocean Region in the form of the Naval Task Group 03 that was constituted as the "East of Suez" operations since 11 September 2001. The NTG 03 was supplemented with the Royal Marines with 19 naval units were deployed in the Persian Gulf Indian Ocean Region. The UK Royal Navy deployments have come in substantial measure in the aftermath of the 11 September 2001 and the War in Iraq. The Royal Navy deployments have been a significant force in the Persian Gulf and Arabian Sea built around the carriers HMS *Ark Royal* and HMS *Ocean.* Its nuclear attack submarines equipped with Tomahawk-TLAM (Tomahawk Land Attack Missiles) cruise missiles. Besides, the units of Commandos 40 and 42 Royal Marines were also involved in operations. The UK Naval forces performed an important role in mine clearing and providing logistical support to the air and land forces.[6]

The Royal Navy deployments are being primed for joint operations with the Army, Royal Marines and the Royal Air Force in the evolution of joint operations with accents on sea basing of its assets and shape an amphibious and expeditionary force that would be deployed for future operations.

The UK has treaty commitments with the Five Powers Defence Agreement (FPDA) in South East Asia (1971) that entails its naval forward presence and joint naval-air exercises with its allies Australia, Singapore, Malaysia and New Zealand. The scope of the FPDA has been changing from its earlier conventional defence obligations towards cooperative threat engagements in terrorism and piracy since 2004.[7] The emergent threat perceptions from transnational threats of maritime terrorism, piracy and the possible disruption of Sea Lanes of Communication that are laden with energy supplies from the Persian Gulf has enhanced the threat perceptions in the region engaging the FPDA in new missions rejuvenating its existence.

The UK maintains a robust forward presence of deployment of Royal Navy warships and submarines and has been conducting joint naval exercises with several Indian Ocean littoral powers and has conducted naval–air operations in the Persian Gulf-West Asia region.

France

France has been an Indian Ocean Power with its standing naval force in the Indian Ocean. The French have been an Indian Ocean power with their military presence in the Reunion, Tromlein and Mayotte, besides they have facilities in the South West Indian Ocean in the sub-Antarctic and Antarctic known as the Eparse Islands. The French forward presence is thus well established. France like the United Kingdom and Japan are dialogue partners in the IOR-ARC. The French forward presence is in Djibouti with a deployment of a rapid reaction force of 2,700 troops, a detachment of the French Foreign Legion and a French Air Force squadron of Mirage F-1 fighters. The French naval detachment has always been two to three combatant vessels of destroyers, one frigate two inshore patrol craft and a reinforcement of two frigates and a Dassault *Atlantique* maritime reconnaissance aircraft that would be tasked with the visiting French carrier force from the Mediterranean.[8]

The French naval deployments in the post 11 September 2001 have been in support of the operations in the Afghan theatre of operations. The French Navy's regional engagement has been in support of the naval–air operations of the "war on terrorism", in Afghanistan, from the Arabian Sea and Indian Ocean, and has been active since October 2001. It is a fact that France opposed the war in Iraq and is not part of the US-led coalition; however their cooperation in the allied operations in Afghanistan continues.

France has been a dominant arms supplier to the region and has been conducting bilateral naval exercises with the Indian Ocean littoral states. Its interest in South-east Asia emanates from its stakes in the South Pacific and its burgeoning trade and military ties with China.

The US, UK and French naval presence is considered to be the dominant extra-regional great power navies in view of their deployed naval orders of battle and the deployment of nuclear propelled platforms in air-craft carriers and nuclear attack and ballistic missile submarines.

Japan

Japan's maritime security concerns in recent times have been focused beyond its territorial waters on the sources of threat from terrorism; piracy and environmental safety. The strategic significance of the post 11 September 2001 has added the gravity of the situation. The concerns over security of SLOCs have been crucial for Japan given its overwhelming reliance on sea-lanes for roughly 90% of its imports.

The Japanese Maritime Self Defence Force (JMSDF) has considerably bolstered its capabilities for patrol and defence of its major ports and key straits as the threat of foreign incursion has risen. The recent incursions of a Chinese nuclear submarine and the earlier North Korean naval incursions have served a powerful reminder of Japanese maritime vulnerabilities.

The Japanese Diet in October 2001 had enacted a set of three new laws addressing terrorism; The Anti-Terrorism Special Measures Law is quite significant that empowers the Self-Defence Forces the right to provide non-combat assistance to US-led military forces engaged in operations related to the global "war on terrorism".[9] The new legal framework has enabled the deployment of several JMSDF vessels in operations in the Indian Ocean since November 2001 to provide escorts and assist with US efforts in Afghanistan.

Japan also has a JMDSF role in Iraq. The deployment plan has emerged after the legislation of the July 2003 Law Concerning Special Measures on Humanitarian and Reconstruction Assistance to Iraq. This has led to deployment of units of the Japanese Air Self Defence Forces and the JMSDF in logistics operations of reconstruction materials and humanitarian relief supplies. Japan had also deployed a 30-member Japanese Ground Self Defence Forces advance unit which arrived in Iraq in January 2004 along with a JMSDF destroyer and troop ship.[10]

Russia

Russia appears to be increasingly interested in asserting itself as a significant maritime power. In April 2003 and August 2005, the Russian navy had deployed a large naval grouping to the Arabian Sea to conduct joint exercises with the Indian Navy. The deployment had about 10 warships of two Udaloy class frigates from Vladivostok, one Slava-class cruiser, one Project 1135 Krivak-class frigate, one Project 61M Kashin-class destroyer, the Project 775 Ropucha-class landing ship from Sevastopol accompanied with the Project 1559V tanker Ivan Bubnov and the Project 712 ocean-going salvage tug Shakhter.

Their passage was into the Mediterranean and through the Suez Canal and rendezvoused with the two Pacific Fleet frigates off Socotra Island. There were three cruise missile-carrying nuclear submarines deployed in support of the group. This show of the Flag presence represented the most significant projection of Russian naval power onto the high seas in recent times.[11]

The deployment included two naval infantry companies reinforced with main battle tanks and armoured personnel carriers. The occasional deployment of the Russian Fleet in recent times since the Cold War is shaping its forward presence as an instrument of its foreign policy. Russia's forward presence in the Cam Ranh Bay has ended in 2002 and its exit marks the end of its forward presence in South East Asia. Its exit has been due to its economical situation and its ill affordability to maintain its presence. However, Russia's support to Vietnam and its supply of military hardware have continued.

Cam Ranh Bay is now a contended spot for forward presence for China, India and the US in a bid to promote their respective maritime forward presence. China has its interests in South China Sea and the Spratly's island disputes are a historical legacy that has not faded away and hence its access is ruled out. The US would like to have places and not bases and hence would like to use as a hop for a surge into South East Asia. India's interests in the region have been keen in view of its expanding naval presence in the region and its countervailing naval presence in the South China Sea for the Chinese naval presence in Myanmar.

Australia

The Royal Australian Navy (RAN) has expanded its roles beyond its territorial waters with maritime support operations in the Indian Ocean in the Operation Enduring Freedom. The forward presence has been in support of coalition operations in the Indian Ocean region. The Royal Australian Navy Maritime Doctrine envisages its Navy operations in support of coalition forces that symbolise the essence of a limited forward presence taking into account Australia's interests and concerns of shipping and sea-lanes security.[12] The RAN has committed an LPA and two frigates in support of Operation "Enduring Freedom", and the RAN ships are serving in the Arabian Gulf as part of the Maritime Interception Operations. The RAN has deployed the LPA, HMAS *Kanimbla* and the two frigates HMA Ships *ANZAC* and *Darwin* along with a team of navy clearance divers for the Iraq war in Operation "Falconer".

The Asia-Pacific is thus a maritime hub of the dominant powers of the US, China, Japan and India rung by the middle-sized powers of South East Asia and Oceania. The US continues to be the anchor of the hub with its overlay of influence and dominance in the region networked with a ring of bilateral alliances with its nuclear umbrella in the region guaranteeing against instability. The UK and France have their extended maritime interests in the region given their colonial linkages and alliances that have staked their presence in the region.

The post 11 September 2001 and the War in Iraq have enhanced the imperatives of the salience of forward presence given the intertwined nature of the high geo-economic and geo-energy stakes in the region and the geo-strategic stakes of West Asia and its contiguous regions.

The persistence of terrorism and asymmetric conflict, the potential of failed states and the emergence of strong littoral resistance to extra-regional presence have accentuated the new roles of the powers.

Forward Naval Presence and naval transformation has been premised with the development of doctrines and capabilities derived from:

(1) The evolution of Joint doctrines and new capabilities that equips forces with enablers to effective intervention.

(2) The new accents on defence transformation that has revolutionised war and intervention operations providing a seamless integration of systems and platforms to prosecute operations on a 24/7 basis.

(3) The stealth and speed in deployments of naval platforms provides subtle overtones in coercive diplomacy and Compellence missions with its leveraging impact in force projection.

(4) The emerging technological possibilities of a sea power doctrine that fuses offensive, defensive and logistical capabilities at sea built on pervasive sea strike capabilities from surface, submerged and aerospace platforms integrated by net-centric platforms constitute the emergent strategic-technological paradigm of power projection that intends to overwhelm the frictions of anti-access and denial strategies and wresting the initiative of the offensive.

The salience of forward presence in the 21st century would be *From the Sea* that would provide enhanced autonomy to the dominant maritime extra-regional powers seeking to reduce their vulnerabilities on land yet persisting with strong littoral intervention capabilities. The US leads the defence transformation process that is being followed by its extra-regional allies and regional partners.

The first implication is the emergence of Joint Forces that would have expeditionary and amphibious capabilities that are increasingly premised on maritime-air-space platforms; the synergies of manned and unmanned platforms in air–sea and submerged terrains and reliant on sea based logistics.

The second implication in the evolving patterns of forward presence is the growing interoperability between the United States forces and its allies in the region. Japan, Australia, South Korea, Singapore, Thailand, Taiwan are in different stages of transformation that is converged on the premise to evolve interoperable standards with US forces in the region.

The third implication of transformation of forward presence is the real time effectiveness in intelligence and surveillance operations of the evolving Command, Control, Communications, Computation, Intelligence, Information Surveillance and Reconnaissance (C4I2SR) platforms and sensors that is integrated into the Joint strike platforms. This integration provides the value addition of the transformed forward presence.

The fourth implication of forward presence is the integration of homeland security concerns with forward presence by way of deploying the sea-based Theatre Ballistic Missile Defences on forward high performance AEGIS cruisers that provides assurance and deterrence against littoral ballistic missile threats in the region. The forward basing of sea-based ballistic missile defences are viewed as vital assurances to regional allies. The sea-based missile defences are also being complemented with the deployment of sea-based nuclear weapons launched from ballistic missile submarines like the Trident D-5 class. The US Nuclear Posture Review 2002 and the adoption of SIOP 04 provides for the flexible targeting of Submarine Launched Ballistic Missiles against hostile regional states.

Issues and Challenges in the Asia-Pacific Maritime Complex

The stakes of the Great Power Navies in forward presence are based on the contentious issues of their extra-regional presence. The critical significance of each of these issues would determine the nature of their forward presence in their competitive and cooperative operational deployments.

Sea Lanes of Communication (SLOCs)

The security of SLOCs in the region is the vital link to the region's access to energy, resources and trade. The SLOCs in the region run through several straits. There are various factors that affect SLOC security:

(1) The unstable political relationship among regional countries.
(2) The varied interpretation over the freedom of the seas principle; islands sovereignty disputes and overlapping maritime jurisdictional claims.
(3) The emergent regional naval build-up; and
(4) The non-traditional threats such as pollution, piracy, drug-trafficking.

The contentions over the SLOCs commence with the Indian Ocean funnelling into the Straits of Malacca and the South China Sea that provides the shortest access for shipping routes connecting North East Asia with South East Asia and the Middle East. The archipelagic profile of the region and the narrow sea gates has complicated the issue of SLOCs in the region.[13] The Straits of Malacca, Singapore Straits, the, Sunda, Lombok and Makassar Straits in South East Asia, and the Straits of Tsushima, Tsugaru, Osumi, and Soya (La Perouse) in North East Asia dot the sea space in the region. The regional SLOCs are well known for their controversies.

The contentious issue is of innocent passage through the territorial waters. The extra-regional powers have always assumed the right of innocent passage also applies to warships. Littoral states have been reluctant to permit passage to warships without prior authorisation or notification given the colonial histories of the region. The littoral countries like Bangladesh, Myanmar, China, India, Indonesia, South Korea, North Korea, and Pakistan require authorisation or notification for the innocent passage of foreign warships.

The fact assumes importance since several warships of the extra-regional powers are nuclear propelled and some carry nuclear weapons. The Indonesian interpretation of the innocent passage imposes some rules to regulate the movements of foreign warships using the Java Sea. Warships sailing outside designated sea-lanes should abide by the norms that govern the rights of innocent passage. It would entail that submarines should sail on the surface, weapons and surveillance radars must be switched off and aircraft-carriers must keep their planes deck-bound.

Indonesia's conditions have been unacceptable to the US. The US has pointed out that maintaining less than battle readiness for more than 300 kilometres for its warships traversing in the Java Seas would not be acceptable.[14] This has been polemical since many of the vessels were nuclear powered and the effects of navigation of nuclear-propelled vessels in littoral waters were politically and environmentally sensitive.

The second issue has been the transit passage through international straits. The UNCLOS defines it in terms of freedom of navigation and over flight solely for the purpose of continuous and expeditious transit in the normal modes of operation utilised by ships and aircrafts for such passage. The controversy persists on the mode of transit of submarines in submerged status in the straits. Yet another dimension of the controversy are the rights of a littoral state to interfere with transit passage due to suspected pollution incidents and the nature and scope of regulatory responsive measures to accidents and pollution taken by a littoral state. Contesting on issues of sovereignty the littoral states want to impose additional restrictions on transit ships like tolls that have been resisted by the international users of civilian and naval traffic.

The third issue has been the differences that have arisen between the littoral states and the extra-regional maritime powers in terms of archipelagic sea-lanes passage. The LOS Convention states that an archipelagic state may designate sea-lanes and air routes suitable for the continuous and expeditious passage of foreign ships and aircrafts through or above its archipelagic waters. These archipelagic sea-lanes must include all normal passage routes and all normal navigational channels. While sovereignty claims are staked by the littoral states, the maritime powers have insisted on free passage.

The fourth issue has been that the contention on the naval activities in the Exclusive Economic Zone (EEZ) constitutes yet another issue. The EEZ regime in UNCLOS balances the competing interests of coastal states for greater control over offshore resources, and those of maritime powers for maintaining traditional freedom of action in waters beyond territorial seas. The restrictive regime of the EEZ poses a threat to the mobility of navies and the ongoing controversy over the EEZ regime includes the freedom of action of foreign navies within EEZ. The issue of extra-regional navies to conduct military manoeuvres within the EEZ without requiring prior notification or authorisation from the coastal state is strong. The future deployment of the US Navy Mobile Operating Base for its sea-based operations in contiguity of the EEZs would further trigger a controversy as the US Navy would deploy the same to conduct pre-emptive action against any of hostile littoral states in the region.

The South East Asia Nuclear Weapons Free Zone (SEANWFZ) Treaty signed by the ASEAN countries in December 1995 has its sensitivities of transit of nuclear propelled nuclear equipped warships of the US and the other major powers in the region. China besides the US would have its nuclear submarines transit the regional waters into the Indian Ocean or to the Sea of Japan.

The fifth issue has been the legal contentions relating to the shipment of nuclear wastes through certain ocean areas and EEZs, territorial seas and straits. Japan has been transporting spent plutonium fuel and receiving reprocessed plutonium from the UK and France. Japan, UK and France have asserted that the shipments are free to navigate through any part of the ocean under the traditional doctrines of innocent passage, transit passage, and freedom of the high seas.[15] The issue has been controversial since the littoral states have been restricting the passage of vessels carrying nuclear or other hazardous cargoes through the Malacca Strait, which can be potential targets of maritime nuclear terrorism.

Maritime Terrorism

Maritime Terrorism in the Asia-Pacific has been an emergent threat since 11 September 2001. Though the maritime designs of the threat in the Asia-Pacific region persisted for over several years with the capabilities of the Liberation Tigers of Tamil Eelam (LTTE), the capabilities of the other groups have remained largely dormant and not experimented.

In the aftermath of the 11 September 2001, maritime terrorism has often been linked with piracy and the nexus between the two have been highlighted. There is yet an incident to prove the linkages though apparent inferences have been drawn.

As a transnational threat, maritime terrorism exposes the vulnerabilities of the SLOCs to disruption with the mass catastrophic incidents that would have serious spiral consequences in the damage of the economies of the region, disruption of energy and trade flows through the narrow sea passages and significantly complicate US bilateral relationships in the region.[16]

The following aspects are considered critical in the light of the threat of maritime terrorism in the region:

(1) The rimland of South East Asia that commences with Thailand, Malaysia, Indonesia, Philippines are now dotted with several radical Islamic groups whose capabilities of terror operations on land have gained strength and have been gradually permeating their presence in the region. With the

exception of Singapore whose Total Defence architecture has been able to successfully foil such infiltration, the other countries of the region are increasingly vulnerable to such disruption.

(2) The targets of the radical Islamic groups like the Al-Qaeda and Jemaah Islamiah (JI) are varied in the region and the regional archipelagic geography seems to provide the terrain advantages to these groups. This is in particular reference to Southern Thailand and the northern Malay provinces that are now infested with radical Islamic violence. It is no coincidence that these are proximal to the Andaman Sea on the west and the Gulf of Thailand on the east. The terror groups in the region have been using the Bangladesh–Myanmar–Thailand corridor and the potential capabilities of future sea-based terror attacks or offshore incidents at sea operating from the coast is increasingly probable.

(3) The Straits of Malacca, the Sunda, Lombok straits are other vulnerable targets that would be targets for the maritime terror groups. The potential targets could be the international users of the sea in the region who could be prime targets much less the littoral users of the sea. Given the existing complications on the SLOCs in terms of the contest of stakes between the littoral sovereign users like Malaysia, Indonesia and Philippines vis-à-vis the international users like Japan, South Korea, US and Australia. Major catastrophic terror incidents at sea in the region targeting the civilian or even naval warships of the international or extra-regional powers could spiral into a regional crisis. Such a situation would necessitate yet another case of pre-emptive action in the region. The probabilities of such scenarios has made the Regional Maritime Security Initiative of the US Pacific Command a necessity as a cooperative threat engagement strategy.

(4) The increasing probabilities of terror at sea could be there, as the US would be realigning its force posture in the region. The evolving US access strategy to develop several access points in the form "places rather than bases" strategy and the new visitation rights that they would be gaining in the region in Thailand, Singapore, Philippines, Australia are all in contiguity of the rimland of the region where the possible bases of terror are located in southern Thailand, Indonesia, and Philippines respectively. The imperative to avert the probability of terror incidents at sea or at ports or on shipping in the international waters would fall as prime responsibilities of the littoral powers who are claiming sovereign rights. In the event of a major sea catastrophe targeting the shipping or the military logistics of the international users (who stake the claims of innocent passage under the UNCLOS) the probabilities of a crisis

escalation in the region is bound to increase. The escalatory possibilities would emerge from: (1) the inabilities of the littoral powers to foil and initiate preventive actions in the region prior to the incident, owing to lacunae in intelligence; (2) the incident would be viewed as an anti-access measure by the extra-regional powers to their rightful innocent passage and hence would insist on their naval patrols and escorts in station for the safety of their SLOCs.

(5) The persistence of the claims of the regional states in the archipelagic waters and their inabilities to curb Islamic militant activities in the region would signal to the terror groups to initiate major catastrophic incidents that would drive further wedge between the extra-regional powers and the regional states.

(6) The vulnerabilities of the region to major catastrophic incidents would be severe in view of the congested geography and the spiral of such incidents could trigger persistent inter-state differences in the region. There could be two opinions that would either invite extra-regional cooperative threat engagement strategy or the hostile opposition to such initiatives.

Thus maritime terrorism has its critical trigger potential that could disrupt the regional stability, trade, energy flows and the security of sea-lanes of communication.

Energy Security

The critical dependence of Asia on the Persian Gulf–West Asia oil supplies and on the sea-borne supply of the same to South East Asia and the Far East has critical implications in maritime security of the sea-lanes and the vulnerabilities of the region to shocks and disruptions. China and Japan, besides South Korea are the predominant consumers and importers of the Persian Gulf–West Asian supplies.

The vulnerabilities of the sea-borne trade of oil supplies from West Asian region has motivated China to consider the options of a limited forward presence of their naval units in the Indian Ocean. Japan and South Korea have been toying with options of their expanded operations in the Indian Ocean as part of their coalition operational efforts in Iraq.

China's Indian Ocean policy has been one of expansion since 2000 with the quest to build access and bases in the region. China has justified that it needs these facilities to secure its oil and trade SLOCs in the region. China has financed and has built the Gwadar port complex with an initial aid of

US$200 million in Pakistan that would entail China's PLA-Navy warships and nuclear submarines to access the port.[17] The Chinese have been building a signals intelligence facility on the Great Coco island, 40 nm from the Andaman Islands, to monitor shipping in the Malacca Straits and Indian missile tests from testing ranges off the east coast. At a cost of over $2 billion China is also modernising Myanmar's naval bases at Munaung, Hainggyi, Katan island, Zadaikyi island and Mergui for its surveillance and monitoring missions and basing its naval units for a surge into the Bay of Bengal with access to the Indian Ocean region.

The Chinese are also constructing a road and waterway link from southern Yunan province to Yangon port in Myanmar to provide Beijing with access to the Indian Ocean through the Bay of Bengal for an alternate route to the Malacca–Singapore straits.

Japan has been concerned about these developments and has since revised its National Defence Program Outline in 2004 and has been augmenting its capabilities for an out of area engagement in the Indian Ocean with respect to the operations in Afghanistan and Iraq. These engagements are perhaps the first steps of the JMSDF for extended operations outside Japan and possibly have given it the opportunities to craft access into the region. Japan has expressed interest in these exercises and has offered to conduct visits by Japanese Coast Guard units. It would involve training and exercise of the regional coast guard forces in counter terror operations with Japanese special operations forces in naval–air coordination exercises. Japan has also contributed about 400 million Yen to a revolving fund called the Malacca Strait Council to tackle and manage disasters in the region that could emerge from oil spills and environmental damages resulting from disruptive attacks.[18]

Given the vulnerabilities of the extended sea-lanes of the oil traffic, Japan, China, South Korea and the ASEAN nations are keen to exploit the Australian and Indonesian natural gas reserves and to venture to exploit the offshore natural gas reserves in the archipelagic waters.

There have been agreements with Russia to have the natural gas from eastern Siberia. China, Japan and South Korea have been rivalling each other in this regard.

Nuclear power for energy generation has been an option to diversify dependence on oil and natural gas for power production. China has been serious on its nuclear power development projects with several European companies aggressively bidding for projects. The US maintains a very strict regimen on exports related to China on nuclear materials in view of proliferation concerns, but has in recent times relaxed to facilitate entry of its entities into the Chinese nuclear energy market.

The energy security concerns in the region could be stabilised with cooperative energy security initiatives that would engage, Japanese, Chinese and Korean energy markets with prospecting and exploiting the natural gas reserves in the region in an apparent move to reduce oil SLOCs from Persian Gulf–West Asia.[19]

Proliferation Security Initiative

The Proliferation Security Initiative (PSI) has emerged as a cooperative maritime convergence in the counter proliferation initiatives that envisages for the proactive and voluntary interdiction of maritime shipping suspected of carrying merchandise of weapons of mass destruction. The PSI is a response to the growing challenge posed by the proliferation of Weapons of Mass Destruction (WMD), their delivery systems and related materials worldwide. The PSI builds on efforts by the international community to prevent proliferation of such items, including existing treaties and regimes.

With the exception of Singapore and to an extent Thailand, the other South East Asian states of Malaysia, Indonesia and Philippines consider the PSI as an extra-regional proposal of interdicting shipping on grounds of suspicion. Given the high sensitivities and strong tendencies in South East Asia to protect national sovereignty, the involvement of extra-regional naval forces in the interdiction of shipping in archipelagic waters is viewed as interference in the sovereign rights of the littoral states.

There are strong divergences on issues of nuclear proliferation and perceptions in regard to the interdiction of maritime shipping carrying the WMD merchandise. One of the major reasons of the divergence has been the domestic constituencies and opinion that countries like Indonesia and Malaysia have to contend. The compulsions of the domestic constituencies have resulted in the opposition to the US led initiatives and US unilateralism. On the hand, other Indonesia and Malaysia have called for greater regional cooperation on security with an emphasis on regional initiatives from the region and a strong disdain of outside interference in littoral issues.

The second perception has been that the provisions of the South East Asia Nuclear Weapons Free Zone (SEANWFZ) Treaty prohibit the countries in the region from developing, possessing, manufacturing, acquiring or transporting nuclear weapons or related materials. Philippines, Malaysia has taken the stand that the provisions of the SEANWFZ hold sufficient statutory enforcement to proliferation concern. The main issue has been that the maritime merchandise of WMD does not emanate from South East Asia, but from North Korea that uses the transit routes of the sea passages of the region in this trade.

The North Korean maritime commerce of WMD in the region has prompted acute concerns for Japan and Singapore to join in the cooperative threat engagement measures.[20]

Japan, Singapore, South Korea have been active participants in the PSI exercises in the region that have demonstrated the capabilities of shared intelligence, tracking and monitoring of suspected vessels carrying the merchandise and have evolved interoperable roles in naval–air coordination for such tasks.

Given the strong divergence and opposition to the PSI, the ability to interdict vessels of suspicious cargo cannot be made in the littoral waters of Malaysia, Indonesia and Philippines, the ability of the United States and its extra-regional allies to interdict vessels suspected of transporting WMD cargoes. They would have to rely on the littoral states to take voluntary action and would not be able to engage in intrusive actions.

The resistance to PSI efforts by Malaysia and Indonesia confirms a pattern of political trend of anti-access to extra-regional presence. The regional rationale to this resistance seems to be pitched from international principles of Maritime Law that prohibit interdiction on high seas and the economic angle to say that it would affect trade and maritime shipping in regions.

The bilateral alliances that the US has with Japan, South Korea, Australia and the access arrangements with Singapore and Thailand serves it to engage with such threats in the region.

Alliance Dynamics

The nature and scope of alliance dynamics in the region has an important role in the assessment of the nature and engagement of extra-regional powers in the region.

Four types of alliances that have emerged in the region:

(1) Formal statutory bilateral treaties, such as US–Japan, US–Korea that are in the form of mutual defence treaties that provide for US Forward Presence and dedicated naval and air commitments to the defence of the respective states.

(2) Allied partners that are not within the realm of bilateral and multi-lateral treaties but are regarded as strategic for reasons of geo-strategic, geo-political considerations — the US conferment of non-NATO allied status to Pakistan, Thailand, Philippines for purposes of strategic expediency.

(3) Strategic alliances that has drawn the regional and extra-regional powers that have the convergence of trade and defence technology relations, such as Russia–China relations, China–France relations.

(4) Multilateral collective security alliances like the Five Power Defence Arrangement.

The nature and salience of these treaties and alliances have been premised on the form and substance of these agreements that have been changing with the changing threat perceptions and the international security milieu.

The Five Powers Defence Agreement was formed in 1971 in anticipation of conventional threats and to enhance the defence capabilities of Malaysia and Singapore with coordinated naval–air exercises in the region. It had served to reinforce regional stability in South East Asia with the extra-regional participation of Australia, New Zealand and the UK with Malaysia and Singapore.

In the June 2004 defence ministers meeting, the Five Power Defence Arrangement reviewed its primary mission objectives with focus on the combat of terrorism in the region.[21] Maritime Security and counter terror operations were considered as new and vital missions of the alliance. The FPDA is an enduring alliance that has nurtured cooperative security concerns and has aided in the build-up of cooperative threat engagement strategies in the region. The new consensus on counter terror and maritime security operations has been aimed to build new capacities for joint operations and increased convergence on intelligence and surveillance operations.

The US–Japan, US–Korea alliance dynamics have been in review with the US Global Posture Review and the renewal and restructuring of these bilateral mutual security agreements have been broadened with the following objectives:

(1) Enhance defence capabilities of its allies Japan, South Korea, Australia, Thailand, Singapore through US arms sales and aid in the defence transformation efforts.

(2) Aid in the development of interoperability of US forces with Japan, South Korea, Australia, Singapore, Thailand and Philippines with the objective to nurture coordinated defence operations in the region with a surge of US forces in the region.

(3) Build access and places in these countries that would enable the US marine and air expeditionary forces to be deployed with minimal footprint while optimising its naval and air strike power for littoral dominance in hostile environments in the region.

China and France, China and Russia have forged bilateral strategic relationships that are centric on strategic cooperation and defence trade relationships.

The China–Russia strategic relationship began in July 2001 that has engaged the two powers in defence technology transfer and arms sales. Russia has been China's predominant supplier of military hardware and naval hardware specifically. By 2006, Russian defence technology transfers and arms sales would include 400 Sukhoi fighters, (SU-27; SU-30 MKKs) many upgraded for multi-role missions; unspecified numbers of Russian anti-air and precision ground-attack weapons for aircraft; several hundred Russian S-300 SAMs; 12 Russian KILO submarines, 8 with CLUB long-range anti-ship missiles; 4 Russian SOVREMENNY class missile destroyers; Russian weapons and electronics packages for three new classes of stealthy warships; Russian 1-meter electro-optical and radar satellites.[22]

The French have been China's emergent strategic partner eager to vie for defence contracts. The French have been lobbying hard in the EU to lift the embargo on arms sales, despite the EU's rejection of the French call. France and Germany are keen to lift the embargo for arms sales to China notwithstanding the enhanced threat to Taiwan. France and China have been exercising in the South China Sea in March 2004 that featured offensive helicopter tactics; ship refuelling at sea and simulated search-and-rescue missions.[23] France has also supplied surface to air missiles and anti-aircraft radars to the Chinese Navy.

The dynamics of alliances and coalitions would be dependent on a host of variables that would interact with the prevalent geo-strategic, geo-economic and geo-political milieu derived from the terms of economic aid, technological transfers, military aid and hardware supplies, infrastructure development ventures, leverages of the extra-regional powers over littoral powers and vice-versa, patterns of intervention, posture and deployment of extra-regional forces and basing patterns.

The convergence and divergence of the alliance patterns would be dictated by the dictates of geo-energy profiles and markets that would drive the geo-political and geo-strategic forces in the region.

Evolving Maritime/Naval Doctrines and Regional Implications

The emergence of new maritime doctrines has been a signal event since the end of the Cold war. The strategic milieu, the regional and global maritime developments, the technological templates and the national interests drive policy that has led to the derivations in maritime doctrines. The forward presence and roles of the extra-regional navies have been driven by these considerations. Maritime doctrines have been significant drivers in the force modernisations of the naval forces. The US, Japanese, PLA Navy, Indian navies have been prominent in the enunciation of new maritime doctrines.

The US Navy had enunciated the Sea Power 21 Concept a follow up of the 1994 *Forward from the Sea* doctrine. The Sea Power 21 advocates the role of forward naval presence that builds capabilities based on net-centric effects based operations. It advocates the elements *of Sea Strike, Sea Shield* and *Sea Basing* that would account for the conduct of littoral dominance operations in the event of littoral powers engaged in hostilities against the US.[24] The US envisions a maritime doctrine that is based on expeditionary forces and projection of power from the sea for a complete littoral dominance overwhelming the undersea, air, surface resistance and anti-access strategies.

The US Navy doctrine is perceived to be transformational and premised on the synergies of joint warfare capabilities and platforms that would project power into the littorals with joint forces enabling strategies of access. The US Navy *Sea Power 21* doctrine envisages the development of new capabilities and platforms that would enhance the agility of US intervention, rapid surge into the region, restructured amphibious and expeditionary capabilities, precision strike and reduced foot print on land bases with increased accents on mobile sea bases.

The JMSDF has developed the out of area deployments in the Indian Ocean for the Afghanistan and Iraq operations. The deployments have been the modification of its National Defence Program Outline. The National Defence Planning Outline (NDPO) revised in 1995, was focused to reorient the Japan Self Defence Forces' (JSDF) missions and capabilities to meet the challenges of the post-Cold War security environment.[25] It was notable in stressing the need for closer US–Japan alliance cooperation — under the 1960 Treaty of Mutual Cooperation and Security — for the defence of not only Japan, but also the surrounding East Asia region. The revised NDPO focuses on power projection beyond the Japanese shores to defensive escort operations in interoperable roles with US naval deployments.

The focus on sea-based Ballistic Missile Defences that would be deployed on its Aegis-destroyers deployed as a missile shield against possible North Korean missile intimidation. Japan's focus is on the creation of a "multifunctional flexible force" capable of inter-service joint operations for its immediate defence and for international cooperation overseas. The revised

NDPO calls for the creation of a standby force — exclusively for overseas dispatch — that can deploy two units, each of 1,300 GSDF troops, to two different locations simultaneously. Japan's power-projection is enabled on the basis of its maritime power with a joint forces focus and interoperable with US forces.

The Chinese maritime outlook views the development of its naval doctrine focuses on the capabilities of "offshore active defence strategy". It aims at the evolution of the new "green water active defence strategy". The span of Chinese naval power projection is envisaged as "Green water" was defined reaching from Vladivostok in the north to the Strait of Malacca in the south and to the "first chain of islands" in the east. Plans involve the creation of a green water navy for early in the 21st century. The Chinese define "blue water" as reaching to the "second island chain". The creation of a PLAN blue water navy is a goal to be realised by 2050.[26]

The PLA Navy has been focused on the operational concept that envisages for an extended strategic depth that projecting the PLAN as a strategic force and the spearhead of China's national defence. The formulation envisages the PLA Navy in warfare strategies that would be focused on littoral operations. The offshore active defence strategy intends to assert China's image of regional maritime power with a robust surface action fleet and formidable submarine fleet with air independent propulsion. Its naval capability is primarily meant to protect its flourishing coastal economic regions and defend its maritime interests. It seeks to generate maritime technological development in both economic and military applications through the navy modernisation programme; and it wants to maximise the navy's strategic functions in national defence planning and establish a sea–air–coast–island integrated defence system.

The Indian Maritime Doctrine is an articulation of the strategic missions of the evolving naval order of battle. The doctrine addresses the coercive and benign dimensions of naval operations and diplomacy enunciating its operational tenets of Security, Offensive Action, Flexibility, Surprise, Containment, Defence in Depth and also Maintenance of Morale. The tenets of India's Maritime Power range from Surveillance and Intelligence, Sea Control, Sea Denial to Fleet in Being and "Guerre de Course". It has the vital missions of convoy, Blockade, Submarine/Anti Submarine Campaign, and Amphibious Operations. The Maritime doctrine highlights the attributes of the Indian Navy and its strengths in mobility, versatility, resilience and poise with the evolving missions and roles that are Military, Diplomatic, Constabulary and Benign. The Indian Maritime Doctrine effectively has translated the objectives of its Strategic Defence Review 1998 into the following three functions: Naval Presence; Preventive and precautionary diplomacy and Pre-emptive diplomacy.[27]

The Indian maritime doctrine emphasises the vital need to secure its maritime environment and to secure its Exclusive Economic Zone. It also addresses its geo-strategic imperatives in terms of the competitive build-up of naval forces in the Indian Ocean, the maritime peacekeeping missions, security of its SLOCs with over 90% of its oil requirements flowing from the Persian Gulf–West Asian region and securing of its off shore oil assets and the performance of Humanitarian missions at sea. Indian Maritime Interests are also very wide ranging, largely due to India's unique geographical position. The primary interests, however, are to protect sea-borne trade, safeguarding the EEZ, protection of, harvesting living and non living resources and keeping the SLOCs open and safe. India's maritime interests are closely bound with India's economic security, as 90% of India's trade is sea-borne.

Operationally the Indian Navy is emerging as a "network centric" force with its evolving dedicated satellite links for its surface naval ships, submarines, aircraft, and shore bases. There are follow-up stages in this process that is built to interlink its long range missiles, radars and sensors on the warships through satellite with the objective of decisive strike force into the littoral of the adversary. The net-centric capabilities would envisage the Indian naval battle order to exchange and transfer real time data providing for a digital tactical battle space view of the dispersed fleet formations, aircraft locations and submarine deployments.[28]

India's nuclear navy is emerging with its procurements from Russia of the lease/purchase of two Akula (Bars)-class Type 971 nuclear-powered submarines (SSNs) and armed with the three-stage, 300 km-range Novator 3M-54E1 Klub-S (SS-N-27) cruise missile, for use against surface ships, submarines and shore targets. The Indian Navy's dominant role would be further augmented by the deployment of its indigenous nuclear submarines that would be armed with the Sagarika missiles, complementing the Russian Akula and Amur class submarines in assortment.[29]

Competitive and Cooperative Maritime Strategies in Asia-Pacific

The analysis of the maritime doctrines and the operational capabilities of the extra-regional navies provide the sense of intents and capabilities of the extra-regional navies in the region.

The common denominators in the *Intents-Capabilities* matrices are the following:

(1) Forward Presence and power projection that serves the military, diplomatic, coercive, cooperative, benign and constabulary missions at sea.
(2) Littoral dominance to exert force to neutralise anti-access strategies.
(3) Combination of coercive and benign naval operations to secure oil SLOCs, containment of maritime asymmetric threats.
(4) Extensive surface, submerged and naval-air capabilities for maritime surveillance, reconnaissance and precision strike capabilities.
(5) Net-centric warfare capabilities.
(6) Nuclear deterrence and nuclear compellence during peace and crisis situations.
(7) Explicit and implicit threat assessments in regard to possible primary and secondary threats in the region and competitive naval build-ups in the region.
(8) Preference for sea-based limited theatre missile defence systems could be the possible indices that determines the competitive naval strategies in the IOR South China Sea region.

The patterns of the competitive naval strategies in the region could likely evolve in the following typologies:

(1) The US led naval concert of the UK, Japan, Australia, India, Singapore, South Korea, and Thailand.
(2) The China naval concert in future could have Iran, Pakistan, Bangladesh and Myanmar.
(3) France would be the opportunistic naval partner to the concert that serves its great power ambitions in the region. In most instances, it would aim at an independent role or would bandwagon with China for their quest for a multipolar naval balance in the region.
(4) Sri Lanka, Philippines provide for the vital access points in the respective regions and hence they could tend to maintain equidistant balance between the rival concerts.
(5) Russia would prefer bilateral naval ties with India and would like to have its occasional presence in the Indian Ocean in the form of show the flag diplomacy but would not be able to sustain regular forward basing and presence.

The patterns of competitive naval strategies in the region could have the access and forward basing facilities in the region in the form of carrier task forces, amphibious and expeditionary formation, naval aviation from carriers and attack submarine deployments typical of the US task forces augmented by the UK, Japanese, Australian naval flotillas.

The second pattern could be the deployment of destroyer-submarine squadrons with frigate and fleet auxiliary support that would have naval exercises in the region and would have semi-permanent basing facilities typical of the PLA Navy in the Arabian Sea, Bay of Bengal with access facilities in Pakistan and Myanmar.

The third pattern could be the forward presence and cooperative naval engagement in forward deployments in support of multinational or US-led coalition naval operations with strong defensive orientation provided by the JMSDF, the RAN and the Republic of Korea Navy.

The fourth pattern would be the forward presence and limited deployment with emphasis on joint naval manoeuvres with regional navies on extended deployment would be typical of the Indian Navy that would have joint exercises with China, Singapore, Indonesia, Malaysia, South Korea, Philippines, Japan and Australia. The Indian Navy would also be the dominant navy after the US Navy in the Indian Ocean in view of its naval order of battle and could play decisive operations in future Indian Ocean naval operations.

Patterns of Littoral Dominance

Littoral operations and littoral dominance would be the accents of the extra-regional naval powers in the region. The scope of forward presence in the 21st century would be centred on the projection of power into the hinterland and the deployment of sea-launched cruise missiles with conventional and nuclear payloads for strike. The maritime doctrines and concept of operations of the US, UK, France, China and India are specific in regard to littoral control operations.

Four factors have led to the quest for littoral control in the respective theatres of operations in the North Arabian Sea, the Indian Ocean, the Bay of Bengal; the South China Sea and in the Taiwan straits.

(1) Surface platforms of the littoral powers evident in the stealth platforms like frigates, missile corvettes armed with supersonic anti-ship missiles and anti-ship cruise missiles has dented the sea control capabilities of the

great powers in the region, enhancing the area-denial effectiveness of the defending powers.

(2) Short range ballistic missiles with nuclear, biological and chemical payloads have increased the retaliatory potential of the littoral powers denting the power projection capabilities of the extra-regional power's surface naval forces that could hypothetically be targeted by land-based missiles.

(3) Submarines in the littorals offer the best-submerged defence of the littoral powers. The enhanced capabilities of the diesel-electric submarines armed with high speed homing torpedoes with fire and forget capabilities provides the effective stealth strike options. In combination with the supersonic cruise missiles, the endurance of the new air independent propulsion submarines offers the potent strike force.

(4) Shore-based naval aircraft armed with anti-ship and air-to-surface attack missiles provide for the emerging platforms for strong littoral defence capabilities that complicate the access and basing operations and the ability to sustain littoral control operations.

Sea basing and joint forces enabling technologies and capabilities are the responses to the increasing frictions of the anti-access strategies that are strengthening the littoral defence operations.

Nuclear Forces and Missile Defences at Sea

Nuclear weaponisation at sea would be the evolving order in the 21st century even as sea-based missile defences would emerge to offer possible limited defence against the ballistic missile forces in the region. Sea-based nuclear weapons on board nuclear submarines counter offers, endurance, survivability and credibility of the assured retaliatory capabilities of the nuclear powers. The substantial deployments of the US SSBN (submerged ship ballistic nuclear) Trident D-5 force, the UK Trident; the French SSBN boats; the PLA Navy Type 94 deployments have been for the maintenance of nuclear deterrence in forward deployments. The advantages of nuclear forward presence are as follows:

(1) Sea-based deterrence provides the optimal policy and strategic solution for the regional powers given its feasibility. Sea-based deterrence would give credence to assured strike capability that could be based on either cruise missiles or ballistic missiles launched from submarines with the advantages of dispersal and stealth.

(2) The saturation of the ground–air defence environment with anti-missile defences would result in newer means of dispersal of land-based nuclear assets of manned attack aircraft and land based missiles to newer locales with the high probability of being tracked and destroyed in pre-emptive strikes. The option of sea-based deterrence as credible and the assured retaliatory capability enhances the deterrence stability of the contending powers. The optimal dispersal of the platforms and payloads would enable the maintenance of a credible deterrence in terms of survivability.

(3) Sea-based deterrence would reinforce the delayed yet assured retaliation in the face of an omni-directional threat. It would provide for sufficient options to retaliate from different locations in the seamless medium of the oceans so as to avoid detection and maintain stealth and precision.

(4) Sea-based deterrence enhances the ability of a viable targeting strategy by and avoids the possibility of a "defanging strike" against a defending power. The operational impact of sea-based theatre missile defences (TMD) deployed to thwart regional ballistic missiles with WMD/nuclear payloads would constitute the shield along with the deployed Submarine Launched Ballistic Missiles (SLBMs). The TMD deployments would be on board the *Arleigh Burke* class destroyers and *AEGIS* cruisers. The emerging US, Japanese and even South Korean AEGIS cruisers with naval theatre ballistic missiles is gaining credence. The obvious implication of substantial sea-based TMD deployments in the Indian Ocean region, North East Asian region in the Sea of Japan would be to target and neutralise the regional nuclear arsenals with ballistic missile inventories in the MRBM/IRBM and extended IRBM ranges of the littoral missile powers. The sea-based Navy Theatre Wide systems would be primarily oriented to intercept missiles as early as possible in flight before countermeasures are dispersed and allow time for secondary attempts.

Sea-based Missile Defence systems provide for mobility and flexibility, and shipboard systems enable a new dimension of power projection ability premised on an offence–defence technology template. Sea-based missile defence systems offer the advantage of mobility in that it makes the defensive missile system less vulnerable to a pre-emptive strike and allows for adaptation on a flexible scale. It also allows for offshore basing without having the deployment in land territory that is vulnerable to pre-emptive ballistic missile strikes and the political consequences of deploying missile defences in allied territory.

Cooperative Naval Strategies in IOR and the South China Sea

The Indian Ocean Region and the Asia-Pacific would emerge as the hub of economic development and a maritime security complex that would have to be based on cooperative maritime strategies to deter and balance the aggressive force build up in the region. The complexities of extra-regional rivalries, aggressive littoral dominance strategies, nuclear weapons and ballistic missiles compounded with persistent archipelagic disputes offer the triggers to crisis escalation. The maritime realm offers scope for cooperation even though competition remains at stake. Cooperative security requires a transnational approach and requires states to build the relevant capacities to transcend primary sources of contention and evolve a functionalist perspective in cooperation for mutual benefit.

Maritime Cooperative security is a functionalist process that has prospects for success. The maritime transnational space facilitates the common goals of cooperation, search and rescue, and disaster management. The accents of cooperative security in the Indian Ocean–South China context lies in the bilateral and multilateral aegis that has scope to be optimised well in the maritime realm.

The transnational concerns and issues of energy, SLOCs, exploitation of the resources in the EEZ, combating and containing of transnational threats of piracy, maritime-based terrorism, interdiction and containment of the spread of WMD technologies can provide the basis for cooperation. In the naval realm, basis for cooperation include Search and Rescue (SAR), Prevention of Incidents in High Sea (INCSEA), combat of narcotics and interdiction, and the maritime initiatives in counter proliferation. There are two issues that attract serious attention in the realm of Cooperative Maritime Security, which is the interdiction of WMD technologies in maritime transit and the combat of maritime-low intensity conflicts.

Joint Naval Exercises

The emerging maritime cooperative trend has been the joint naval exercises that have been institutionalised on bilateral and multilateral aegis. Joint naval exercises provide the cooperative naval engagements in interoperability and exercise of capabilities that provides the basis for future contingency operations. Joint naval exercises in the region have enhanced cooperative engagements.

Joint Patrols of the Straits

A contentious yet vital aspect of cooperative maritime engagement has been the patrolling of narrow sea gates like the Straits of Hormuz and the Straits of Malacca. Contestations have emerged in terms of sovereignty controls and archipelagic disputes persist. The trilateral MALSINDO patrols of the Straits of Malacca are an emergent trend in joint patrols in the region. Joint patrols have also been in the form of engagement of regional coastguards that have more salience in counter-terror and counter-piracy operations than navies. Naval deployments are viewed more in terms of offensive power projection and coast guards in defensive formations.

Maritime Intelligence Sharing

Transnational threats and the imperatives to maintain maritime stability have endeavoured the countries of the region towards institutionalising mechanisms for intelligence collection and sharing on a real-time basis.

Maritime Capacity Building

Regional maritime initiatives have gained significance with emphasis on (a) better situational awareness fostered through sensors networks, coordinated patrols with overlaps; (b) effective interagency coordination and the dedicated agencies that has effective lateral linkages for coordinated interdiction and containment of asymmetric challenges at sea; (c) joint coast guard exercises.

Conclusion

The maritime strategic trends in the Asia-Pacific portray a chequered picture of intense competitive rivalries with strands of cooperative maritime partnerships that have emerged in recent years. The competitive–cooperative maritime strategies are the dichotomous outcome of the evolving balance of power in the region that features a rising China and the emergence of Japan as a "normal" power. The region's adaptation to a Rising China is considered to be a crucial challenge even as China expands its military prowess especially its naval prowess commensurate to its economic capabilities and strength. The balancing role of India's navy in the Indian Ocean in response to the emergent Chinese naval posture would be crucial even as the Asia-Pacific contends with the expanding PLAN fleets from the second island to the third island chain capabilities and for a evolving blue-water capability that would radiate beyond the Straits of Malacca into the Indian Ocean in the west.

The US continues as the dominant hegemonic power that provides the crucial stabilisation influence in the region that has several potential territorial contestations and asymmetric challenges.

The maritime balance of power in the region would be driven significantly by the process of naval transformation derived from defence transformation.

Naval transformation would be determined by the emergent strategic milieu that conditions the balance of power in the region. The accents would be in the nature of a multipolar structure that would evolve with economic growth and strategic capabilities that would be in the form of competitive–cooperative relationships. The United States would emerge as the offshore balancer that would provide the stabilising influence in the region.

Naval transformation would be determined by the evolving maritime doctrines that provide the basis for seamless integration of operational roles and emergent technology and maritime capabilities of the powers. Maritime/naval doctrines would determine the process of transformation and the strategic milieu of the powers in the region.

Naval transformation would be crucially determined by technology that would be in the accents of *jointness. Jointness* of the armed forces would be the future paradigm even as the conduct of operations would be tailored to suit the requirements of the architecture of the armed forces. The navies would be the enablers in the process of jointness. Jointness would be enhanced in effectiveness by the net-centric capabilities of the naval forces. Net-centric capabilities would be the ultimate platforms that would integrate the "sensors" and "shooters".

In summation, the maritime strategic trends in the Asia-Pacific portray strong evidence towards a technology centric naval transformation process that is increasingly in the competitive–cooperative dichotomy of interests that would under grid the evolving balance of power in the region.

Notes

1. Paul Dibb, "Towards an Asian Balance of Power", *Adelphi Paper* 295, 1995.
2. Paul J. Bracken, *Fire in the East: The Rise of Asian Military Power and the Second Nuclear Age* (New York: Harper Collins, 1999).
3. Geoffrey Till, *Seapower: A Guide for the Twenty-First Century* (London: Frank Cass, 2004).

4. United States Government, Department of Defense, "A Framework for Strategic Thinking: Building Top Level Capabilities", *FOUO Working Papers*, 19 August 2004.

5. Admiral Vern Clark, "Sea Power 21: Projecting Decisive Joint Capabilities", *Proceedings*, October 2002.

6. United Kingdom, Ministry of Defence, *Delivering Security in a Changing World* (*Defence White Paper*) (London: UK MoD, 2003).

7. "Five-nation regional defence pact to expand to counter terrorist threat", *Agence France Presse*, Singapore, 7 June 2004.

8. "Navy: France", *Jane's Sentinel Security Assessment — Western Europe*, 15 November 2004. Available at: http://www.jni.janes.com

9. See the detailed analysis by Christopher W. Hughes, "Japan's Re-emergence as a 'Normal' Military Power", *Adelphi Paper 368–9*, 2004.

10. Ibid.

11. "Navy Russian Federation", *Jane's Sentinel Security Assessment — Russia and the CIS*, 3 June 2003. Available at: http://www.jni.janes.com

12. "Navy Australia", *Jane's Sentinel Security Assessment — Oceania*, 2 February 2004. Available at: http://www.jni.janes.com

13. Ji Guoxing, "SLOC Security in the Asia-Pacific", *Asia-Pacific Center for Security Studies Occasional Paper*, Available at: http://www.apcss.org/Publications/Ocasional%20Papers/OPSloc.htm

14. Stanley B. Weeks, "Sea Lines of Communication Security and Access", in Sam Bateman & Stephen Bates (eds), *Shipping and Regional Security*, Canberra Papers on Strategy and Defence No. 129 (Canberra: Strategic and Defence Studies Centre, Australian National University, 1998).

15. Marco Rosini, "The Navigational Rights of Nuclear Ships", *Leiden Journal of International Law*, Vol. 15, No. 1, March 2002, pp. 251–265.

16. See the analysis of Rohan K. Gunaratna (2001), "Transnational Threats in the Post-Cold War Era", *Jane's Intelligence Review*, 1 January 2001. Available at: http://www.jir.janes.com. Also see Rohan K. Gunaratna, "The Asymmetric Threat from Maritime terrorism", *Jane's Navy International*, October 2001, p. 28. Available at: http://www.jni.janes.com

17. John Garvar, "The Future of the Sino-Pakistani Entente 'Cordiale'", in Michael R. Chambers (ed), *South Asia in 2020: Future Strategic Balances and Alliances* (Carlisle: Strategic Studies Institute, U.S. Army War College, November 2002).

18. Toshiki Sakurai, "The Straits of Malacca Challenges Ahead: Japan's Perspective", *Paper presented at the International Conference on the Straits of Malacca*, Kuala Lumpur, October 2004.

19. Tsutomu Toichi, "Energy Security in Asia and Japanese Policy", *Asia-Pacific Review*, Vol. 10, No. 1, 2003, pp. 44–51.

20. Tamara Renee Shie, "The Nexus between Counterterrorism, Counterproliferation and Maritime Security in South East Asia", *Issues & Insights*, Pacific Forum, CSIS, Vol. 4, No. 4, July 2004.

21. "Five-nation regional defence pact to expand to counter terrorist threat", *Agence France Presse*, Singapore, 7 June 2004.

22. Richard D. Fisher Jr., "Foreign Military Acquisitions and PLA Modernization", Testimony of Richard D. Fisher, Jr., Center for Security Policy, Before the U.S.–China Economic and Security Review Commission, Washington D.C., 6 February 2004.

23. "France and China: Cozying Up for Mutual Gain", *STRATFOR*, 11 October 2004. Available at: http://www.stratfor.com

24. Several analyses that highlight the various issues of the US Navy transformation have been made. See Ronald O'Rourke, "Transform and roll out: the USN's approach to change", *Jane's Navy International*, 4 March 2004; Scott C. Truver, "Sea Basing; more than the sum of its parts?", *Jane's Navy International*, 5 February 2004; Andrew Koch, "US Navy outlines vision for Sea Power 21 Concept", *Jane's Defence Weekly*, 11 December 2002; "Navy: United States", *Jane's Sentinel Security Assessment — North America*, 11 November 2004. Available at: http://www.janes.com

25. "Japan's New Defence Posture: Towards Power Projection", *Strategic Comments*, Vol. 10, No. 8, October 2004.

26. "Navy: China", *Jane's Sentinel Security Assessment — China and Northeast Asia*, 27 May 2004. Available at: http://www.jass.janes.com

27. Integrated Headquarters, Indian Navy, Ministry of Defence, Indian Navy, *Indian Maritime Doctrine*, INBR 8 (New Delhi: Indian Ministry of Defence, 2004).

28. Vijay Sakhuja, Naval Diplomacy: Indian Initiatives, *Bharat Rakshak Monitor*, Volume 6, Issue 1, July–August 2003.

29. Vijay Sakhuja, "Change But Continuity: The Indian Navy Marches Ahead", IPCS Article 1457, 10 August 2004. Available at: http://www.ipcs.org

III. *National Maritime Doctrines and Capabilities*

Chapter 4

China's Naval Strategy and Transformation

You Ji

Twenty five years have passed since the Peoples' Liberation Army Navy (PLAN) put forward its blue water maritime strategy.[1] It is a three-phase 50 year grand plan. According to PLA researchers' projection the navy should have by 2000 acquired sea-control power within its coastal waters and have achieved a kind of sea-denial capability within the first island chain in the West Pacific in 2010–2020.[2] Now it may be a good time to review the progress that the PLAN has made in translating an ambitious plan into practice. We all know that maritime strategy is a rather abstract concept if it is not discussed in association with operational models and order of battle. The review is straight-forward as we evaluate what the PLAN has done to achieve its objective of each phase. The Chinese may have failed to attain the goal of the first phase on time, as the overall growth of naval capabilities remained flat between 1990 and 1999. Since 2000 the progress of PLAN transformation has been visibly accelerated, and there is no doubt that it has increased its operational readiness. The number of new major surface combatants and submarines that has entered service between 2000 and 2004 has more than doubled that of the entire decade of the 1990s. After a delay of half a decade the goal of the first phase of development has been met. The PLAN has now entered the fast track of modernisation and if the current trend of growth continues, China can attain its Second and Third Phase objectives, that is, that of exercising maritime influence beyond the second island chain by the year 2020, and becoming a naval power capable of making its presence felt globally by 2050.

The Evolution of China's Maritime Strategy

Does a blue-water strategy matter? As far as the PLAN is concerned, for some time the answer was *no* because there is a big gap between its blue water rhetoric and its real capabilities to practice it. In the late 1990s there were doubts among western analysts how meaningful China's blue water strategy really was.[3] The navy's structure and weaponry prohibited it to take any blue-water combat missions: the number of larger platforms was too small and proper logistical and surveillance systems were seriously lacking. It lacked crucial capabilities, such as area air-defence and ASW systems, for its very survival in deep ocean missions. However, if we see PLAN development as a continuum, that is, if we do not base our evaluation on comparing its current inventory with the final goal of its blue water strategy, we will see that a good strategic guidance does matter in a navy's long term transformation.

The Revolutionary Change in Naval Doctrine

The PLAN celebrated its 55th birthday in April 2005. In the last five decades it has experienced a gradual revolution in strategic thinking. 1979 was an important year for the navy, as Deng Xiaoping approved the navy's request to extend its activities from coastal waters to adjacent seas (the Yellow, the East and the South China Seas).[4] After Liu Huaqing became naval chief (1982–1988) he systematically enriched the various ocean-going ideas proposed by PLAN war planners and, according to his perceived external threat and combat needs, elevated them into a grand strategy. On 13 February 1987, he and his commissar Li Yaowen co-signed a doctrine entitled *Guanyu mingque haijun zhanlüe de wenti* (On the question of establishing the naval strategy) and formally submitted the doctrine to the Central Military Commission for approval. This document has been the guiding doctrine for China's naval development to this day.[5] This strategy has been the country's first ocean-going strategy. It extended the navy's combat mission from coastal defence to blue water power projection with corresponding alteration in operational objectives, weapons research and development (R&D) and battle tactics. Under Liu the navy changed its total subordinate position vis-à-vis the Army and was officially recognised as a strategic force assuming independent campaign tasks.[6] More fundamentally, a sense of ocean (*haiyang yishi*) was advocated to inspire the Chinese to look beyond their land territories, the sense that has been buried by China's continental mentality since the end of Zheng Ho's voyage.[7]

Some naval analysts have regarded Admiral Liu as China's Gorshkov.[8] This can be substantiated given the fact that both commanders regarded high-technology equipment as essential for the conduct of sea battles. Furthermore, Liu's strategy clearly reflected Gorshkov's influence on his military thinking. Liu had studied in the Voroshilov Naval Academy in the second half of the 1950s. This was at a time when the Soviet Union endeavoured to become a global naval power under Gorshkov's theoretical guidance. The Soviet effort to expand maritime defence from coastal waters to deep oceans could not have failed to make an impact on Liu, as was demonstrated by his recommendation to his colleagues that they should all read Gorshkov's book, *Sea Power of the State*, carefully.[9] Indeed, when the PLAN took similar steps under Liu, the Soviet example became relevant to China's naval build-up. More specifically, Gorshkov's influence on Liu can be seen from the following doctrinal changes.

Defence in Great Depth

Under Gorshkov's leadership, the Soviet navy built a layered defence line radiating from coastal waters to deep oceans. The initial goal was to cover Moscow against US Polaris missiles which had a range of 1,500 nautical miles (nm). This defence line was then extended to the Norwegian Seas where the Soviet nuclear submarines posed a strategic deterrent against the US. In the 1970s as the Soviet offensive fleets became operational, the defence line was further broadened. The purpose of this layered defence was clear from the very beginning — it would make it harder for an attacking force the closer it approached the Soviet coast.[10] Gorshkov also reoriented the Soviet naval focus from coastal protection to threatening the enemy's heartland, especially with the submarine-based nuclear retaliatory capabilities.[11]

In the 1980s, Admiral Liu made a similar doctrinal change for the PLAN. He expanded its defence line from *jinan* (in-shore) to *jinhai* (off-shore), setting up also a kind of layered defence of the Chinese style. The Chinese term "*jinhai*" has generated differing interpretations by researchers. Some researchers use the word "green-water", located between the "brown waters" (the coastal waters) and "blue waters" (beyond the first islands chain).[12] Others use the term "blue-water", indicating the geographic area beyond the East China Sea and South China Sea.[13] The different interpretation may be attributed to the phased objective of the naval strategy: green water for the first phase and blue water after that. The distance of *jinhai* (off-shore) can be flexible, while the concept of *jinan* (in-shore) covers only a fixed scope.

At the core of the concept of *jinan* are three of China's internal straits: the Bohai, Taiwan and Qiongzhou. Among these straits, the Bohai Channel would be defended at all cost since it is the last line of defence for Beijing and Tianjing. The Qiongzhou Channel is critical for its role of protecting China's second largest island and strategic heartland of Southwest China. The Taiwan Strait is the choke point for several key international pathways. Within this radius the main purpose of the coastal defence (the first layer) is to defeat the enemy's amphibious operations. It also shields Chinese coastal land up to 200 km inland from the sea where 41% of Chinese population and 50% cities are located, 70% GDP is yielded, 84% FDI is attracted and 90% export is made.[14]

The second layer of defence is 200 nm from the Chinese coastal defence, reaching to vast expenses of waters in the West Pacific. As specified by Admiral Zhang Xusen, former naval Chief of Staff, the combat zone of this layer covers all of China's sea territories and the islands scattered in the East China Seas. Although part of the South China Sea, embracing the Nansha (Spratly Islands) and Xisha (Parecel Islands) is beyond this line, given China's claim on their sovereignty; it has to be defended with all efforts.[15] Geographically, this area stretches from the Chinese waters adjacent to Vladivostok in the north to the Straits of Malacca in the south, and continues to the first island chain of the West Pacific in the east. Obviously, this incorporates a vast area of the Pacific including Japan, the Liuqiu (Ryukyu) Islands and the Philippines. Given the long distances from the Chinese mainland, the concept is certainly a blue water one and constitutes a leap in Chinese naval strategic thinking.[16]

The importance of this defence line is to break any maritime blockade against the PLAN, which was the West's practical policy against China during the Cold War era.[17] Moreover, in a posture of defence this distance of 200 nm provides critical defence depth for China to protect its key economic centres. In a posture of offence, the area covers key international Sea Line of Communications (SLOCs), such as the Spratly Islands and the Malacca Strait where 70% of Japan's oil tankers go through. Therefore, it is crucial for the PLAN to achieve a degree of freedom of movement in this geographic area if it is to become a credible navy.[18]

The Notion of a Regional Naval Power

In addition to the enlarged defence depth, the meaning of China's maritime strategy evolves over time in accordance to the changes of its perceived national interests. The Central Military Commission (CMC) has recently enriched the contents of the naval strategy by injecting a new geo-political and economic element into it. It should cover "all maritime areas that have any important bearing on China's national security and fall within the effective reach of the PLAN".[19] Clearly the naval policy has become more closely linked to China's overall national security strategy and is no longer just an operational defence plan. This has offered a new angle to analyse China's maritime strategy. Thus *Jinhai* defined by green water is seen as inadequate to plan its naval missions.

From the Chinese point of view, the US is the only navy with a global naval strategy. All other major powers have only a regional navy, adopting a *Jinhai* (defined by *blue water*) maritime strategy. However, the contradiction is that their maritime interests far exceed the geographic range of their normal blue water naval activities. To resolve the contradiction, the Chinese emphasise the strategic employment of naval power beyond the region. This is reflected by their effort to build combat platforms that can deliver strikes beyond the geographical limits of the region. For instance, the British navy is a regional navy but is capable of launching strategic campaigns in Latin America. This category of the regional naval power offers a roadmap for China to follow in its future transformation.[20]

What this means is that the PLAN as a regional navy should not only have a certain prescribed geographical scope of activities but should possess power projection capabilities capable of dealing with situations that depart from this geographical scope, as the country becomes a global economic power. Specifically, the combat zone for the Chinese navy as a regional power will move beyond the second island chain, to cover the bulk of the areas in the Northwest Pacific, when capabilities permit.[21] This will represent the third layer of maritime defence for China. To the PLAN, being a regional navy means the possession of an ocean going fleet with access and the ability to manoeuvre within a vast expanse of water. Only when the PLAN have acquired such a capability can it claim to be a true blue-water navy.[22] Logically the notion of China as a regional naval power unifies the time, the PLAN's second phase of development to 2020; the space, a geographical coverage of 1,000 nm requirement of the geographic scope; and the capabilities required, both in hardware and software, for China. The three components of time, space and capability are useful gauges to evaluate the expansion of the PLAN.

The notion of a regional naval power testifies to the nature of China's maritime strategy. It is not global, not expansionist and not pre-emptive in accordance to Deng's prescription of building a defensive navy.[23] Yet in terms of strategic missions, combat ranges and force structure/strength, it will increasingly differ from that of an off-shore navy. For instance, it stimulates the construction of naval presence and facilities away from home (*zhanchang jianshe*) to include underwater surveillance networks in deep oceans, and ambush sites beyond the off-shore waters. It is interesting to note that the adjustment of the timeframe work for realising the goal of the three-phase naval development, as mentioned at the beginning of the paper has some strategic significance. When China's blue-water strategy was first raised in the mid-1980s, the task of securing the first and second layer of defence was planned to be attained at 2000 and 2010 respectively. However, the slow naval modernisation process in the 1980s and 1990s meant that the PLAN had to postpone the attaining the goals of each phase by a decade.[24] What this means is that if a war in Taiwan can be avoided and no major territorial disputes occur, the PLAN will basically adopt a defensive defence posture vis-à-vis major powers before 2020. When it becomes a regional navy capable of operations beyond the first island chain, this defensive posture may become difficult to sustain. Its eastward movement may overlap Japan's westward movement, as Japan also seeks to have a 1,000 nm span of maritime control, which may make some kind of encounters inevitable.

Clearly the extended radius for the PLAN as a regional navy implies a forward defence posture and the range of 1,000 nm is viewed as necessary by the PLAN. Conditioned by China's coastal geographic make-up, the bulk of PLAN forces have to be stationed in first-line ports, whose defence depth is very shallow. As these ports are easy to seal off, the navy must deploy some of its combat units *elsewhere* to broaden the defence depth in order to give the top command more options.[25] This dictates that the PLAN create as large a space for fleet manoeuvrability as possible. As Admiral Zhang reasoned, forward defence is essential to the navy's survival, not to mention the fulfilment of its strategic tasks. Only when forward defence is achieved can the navy have a chance to win sea battles.[26] Indeed, this conclusion was drawn from the painful lesson from the Sino-Japanese War in 1894. The Qing Navy was ordered by Li Hongzhang, the founder of the navy, to passively defend the ports and narrows of the coast as a way of survival. As a result, the fleet was blocked in the ports and used only as gun battery. Its demise was only natural. To the PLAN the historical debate of whether to defend the coastal passes or engage the enemy in open seas has current significance. Going blue water is the only way to avoid the same fate of the Qing Navy, and determined engagement in the ocean is probably the only way to win the sea battle.[27]

In order to become a regional navy the PLAN has taken an even longer view on its modernisation. This starts from redressing some legacies of the previous doctrine. During the Mao era the navy had built few forward bases because of its obsession with defensive missions. Forward airports and navigation facilities were especially scant. Preparations for action in deep seas, such as information about marine meteorology, magnetic field intensity and nautical charts of likely combat zones were largely neglected.[28] These have since become priority objectives for the navy since the 1990s. More recently, the navy has sought potential sites for facilities in areas its ships cannot yet reach. These footholds may be critical for its future movements and even deployment. The observation stations that the PLA built in Indian Ocean may help to achieve this objective.[29] China's investment in the Pacific islands may also pave the way for naval port calls in the future when needed. The Chinese have realised that besides the possession of ocean going ships, a regional navy also needs access to ports.

The Missing Links between Strategy and Capability

Admiral Liu had raised the PLAN's hope to achieve the status of a major sea power. But this has also exposed the PLAN's inadequacies. Although the navy has made steady progress in modernisation over the last two decades, it is still in a transitional phase. 20 years have elapsed but the PLA's blue water dream remains unfulfilled. Only in the last five years have the navy's capabilities improved significantly. This contrasts sharply with the success of the Soviet navy under Gorshkov. Within 15 years from the time he took the helm of the Soviet navy, it had fully transitioned to blue water status.

The gap between the strategic ambition and real capability is the first missing link in the PLAN's transformation. Until recently the expansion of the PLAN's combat power has been dismal. In the 1990s, only four new destroyers entered service; 112, 113, 165 and 167. The acquisition of the two *Sovremenny* destroyers has not increased the navy's overall strength either. Many plans for hardware upgrading remain uncompleted. For example, the aircraft carrier project was aborted and the design of arsenal cruisers (for launching a great number of long-range missiles) has been shelved.[30] The production of the new class conventional submarines has been slow in coming. The replacement of 091 nuclear attack submarines has also been delayed over and over. With only one crippled nuclear-powered strategic missile submarine in service China's nuclear triad capability exists only in theory.

The PLAN's light force structure is the second missing link that restricts its qualitative change. The large number of small naval crafts and obsolete major combatants absorb manpower and resources. But to scrap them would dramatically reduce operational readiness, as the navy cannot quickly replace them with sufficient numbers of large and modern platforms. As the navy may be dragged into an unexpected war given the tense situation in the Taiwan Strait, it is forced to keep many of these "junks". The requirement to conduct current operations prevents the PLAN from increasing the numbers of advanced large warships in its inventory. A vicious circle seems to have set in with priority given to the conduct of current operations over force modernisation requirements.[31]

The acquisition of technology is another major problem. Theoretically speaking, China, which has the world's third largest ship-building industry, should be capable of constructing more major combatants than it is currently doing. But it realises that numbers alone do not count and that real combat power lies in advanced information technology which integrates the systems together and that future operations will be centred on information warfare.[32] The biggest challenge for the PLAN in the IT age is not how to add more hardware platforms but how to network them in a seamless manner. The PLAN suffers from a lack of good IT assets and C4ISR systems. Without these crucial technologies, warships are little better than junks.[33] As a result, the PLAN has been reluctant to merely boost its numbers of unsophisticated large warships. The current weapons equipment policy highlights the development of a software technological capability as a way to transform the PLA into the era of network-centric warfare. However, this will be a gradual process. In the meantime the gap between strategic requirement and real capability will remain for a long time to come.

Foreign procurement serves only as a quick fix and large quantities of foreign acquisitions are out of the question for a number of reasons. First, the PLA would not want its modernisation to be influenced by any foreign power. Secondly, the economic cost is prohibitive. Thirdly, the difficulty of integrating the various foreign components into a complete and effective weapon system is tremendous. In short, the PLA cannot count on overseas purchases to improve its overall capabilities.[34] One painful lesson is China purchasing rights to assemble 200 S-27SK (J-11 in Chinese), an early version of the plane. It is reported that China has stopped producing the aircraft half way through due to its backward avionics. It cannot launch R-77 anti-aircraft (AA) missiles and KH-31 anti-ship missiles, and has no beyond-visual-range (BVR) capability. The S-27K is inferior to the S27-MK. There are a lot of pitfalls in buying Russian arms.

Due to these inadequacies, the PLAN's maritime strategy is blue-water in name only. Its operational principles are still largely based on the doctrine of coastal water defence and on an inshore force structure. The training programmes are those of a coastal navy: almost no combat exercises at the fleet level have been staged so far. This may be the reason why the navy does not want to talk about sea control and sea denial capabilities and talks mainly about strategies. Some of the missing links are elaborated in the subsequent paragraphs.

The fundamental problem for the PLAN is that it lacks major capabilities to cope with a fast moving, long ranging and information-dominated war.[35] What follows is an incomplete list of missing capabilities that impedes the process of PLAN modernisation.

Weak Anti-Submarine Warfare (ASW) Capabilities

For a long time the Chinese believed that submarine warfare would not fit its naval operations in the shallow brown waters which do not provide favourable conditions for the enemy submarines. As a result, the PLAN did not invest much to enhance its anti-submarines capabilities. There are only two destroyers (112 & 113) that are equipped with the towed body sonar systems in the PLAN. Each time there is a major ASW exercise elsewhere they would be dispatched. As McVadon has pointed out, the PLAN is still using rudimentary direct communications between ASW aircraft and surface ships. There is no interface to harmonise the disparate components. Furthermore, the PLAN lacks effective ASW platforms, such as aircraft, naval vessels, and land-based or sea-based anti-submarine missiles.[36]

Weak Air-Defence Systems

The PLAN restricts its ocean-going activities mainly due to the lack of effective air cover in a combat situation. For a long time only a small number of major surface combatants had surface–air missiles that are capable of point air defence. This confines its fleets within the radius of the land-based air force which does not go far beyond the first island chain. The ship-born area air-defence missile systems have only recently been installed in a few destroyers, on a trial basis. As result the out-going fleets as a whole cannot handle saturated air and missile attacks.

Weak Logistical Supply Capabilities

The PLAN is short of ocean-going transports, a problem which it regards as a handicap in its naval modernisation.[37] Without sufficient supply ships, the PLAN cannot establish battle groups composed of large and medium sized combatants. At high speed, a destroyer consumes 30 tonnes of fuel a day and needs to be re-supplied daily.[38] If a battle group comprises five or six such ships and the navy has three or more such groups, the current number of such supply ships would have to be several times more but there is no sign that the PLAN would have this required number any time soon.

The New Era of PLAN Transformation

The pattern of flat growth was finally broken in 1999 when the top Chinese leadership adopted a far-reaching decision to accelerate preparation for "military struggle", following the US bombing of China's Belgrade Embassy and the worsening situation in the Taiwan Strait.[39] In the first decade of the new century the PLAN has visibly accelerated its modernisation drive. New, more sophisticated and diversified major combatants have entered the service in large numbers. For instance, compared with the only four destroyers entering service in the 1990s, four rolled out in 2003/2004 alone. There is also a great leap in technological quality for the new ships. Such a phenomenal growth in both numbers of ships and their technological sophistication is unprecedented in PLAN history. Analysts still debate whether such a visible change represents a normal trial/production cycle or a new era of sharp rise. Whatever the answer to the debate, the on-going leap forward of Chinese naval power marks the end of the flat growth in the 1990s, although the decade was one of strength and technological accumulation for the PLA to kick off a big jump in naval capability.

There are several reasons why this is the case. Firstly, China's rapid economic expansion can now provide greater material and technological support for a speedier naval modernisation. Secondly, the leadership's conclusion that China's future war will be fought in its maritime regions has given a tremendous boost for naval development, in terms of budget and foreign procurement.[40] Thirdly, for about 20 years the PLA's R&D guiding principle has been "more research and trial, less series production and equipment".[41] There has been a period of technological foundation-building before any major effort of scaled production. Since the late 1990s, partially due to the changed situation in Taiwan and partially due to the perceived technological maturity, the equipment policy has been adjusted to allow more hardware and software acquisition. Fourthly, after 20 years of study the PLAN has obtained a better understanding of the blue-water strategy as a way to overcome the legacies of the past. More concretely, this means a better understanding of what force structure and weaponry the PLAN should have to qualify for a true blue-water navy. Finally the PLAN has proved to be a good student in learning the best naval ideas of the western powers. It has embraced the IT-RMA concepts and rightly identified that network-centric warfare as the type of war it has to fight in the future.[42] In the minds of naval commanders the blue-water strategy merely based on major platforms is an obsolete idea of the industrial age. Now the PLAN has placed equal emphasis on both the hardware and the systems integration in building its modern fleets. The current IT driven PLA transformation has injected powerful impetus to the process of naval modernisation.[43]

The New Capabilities Added to the PLAN Since 2000

The PLA Navy's capability build-up has been quite impressive in the last five years. Qualitative progress has been achieved simultaneously with improved quantity. Major surface combatants developed since 2000 include the following:

- *Two Sovremenny Destroyers (136 Hanzhou and 137 Fuzhou) (2000).* For the first time the PLAN acquired some area air-defence capabilities. The ship's super-sonic anti-ship missiles, the Sunburns, (SS-N-22), are believed to have been developed by the Soviets to strike US aircraft carriers. The ability to conduct area air-defence missions and strike carriers is the primary reason why the PLA purchased the destroyers.

- *Two 052B (Luhu class) Destroyer (168 Guangzhou and 169 Wuhan) (2003).* With the displacement of 8,000 tonnes and stealth features, this series will be the PLAN's mainstay sea-control destroyers assuming blue-water missions (though as the low-end in the high/low mix in a fleet formation). Probably four more ships will be built in the next few years. They are also specialised combatants, with anti-ship and ant-submarine warfare (ASW) as their major missions with each of them having some area air defence capability.

- *Two 052C (Luyang class) Destroyers (170 Lanzhou and 171 unknown) (2004).* These are the first PLAN ships equipped with the Chinese *Aegis* systems. Also they are installed with China's first indigenous cool-launch vertical launch systems (VLS), capable of intercepting targets over 100 km away. With 48 launchers (HHQ-9 long-range SAM) they provide the PLAN blue water fleets with a shield against saturated attacks. They are at the high-end in the high/low mix in an ocean-going fleet.

- *051C Destroyer (115) (December 2004).* This is also a large ship with displacement of about 7,000 tonnes. The details of the weapons systems are not clear yet. Some sources revealed that the ship will be equipped with Russia's RIF-M (SA-N-6) VLS for fleet air defence. It is more likely that the ship will follow its identical predecessor 167 to become the command ship for the North Sea Fleet. As such it will be installed with the advanced C4ISR systems, (i.e., the LINK systems) aiming at capabilities of network warfare. The difference is that 167 is an embodiment of foreign technologies, while the bulk of the systems integration equipment of 115 is said to be developed by the Chinese.
- *054 Frigate 525 & 526 (Maanshan class) (2003).* These are latest frigates of the PLAN, which have strong stealth features. Its design has broken away from China's Soviet tradition and is more similar to the European style. With an enlarged displacement (over 4,000 tonnes) as compared with the PLAN's existing frigates, it is able to keep pace with larger platforms (destroyers or cruisers) in a deep ocean combat mission. The ships are either equipped with HHQ-7 long range anti-ship missiles or HQ-16 mid-range anti-air missiles. There is space reserved for replacing the current systems with VLS.
- *053H3 524, 564, 565 & 566 (Jiangwei 3 Class).* With similar weapons systems in 054 FFG-2. However, because the ships' displacement is smaller (2,800 tonnes), they are not suitable for sustainable deep ocean operations. However their good stealth feature distinguishes them from the early classes of frigates in the PLAN.

From the list we see that in the first half of this decade seven destroyers and six frigates have been committed, although many of them have not become truly operational. This compares sharply with the entire 1990s. Also in this decade the PLAN has acquired other major combatants that have given it tremendous blue-water capabilities. These include two 093 nuclear attack submarines, of which one is operational, one 094 strategic nuclear missile submarine, which is in the middle of the trial period), one new class conventional submarine (*Yuan* class), and no less than four 039 (Song class) submarines. By the end of 2005 there should be four more Kilo (636) submarines to join the PLAN. These acquisitions may have fully changed the image of the PLAN submarine fleet, previously made up of noisy, ill-equipped and accident ridden vessels of

Soviet origins. The *Yuan* class with air independent propulsion (AIP) technology is an advanced attack platform. Together with a rising number of Kilo
submarines in the PLA inventory, the PLAN submarine fleet may pose a real
threat to any major naval power in the region.[44]

Evaluation of the Speedy Modernisation Since 2000

The Chinese naval build-up has entered a fast track of expansion in the last
five years. And the pattern of growth looks sustainable: intensive research and
development of many years has culminated in a season of harvest. Domestic progress is propelled by foreign acquisitions, despite the continued arms
embargo against China by the West. Most importantly, China's powerful economy will provide unprecedented financial support to speed up naval modernisation. In this decade about an additional US$10 billion will be spent for this
purpose.[45] It seems then that the PLAN transformation is aimed at plugging
the gaps that will enable it to progress from a brown-water to a blue-water
naval capability.

Technological Breakthroughs

Certainly the PLAN is still a second rate navy as compared to the top naval
powers, including Japan. The accomplishment of the last five years is very
impressive but does not go beyond the characterisation of "pockets of excellence" because the overall force structure is still out-of-date. The gaps between
a blue-water strategy and capabilities remain. On the other hand, the PLAN
now has at its disposal capable ships and weapons that will allow it to extend
its combat range. To some extent it may have already possessed the capability
to survive a relatively large scale campaign beyond its traditional battlefield of
the Bohai Sea. Depending on the nature of operations it may already be able
to carry out blue-water missions around the first islands chain.[46]

These capabilities are provided by China's new major combatants. The Chinese *Aegis* and Russian Sovremenny destroyers give the PLAN fleets enhanced
fatal punches. Its new submarines, indigenously developed or purchased from
the Russians (Kilo and *Yuan*) are quiet and equipped with long range anti-
ship missiles, anti-submarine missiles and the new generation torpedoes. The
destroyers and submarines will be the major forces used to fulfil the sea control tasks in China's coastal maritime regions, as well as the sea denial missions
within or beyond the first island chain in the West Pacific. They are especially
effective when used to conduct a blockade against Taiwan's ocean liners.[47]

To be more concrete, the PLAN's new assets are the product of an impressive number of technological breakthroughs by China in the last two decades. These breakthroughs will constitute a solid foundation for the naval transformation in the years ahead. With this technological advance the Chinese naval leap forward will not be a one-off show. Examining some major breakthroughs made by the Chinese may give analysts an impression that in major military R&D areas China may have finally caught up with current Western technology. This is contrary to the long-held views that the Chinese is generations behind the West in the adoption of technology in the navy. The following are worth mentioning in brief.

- The ship-born track-while-scan phased array radar systems in 170 and 171 are certainly one of the surprises. Very few countries can develop such advanced surface-to-air systems independently.
- The Chinese-made cool launch VLS of long range anti-aircraft missiles in a number of Chinese latest destroyers.
- AIP technology that is installed in the *Yuan* class submarines.
- Sound absorbing tiles used by the 039, 091, 093 and 094 submarines.
- Length/width ratio of 8.5 achieved by 054 frigate (8 is western standard).
- Module design for ship-building and installation of weapons systems.
- Initial success in producing CODOG that will allow more large ships to be built.
- The battle-field management system based on the LINK technology, for instance in 167.
- 730 Close-in weapon system (CIWS) in 170 & 171.

There are also other new military technologies that are closely related to naval transformation. For instance, China's military space technologies have become increasingly mature, and can help provide precision positioning and real time C4ISR information for PLAN combatants. The PLA Air Force's *Yujing* 2000 AWACs can help the navy to identify, coordinate and attack unfriendly targets.

Trend Assessment

We can see that most of the above-mentioned technological breakthroughs are meant for blue-water missions, with an emphasis on fleet air defence and anti-submarine warfare capabilities. The new major surface and submarine assets can substantially improve the combat effectiveness of the PLAN fleets at large distances from home waters. The following trends and issues arising from the PLAN's modernisation can be identified for examination.

Larger Platforms

Almost all the new warships introduced in the last five years are large platforms. The displacement for new destroyers is over 7,000 tonnes and for new frigates, 4,000 tonnes. The PLAN understands the close relationship between blue-water capabilities and the need of large platforms as carrier of various sophisticated weapons systems. To the PLAN its largest ship, 170, is still not large enough to place a number of badly needed weapons systems after the phased array system is installed. For instance, there is no room for medium range air-defence systems on board, leaving the ship dangerously unprotected in-between the long range and close-in protection. It is quite vulnerable if it sails alone. According to the Chinese media, the navy has already tried to acquire cruisers of over 10,000 tonnes that are capable of area air defence, comprehensive ASW and land attacks with long range cruise missiles of 3,000 km.[48] If the widely rumoured news are proven to be correct, the Chinese navy is targeting Russia's Slava class cruisers to fulfil its plan of possessing a number of capital warships.

If the current effort to build large platforms continues, we may see no fewer than eight more major surface warships that will be built by 2010. These may include one more 051C destroyer, two more Sovremenny destroyers, and one or two more 170 type of Chinese *Aegis*. In addition a number of new frigates will enter service. When the major surface combatants that were completed between 2000 and 2004 become truly operational in the next few years, the PLAN will have at least a dozen modern surface combatants and will take on a new look.

Restructuring

These warships will fundamentally change the light nature of the PLAN structure. In fact the restructuring has gone on for some time now. For instance, a large number of missile boats have been removed from service (from about 100 in 1984 to only half of the number expected in 2008). Type 033 submarines will be out of service by the end of 2010, thus cutting the number of Chinese submarines to about 60. However, the new inventory will consist of about 14 nuclear submarines (including five Han 091 in reserve), 16 Kilos, 17,039s and five *Yuans*. The technological sophistication will be an improvement over those developed at the beginning of the decade. The number of the major surface combatants will remain steady but all frigates with displacement of below 1,900 tonnes, Jiannan and Chengdu classes will be decommissioned.

The number of Type 051 destroyers will be slight smaller. All of them that entered the service in the 1970s and 1980s will undergo major substantial retrofitting with an emphasis on installing information warfare measures. By 2010, the overall quality of Chinese destroyer and frigate fleets will be dramatically improved. On the other hand, the slow reduction of obsolete major combatants shows that it is difficult for the navy to proceed with the restructuring. As it will not have a sufficient number of capital ships in the foreseeable future, the navy tends to keep many old vessels in service. Numbers are important not only to make up for quality, but also to avoid trading off crucial strength in strategic directions.[49]

The restructuring has clear objectives. The priority is to form ocean-going battle groups, which are the foundation of China's maritime strategy. These task fleets are essentially created for sea control and sea denial missions. In due time they will be able to initiate independent campaigns in the West Pacific. They would be supported by long-range aircraft and nuclear submarines. When the conditions are ripe, they would be incorporated into aircraft carrier (or large cruiser) battle groups.[50] The PLAN's blueprint was drawn at about the same time when its maritime strategy was changed from that of brown-water defence to blue-water defence. However, the lack of large and specialised platforms like area anti-air warfare ships continues to delay the plan. Now with larger combatants continuously commissioned to the service, the navy is finally able to plan several fast response units capable of launching campaign level battles around the first islands chain. This is the landmark indicator to evaluate whether the PLAN is up to the task demanded by its blue-water strategy.[51]

As a weak navy the concept of fleet in being is very important for the PLAN. This means that the navy would form a number of flotillas with a variety of specialised combatants to assume tactical campaign missions far away from home. Dividing the PLAN into relatively small formations allows for a degree of survivability and ensures that it will not be eliminated in a few sea battles at the beginning of the war, in any confrontation with the US, the sole global superpower. The formation is organised flexibly as ships can be transferred across the PLAN's three fleets.[52] When the PLA has more capable and larger platforms it will plan strategic campaigns in the West Pacific. It is suggested that its current three fleets should then be restructured into two major fleets, the Pacific Fleet and the South China Sea Fleet, for the decisive sea battles in deep oceans. Each of them will command a few small specialised, highly mobile and functionally integrated formations. At the same time a coastal navy will be created for the defence of home waters.[53]

More concretely, the PLAN may follow the Japanese 8.8 flotilla structure, which is with eight helicopters on board eight destroyers, in forming four small groups in the near future. China has purchased four Sovremennys and constructed four 054 FFGs. These are added with 052B and 052Cs, two each, and possibly an equal number of 051Cs. An initial picture of four small groups becomes clearer: the core of each will be composed of one area air-defence destroyer, one sea-control destroyer, one ASW destroyer and one new class frigate. They would be supported by a number of old surface ships and submarines. If China can successfully develop four cruisers of the Slava type, it will further enhance the combat capability of the flotillas. In dealing with different combat scenarios the ships in the four groups can be "borrowed" at short notice, which means that there is no urgent need for the four Slavas. In the long term, these ships will constitute the base for an enlarged ocean-going fleet, as the Chinese acquire the cruisers or, potentially aircraft carriers in the second phase of naval development that will span from 2010 to 2020.

Comprehensive Transformation or Still Trial and Error?

Is this rapid naval expansion the end of the era of "concentrated research, minimum equipment", briefly mentioned earlier? The answer to the question is of strategic importance. A yes answer will quickly add blue-water power to the navy, while the no answer will continue to produce "pockets of excellence". One important fact is that since the early 1990s each class of the destroyers that China has developed contains only one or two ships, a typical phenomenon of trial production rather than series production. This paper argues that the PLAN is still tossing with the idea of more research, less production. Despite all the technological breakthroughs, many of the platforms are obsolete in the West. The major powers can move to a new level of technological development, rendering the new ships in the PLAN junks again in a short period of time. This means that technologically the PLAN has not come to the stage of comprehensive transformation.

The first reason for the argument is that any comprehensive transformation has to be built upon a domestic technological foundation. This is far from the case in China. One key indicator is that China continues to import major weapons systems.[54] Secondly, the relatively fast improvement of basic research and development in laboratory cannot be matched by engineering and manufacturing maturity. Thirdly, although the Navy has greatly raised its fire power, its C4ISR systems and combat management systems are still far behind the world standard, partly due to China's weak space and IT industries.

The impact of past emphasis on mechanisation in force modernisation is heavily felt, as the pace of informatisation is greatly hampered.[55] Fourthly, China's financial situation does not allow the navy to expand too quickly. Although the navy is the beneficiary of China's priority allocation, the current budgetary levels is hardly enough to sustain the abnormal pace of introduction of new ships in the first half of the decade. Finally a deep transformation begins with a scale of series production of certain advanced warships. There is no sign of this in the introduction of China's new classes of ships.

For instance, by design 052Cs are capable area air-defence assets. However, 170 and 171 look more like experimental ships. The phased array system is too large and heavy, allowing only 48 VLS units on board (in comparison to 90 of Japan's Kongo class with a similar displacement). Due to the limited space left, the ship cannot install defence systems against targets below 500 m such as skimming aircraft and missiles. Major defects exist in other new ships. Poor propelling power and rudimentary ASW capabilities may cripple the new FFGs when they join the larger platforms for a campaign level battle in the open-ocean. Even if the Chinese have some technologies of the same generation of the West, these are at the lowest end. Any series production of the new class will take a number of years. When the process finishes, the West may well have reached a new technological level. Therefore, the safest way for the PLAN to catch up is to continue to explore the technological frontier. Series production is implemented only when some mature designs can be formulated that is comparable with what the major powers possess. This so-called generation-leap strategy is at the core of China's 2002 national defence strategy aimed at informatising the PLA in the next 30 years.[56] If peace can hold on for a few more decades, then China will not be in a hurry to level the gap with the West. Yet such a leap strategy is untested in the history of military modernisation and is a risky attempt. Mechanisation, in terms of ship-building, may be further delayed due to shrinking resources and comprehensive informatisation is beyond reach due to China's thin technological foundation. The double whammy of mechanisation and informatisation may mean falling between two stools.[57]

Conclusion

The PLA Navy has not experienced any major sea battle. Not being battle-tested, it is difficult for us to assess the capability of the PLAN. Some analysts regard the warships of the PLAN as little more than junks but others believe that the Chinese navy is an increasingly formidable fighting force and a key regional player.[58] Liu Huaqing's contribution was in setting the right direction of development for the PLAN, through the formulation of a blue-water strategy as the blueprint for PLAN development. Under this strategy, the navy has broadened its defence depth, built large platforms, and lifted its profile in the armed forces. This strategy is long term with the open ended goal of advancing the navy to a blue water status. But for the time being, this grand goal remains elusive.

Practically, Chinese naval operations are not grounded in blue-water intentions, but in more realistic combat models. If the concepts of sea control and sea denial are used to explain these models, we see that the PLAN has tried to exercise sea control within its coastal waters. Given its current capabilities, the combat zone for control is limited. Specifically, the combat zones are centred on the country's three internal channels, the Bohai, Taiwan, and Qiongzhou Straits. In the outer waters, radiating gradually to the first island chain, the navy is trying to project a sea denial capability meant to inflict heavy losses on the enemy if it tries to blockade China and helps Taiwan's *de jure* independence. This posture of defensive-offence suits the navy's regional role and indicates that it sees sea control and sea denial more in tactical than in strategic terms. When the PLAN reaches its second stage of development, it will look at the second island chain. The two chains are geographically and strategically important for China in its effort to break a naval blockade and to secure a safe passage for their shipping to the world.

Right now there is still a missing link between the PLAN's strategic ambition and its actual operational capability. As the PLA believes that a war with Taiwan is not entirely avoidable, it has invested heavily to modernise its navy, which will bear the first brunt of a cross-Strait conflict. The pace of naval modernisation has been visibly accelerated since 2000. Driven by breakthroughs in key technologies and with much more financial allocation, new and more sophisticated combatants have entered service in unprecedented numbers. Especially with ship-born area air-defence systems, the PLAN has gained more confidence in assuming ocean-going combat missions. The better submarines, nuclear or conventional, have also generated a higher level of deterrence against an external military threat. As this naval modernisation picks up momentum, more and more Chinese naval vessels will be seen operating in-between the two island chains in the Western Pacific in the years ahead.

There is still a long way to go before the PLAN can be considered a true blue-water power. There are numerous difficulties to overcome: its lopsided force structure, the slow growth of its ocean-going fleets, its lack of progress in building strategic nuclear submarines, its obsolete air force, and the low quality of its personnel. But the navy has started on the right path: it has got its strategic vision right. Its leaders have absorbed the best thinking of the world and have worked out a set of realistic long term plans. If China's phenomenal economic growth continues, it will have the material resources to finance its military modernisation, and it will only be a matter of time before the navy achieves its ambition of becoming a true blue-water power.

Notes

1. I first delved into the subject of China's blue-water strategy in 1989 when I sensed that its navy was aiming for a big increase in its sea power. Looking back, the Chinese effort is more illusionary than real. See You Ji, "In Search of Blue Water Power: The PLA Navy's Maritime Strategy in the 1990s", *The Pacific Review*, No. 2, 1991, pp. 137–149. See also Tai Ming Cheung, "Growth of Chinese Naval Power", *Strategic Papers*, Institute of Southeast Asian Studies, 1991.

2. Bai Keming, "Zhongguo Haijun De Weilai Fazhan (The future development of the PLA Navy)", *Jianchuan Zhishi*, No. 12, 1988, pp. 2–4. The PLAN has identified two island chains that figure prominently in the seaward defence of China. The first chain begins in Japan, passes through the Liuqu Islands to Taiwan, and then to the Philippines. The second island chain stretches from Japan's Ogasawa-gunto Islands, through to the Io-retto Islands, and from there to the Mariana Islands. It is 200–300 nm eastward to the first.

3. Views expressed by a participant of the specialist workshop *China's Navy in the 21st Century*, Center for Naval Analysis Corporation, Washington DC, June 27–29, 2001.

4. On 4 March 1979, Deng summoned naval commanders to his residence where he endorsed, on the spot, the navy's request that China's maritime defence should extend to the *jinhai* (off-shore waters) rather than *jinan*, (in-shore waters). *Dangdai Zhongguo Haijun (Contemporary Chinese Navy)* (Beijing: Zhongguo shehui kexuechubanshe, 1987), p. 709. See also Tang Fuquan, Du Zuoyi and Zhan Xiaowu, "Deng Xiaoping Xinshiqi Haiyang Zhanlie Sixiang Yanjiu (The study of Deng's strategic maritime ideas)", *China Military Science*, No. 2, 1997, p. 76.

5. Admiral Liu Huaqing, *Liu Huaqing Huiyilu (The Memoirs of Liu Huqing)*, (Beijing: PLA Publishing House, 2004).

6. It is interesting to note that in China's *Defence White Paper* of 2004, the Navy is named before the Army and Air Force, which is seldom seen in PLA's history. Obviously this follows the international practice.

7. Zhang Shiping, *Zhongguo Haiquan (The Chinese Sea Power)* (Beijing: The People's Daily Press, 1998). Zheng Ho, an official in China's Ming Dynasty, commanded the world's largest naval force (with over 150 ships and 20,000 sailors) at the time.

In 1405 he started the blue-water missions to reach Africa and some analysts have even said that he discovered North America.

8. Branley Hahn, "Hai Fang (Maritime defence)", *US Naval Institute Proceedings*, March 1986, p. 119. Under Liu's instruction, Gorshkov's book was translated into Chinese by Haiyang Chubanshe in 1985 and was presented to all senior naval commanders.

9. Zhao Wei, "Admiral Liu Huaqing — The New Vice-Chairman of the CMC", *Mingpao Monthly*, No. l, 1990, p. 39.

10. John Downing, "China's Maritime Strategy", *Jane's Intelligence Review*, April 1996, p. 187.

11. For a detailed analysis, see Derek da Cunha, *Soviet Naval Power in the Pacific* (Boulder: Lynne Rienner, 1990). For the Chinese analysis, see Yan Youqiang, Zhang Dexin and Lei Huajian, "Haishang zhanyi de fazhan qishi jiqi duiwojun zhanyi de yingxiang (The development of maritime campaign theory and its impact on the PLAN's campaigns)" in the Editor Group (ed.), *Selected Papers of the PLA's First Conference on the Campaign Theory: Tongxiang Shengli De Tansuo (Exploring the Ways to Victory)* (Beijing: PLA Publishing House, 1987), p. 993.

12. Zhang Shiping, p. 5. However, the official Chinese translation of Liu's strategy is still "coastal defensive strategy". The word "coastal" here is somewhat puzzling. The term may have been used to defuse any international repercussions that may result from adopting a more aggressive term. Also see, Chieh-cheng Huang, "The Chinese Navy's Offshore Active Defence Strategy: Conceptualisation and Implication", *Naval War College Review*, Vol. XLVII, No. 3, Summer 1994, pp. 16–19. To this author, the green-water scope is only a transitional one leading to something else later.

13. The PLAN (ed.), *Zhongguo Renmin Jiefangjun Junguan Shouce: Haijun Fence (The naval part of the manual book for PLA officers)* (Qingdao: Qindaochubanshe, 1991), p. 345.

14. Remarks by Senior Colonel Jin Yinan of the PLA National Defense University on the *Program of Across-the-Strait*, CCTV, 31 January 2005.

15. Huang Caihong, "Zhongguo Haijun De Fazhan Zhahanlie (The PLA Navy's development strategy)", *Jianchuan Zhishi*, No. 4, 1989, pp. 2–3.

16. You Ji, "A Test Case for China's Defence and Foreign Policy", *Contemporary Southeast Asia*, Vol. 16, No. 4, March 1995.

17. Lu Rucun *et al.* (eds.), *Dangdai Zhongguo Haijun (The Contemporary Chinese Navy)* (Beijing: Zhongguo Shehui Kexue Chubanshe, 1987), p. 47.

18. Senior Colonel Liu Yijian, *Zhihaiquan Yu Haijun Zhanlie (The Command of Sea and the Strategic Employment of Naval Forces)* (Beijing: The PLA National Defence University Press, 2004), p. 233. Commodore Liu teaches at the PLAN Command College and is one of the first naval officers to have obtained a doctoral degree in military science in the 1990s.

19. "The Chinese Aegis destroyers marks the subtle changes of the PLAN's off-shore water strategy", 20 January 2005. Available at: http://www.wforum.com/specials/articles/07/12989.html
20. Liu Yijian, *Zhihaiquan*, p. 230.
21. Ibid., p. 232.
22. Admiral Zhang Xusen, "Shilun Weilai Haishang Zhanyi De Zhidao Sixiang (On the guiding principle of our campaign tactics in future wars)" in Editor Group (eds.), *Selected Papers of the PLA's First Conference on the Campaign Theory: Tongxiang Shengli De tansuo (Exploring the Ways Towards Victory)* (Beijing: the PLA Publishing House, 1987), p. 1000.
23. *Deng Xiaoping on Military Affairs* (Beijing: the PLA Academy of Military Science, 1992).
24. Liu Yijian, "Zhongguo Weilai De Haijun Janshe Yu Zhanlie (China's future naval build-up and strategy)", *Zhanlie yu Guanli*, No. 5, 1999, p. 96.
25. Chen Fangyou, *Haijun Zhanyixue Jiaocheng (The Textbook for Naval Campaign Theory)* (Beijing, PLA National Defence University Press, 1991), p. 66.
26. Zhang Xusen, p. 979.
27. Jiang Ming, *Longqi Paoyang De Jiandui (The Fleet Under the Dragon Flag)*, (Beijing: Sanlian Publishing House, 2002), p. 362.
28. Ibid., p. 980.
29. See for instance, Tarique Niazi, "Gwadar: China's Naval Outposts in the Indian Ocean", *China Brief: a Journal of News and Analysis* (The Jamestown Foundation), 15 February 2005, Vol. V, Issue 4; Ashton William, "Chinese Bases in Burma: Fact or Fiction", *Jane's Intelligence Review*, October 1997, pp. 84–88. According to DoD sources, the PLAN is planning a series of outposts along its oil transportation lines from the Middle East. *International Herald Tribune*, 31 January 2005.
30. Liu Huaqing, *Liu Huaqing Huiyilu.*
31. Chen Fangyou and Li Shuyu, *Haijun Zhanyixue Jiaocheng (The Textbook for Naval Campaign Theory)* (Beijing: The PLA National Defence University Press, 1991), p. 51.
32. Wu Renhe, *Xinxihua Zhanzheng Lun (On Information Warfare)* (Beijing: The PLA Academy of Military Science Press, 2004), Chapter 1.
33. Eric McVadon, "Systems Integration in China's People's Liberation Army", in James Mulvenon and Richard Yang (eds.), *The People's Liberation Army in the Information Age* (Santa Monica: RAND, 1999), pp. 217–256.
34. See You Ji, *The Armed Forces of China* (Sydney, London and New York: Allen & Unwin and I.B. Tauris, 1999), Chapter 3.
35. Wang Ziqiang, "Xinshiqi Haijun Jianshe De Liangge Wenti Chutan (The two major questions concerning the navy's buildup in the new era)", in PLA NDU (ed.), *Jundui Xiandaihua Jianshe De Sikao (Ideas for the Development of a Modernised Military)* (Beijing: PLA NDU Press, 1988), p. 384.

36. McVadon, p. 226.
37. Wu Qisheng, "Nuli Tansuo Haijun Houqing Xiandaihua Jianshe de Luzi (Strive to modernise naval logistics systems)", *Journal of the PLA National Defence University*, No. 8, 2000, p. 73.
38. Chen Fangyou and Li Shuyu, p. 285.
39. General Qian Guoliang (Commander, Shenyang Area Military Command), "Quanmian Luoshi 'Silinbu Jianshe Gangyao', Gaobiaozhun Zhuahao Silingbu Jiguan Jianshe (Comprehensively implement the guideline of headquarters construction, and do a good job in headquarters construction)", *Journal of the PLA National Defence University*, No. 6, 2000, p. 4.
40. Yu Shouguo, "Jiaqian Zhanliexin Kongjun Jianshe De Jidian Sikao" (Some thoughts on the enhanced effort to build a strategic air force), *The Journal of PLA National Defence University*, No. 1, 2004, p. 21.
41. General Zhen Wenhan, "Guanyu Changbeijun Jianshe Wenti (On building standing armed forces)", in PLA Academy of Military Science (ed.), *Xinshiqi Changbeijun Jianshe Yanjiu (Study on Standing Armed Forces in the New Era)* (Beijing: PLA Academy of Military Science, 1990), pp. 1–5. See also You Ji, *The Armed Forces of China* (Sydney, London & New York: Allen & Unwin and I.B. Tauris, 1999), Chapter 3.
42. Li Jie, *GaoJishu Yu Xiandai Haijun (Hi-tech and Contemporary Navy)* (Beijing: PLA Academy of Military Science Press, 1994). Lu Xin, "Xinxi Jishu De Fazhan Dui Lianhe Zhanyi Liliang De Yingxiang (The impact of IT on services in joint operations)", *Journal of the PLA National Defence University*, No. 8, 2004, p. 32.
43. For the PLA's new IT centred transformation, see You Ji, "Learning and Catching Up: China's RMA Initiative", in Emily Goldman and Thomas Mahnken (eds.), *The Information Revolution in Military Affairs in Asia* (New York: Palgrave Macmillan, 2004), pp. 97–124.
44. For submarine operations, see Lyle Goldstein and William Murray, "Undersea Dragons: China's Maturing Submarine Force", *International Security*, Vol. 28, No. 4, Spring 2004, pp. 161–196.
45. Rear Admiral Eric McVadon's article to *Washington Post*. Available at: http://www.wforum.com/wmf/. <Accessed on 21 February 2005>.
46. Rear Admiral Eric McVadon's keynote speech to the workshop *US Defence Transformation: Implications for Security in the Asia-Pacific Region*, Asia-Pacific Centre for Security Studies, Honolulu, 2 December 2004. This is also the view of a number of participants at the conference *Escalation Control of Taiwan Crisis*, RAND/CAPS/Carnegie Foundation, Taipei, 20–23 October, 2004.
47. Lyle Goldstein & William Murray, "Undersea Dragon", pp. 161–196.
48. *The Programme Following Military Affairs*, Phoenix TV, 19 December 2004.
49. You Ji, "A Blue Water Navy, Does it Matter?", in David Goodman and Gerry Segal (eds.), *China Rising: Interdependence and Nationalism*, (London: Routledge, 1997), p. 81.

50. Chen Fangyou and Li Shuyu, p. 164; Hu Guangzheng, "20 Shiji Jundui Tizhi Bianzhi De Fazhan Jiqi Qishi (The development and lessons of force structure and establishment in the 20th century)", *Zhongguo junshi kexue*, No. 1, 1997, p. 124.

51. Su Yingrong, "Haijun Zhanyi Ying Guanche 'Xiaojiqun Jidong Zouzhan' De Zhidao Sixiang (The guiding principle of small task force and mobile tactics in projecting naval campaigns)", *Journal of the PLA National Defence University*, No. 3, 2004, p. 31.

52. At the moment the structure of the three fleets is quite odd. For instance, all the best ASW ships are deployed in the North Sea Fleet, all the best sea-control ships (Sovremenny) in the East Sea Fleet, and the 170 and other new air-defence destroyers in the South Sea Fleet. The advantage of this organization is easy maintenance and logistical supply during the time of peace but the need of specialisation would force the PLAN to move the ships around for routine across-fleets training of integrated warfare.

53. Liu Yijian, p. 236.

54. Senior Colonel Zhang Tianping, *Zhanlie Xinxizhan Yanjiu (Study of Strategic Information Warfare)* (Beijing: the PLA National Defence University Press, 2001), p. 253.

55. Senior Colonel Sheng Weiguang, *Xinxi Junshi Cankao (Reference of the Military Information Systems)* (Beijing: Xinhua chubanshe, 2003).

56. Li Zhiping, "Laogu Shuli Kexue Fazhanguan Tuijin Budui Xiandaihua Jianshe Kuayieshi Fazhan (Establishing the principle of scientific development and promoting generation leap for the PLA modernisation)", *Journal of PLA National Defence University*, No. 8, 2004, p. 52.

57. You Ji, "A Bird Eye View of China's New National Defence Strategy", *East Asian Institute Background Brief No. 226*, Singapore.

58. For the latter view, see Lee, Ngok, *China's Defence Modernization and Military Leadership* (Canberra: Australian National University Press, 1989), p. 68. See also Duk-Ki Kim, *Naval Strategy in Northeast Asia: Geo-strategic Goals, Politics and Prospects*, (London: Frank Cass, 2000), p. 132.

Chapter 5

Indian Navy: Keeping Pace with Emerging Challenges

Vijay Sakhuja

Introduction

After independence in 1947, the Royal Indian Navy was divided into two different entities, the Indian navy and the Pakistan navy. The Indian navy continued to be commanded by British Royal Navy officers due to the absence of experienced senior Indian naval officers. As the ruling elite in India was conscious of the fact that the absence of sea power had led to the colonisation of India, it was generally agreed that a strong navy was essential for India.

The Indian navy of the 1950s was perhaps the most powerful in Asia, given the defeat of the Japanese navy during the World War II, its near total disarmed status, and that the Chinese navy was still fighting the US and the nationalist navy in Taiwan. Despite this, Indian naval growth did not progress as projected at the time of independence as continental threats dominated the minds of the government and ruling establishments in India as evidenced by the subsequent wars with China and Pakistan in the 1960s and 1970s over boundary disputes and perennial tension between New Delhi and Islamabad.

Today, however, the Indian navy is the largest in South Asia and the third largest in the Asia Pacific region after the People's Liberation Army Navy (PLAN) and the Japanese Maritime Self Defence Force. The Indian navy has grown in numbers and the quality of weapons and sensors has also improved. The Indian navy has also conducted advanced exercises with several advanced navies involving multiple platforms. The chapter examines the geostrategic imperatives that are shaping the growth of the Indian navy and highlights the Indian navy's strategy and force structure as well as its roles and missions.

Geostrategic Imperatives in the Indian Ocean

Today, the Indian Ocean is the most dynamic region in strategic and economic terms. Maritime developments are integral to the regional economic and security environment. For many countries, economic vitality is dependent on relatively long and vulnerable sea lines of communication (SLOC). The Indian Ocean waterways therefore have strategic significance for both merchant and naval shipping. Coastal and offshore resources provide a principal means of livelihood for many countries in the region. Thus, security is intertwined with maritime affairs.

With the end of the Cold War and the disintegration of the Soviet Union, the United States remains the only superpower in the world. Though being both a Pacific and an Atlantic power, it has not turned its attention away from Indian Ocean. Interestingly, whatever is the future strength of its presence and commitment in the Atlantic and the Pacific Oceans; it remains deeply involved in the Indian Ocean region.

The current US military presence is conspicuous in the entire swath of the Indian Ocean: from Iraq in the Persian Gulf to the Horn of Africa, and South Asia to Southeast Asia. The US is also combating Al-Qaeda and other terrorist groups linked with it in the Arabian Sea and Malacca Strait. Besides, it remains concerned about safeguarding its long-term energy and security interests. In short, it continues to play a dominant role from the Red Sea to the South China Sea. The United States also has military alliances, treaties and bilateral cooperation mechanisms with several countries in the region.

France has consistently emphasised its independent role as an Indian Ocean power. Its strategy is shaped by its own perception of an independent "Great Power" based on its economic and security concerns that include protection of its island territories in the Indian Ocean. The French navy has a near continuous presence in the Indian Ocean. Paris has consistently rejected the idea that it is an extra regional power since its security interests lay in the island territory in the Indian Ocean. This strategic thought is further reinforced by the fact that French naval vessels have taken an active part in the US led "Global War on Terrorism", or GWOT for short.

As far as China is concerned, it has long understood the strategic importance of the Indian Ocean. The Indian Ocean figured in the strategic thinking of ancient mariners in China who sailed in these waters first for trade and then suzerainty. Chinese maritime planners and practitioners are convinced that the Indian Ocean dominates the commercial and economic lifelines of the Asia-Pacific region. China has long been seeking an outlet into the Indian Ocean to safeguard its oil supply routes from the Persian Gulf and the markets of the region. It is also well aware of the importance of choke points in maritime strategy. Towards that end, it has consolidated itself in Pakistan[1] and South East Asia and has encircled the Malacca Strait by establishing a strategic staging/listening post to control the western approaches of the Malacca Strait.

In recent years, Japan's military has increasingly begun to bridge the gap between being a self-defence force and a military power. By participating in the US led war on terrorism in Afghanistan, Japan is prepared to be involved in coalition operations as far as 3,000 nm from the homeland even though its area of interest is officially stated to be 1,000 nm around Japan. Distant and joint naval operations once unthinkable are now accepted as part of national defence. The changing role clearly reflects the creeping assertiveness of the Japanese navy and a desire to shed the symbolic pacifism attached.

Since independence, India been actively engaged in building closer relations with countries across the globe. The Indian navy has participated in international fleet reviews, offered humanitarian assistance, carried out disaster relief activities, search and rescue, anti piracy patrols and joint exercises with several navies aimed at building confidence and trust. Currently, India is an active member of several international and regional arrangements for maritime cooperation. New Delhi is, however, concerned about the future role of extra regional powers in the Indian Ocean and their impact on stability and security of the region, but it sees itself as an active participant in maintaining order at sea, challenging forces inimical to growth of maritime enterprise and economic prosperity.

Understanding Indian Naval Strategy

According to an Indian navy's official briefing, the navy is required to "provide maritime security in all directions — the classical doctrine of '*tous azimuth*' — and during hostilities, it should have the capacity to take the battle into the adversary's zone. The navy's foremost task is to provide deterrence from a position of strength and the carrier task force must be able to execute sea control in a zone that extends up to 1,500,000 square kilometres around it at any time".[2]

It has also been argued that the Indian navy's strategy is based on its ability to exercise control of sea areas in waters around it.[3] These sea areas have been termed as: (a) Zone of Positive Control (ZPC), (b) Zone of Medium Control (ZMC), and (c) Zone of Soft Control (ZSC).[4] These zones are based on the Indian navy's ability to engage a given enemy before it can endanger or damage national assets ranging from national sovereignty to resources at sea. In simple geographic terms, these zones encompass large sea areas from the coast to the deep seas covering the entire Indian Ocean.

In the ZPC, the navy should have the ability to execute sea denial using its sea-based assets and shore-based aircraft. The coast guard units must also be included in tactical plans. In the second zone, the ZMC, stretching 500 km from shore to 1,000 km into the high seas, the Indian navy must have the capacity as also capability to exercise sea denial. In the ZMC, the Indian navy should be able to engage. The forces that need to be deployed should include submarines, long-range maritime aircraft and shore based strike aircraft. Operations in this zone should be supported by intelligence, over the horizon targeting and surveillance. In the outer zone, the ZSC, nuclear submarines, aircraft carrier supported by oil tankers and long-range maritime patrol aircraft should be deployed.

The Andaman & Nicobar and Lakshadweep group of islands fall in the ZSC. This requires the Indian navy to have the range and endurance for extended deployment and interdict enemy forces approaching the island groups. The islands will then act as unsinkable carriers and serve as forward bases to host combat aircraft, shore missile batteries, electronic pickets as also provide logistics support to forces operating far from the mainland.[5]

The Indian navy's *Strategic Defence Review* published by the Naval Head-quarters in 1998, notes that "the navies enjoy complete international legality over two-thirds of the earth's surface and therefore can operate well beyond the territorial limits of a nation in different situations covering a variety of contingencies both during war to peace".[6] It also notes that the navy is an important tool that can be employed for "cooperation, conflict resolution and achieving competitive advantage in economic activity". Besides, naval forces are capable of performing multiple tasks whether they be military, constabulary or benign in nature. Given these conditions of naval utility, the Indian navy should have the capability to be regarded "as of consequence in the region".[7]

The Indian Maritime Doctrine, INBR 8, published in 2004, notes that while the fleet battles of the past are part of history, but the *raison d'etre* of the navies will be to protect the sovereignty and national interests of their states.[8] The navy's military role will continue along with its constabulary and politico-diplomatic duties. The latter will shape multinational naval cooperation to strengthen confidence-building measures among states. Navies will increasingly cooperate and work together to preserve order at sea even when they are not part of any military alliance. The Indian Maritime Doctrine also notes that with the end of the Cold War, the focus has shifted from large armies and their bases to maritime forces in support of littoral warfare. Such forces will be centred on carrier battle groups and long-range precision guided munitions as power projection shifts to the seas with a greater emphasis on the littorals. The Doctrine highlights that the Indian maritime vision for the first quarter of the 21st Century must look at the arc from the Persian Gulf to the Straits of Malacca as a legitimate area of interest.[9]

Given these varied perceptions and requirements, Indian naval thinking is primarily concerned with: (1) establishing powerful forces for deterrence, (2) conducting naval diplomacy, and (3) preserving order at sea. In operational terms, the conduct of joint operations, information warfare and littoral warfare are the mantras of the Indian navy.

Towards that end, the navy has followed a judicious force acquisition programme aimed at safeguarding national interests and supporting naval strategy. The current force structure is centred on one aircraft carrier, eight destroyers, 33 frigates/corvettes, 17 conventional submarines, a large number of smaller combatants, support vessels and a host of long range maritime patrol aircraft, fighters and helicopters.[10]

Force Structure

Indian naval practitioners believe that aircraft carriers are power projection platforms that can act as a deterrent. They are also powerful political weapons that have the ability to influence events short of war. Indian national security interests include enabling the country to exercise a degree of influence over nations in the immediate neighbourhood as well as to promote harmonious relationships in tune with national interests. To that extent, the aircraft carrier is an important tool for influencing events in the maritime neighbourhood. From a tactical perspective, there is no doubt that the Indian navy requires aircraft carriers. It needs these platforms to serve as a deterrent, defend the fleet on the high seas against air strikes, conduct anti-submarine patrols and execute strikes against targets ashore as was demonstrated during the India–Pakistan war in 1971.

Soon after independence, a ten-year naval expansion plan was unveiled and it was decided that two fleets be built with aircraft carriers as their nuclei.[11] It was in the 1950s that the Indian navy first unveiled its blueprint for a three-carrier force. Naval planners at that time had studied and understood the relevance of aircraft carriers during the Second World War. Besides, the navy's blue water ambitions were very clear and Indian naval leadership has often argued that aircraft carriers were a deterrent to an invading force.[12]

Unfortunately, funding problems have been a major concern and have affected the progress of acquisition projects. Notwithstanding that, India acquired the *Vikrant* and *Viraat* (ex-British *Hermes*) from the United Kingdom in 1961 and 1986, respectively. By the early 1990s, *Vikrant* had been laid alongside and decommissioned in January 1997 and *Viraat* served as the only power projection platform.

In the late 1980s, the Indian navy had also begun to look for a replacement for the ageing carriers. The plans envisaged the building of a 30,000-ton "Sea Control Ship" for which assistance was sought from DCN International of France. But by 1991, the plans were shelved for a lighter vessel, which was designated as the Air Defence Ship (ADS). In 1999, the Indian Government finally sanctioned the ADS to be built at the Kochi Shipyard. It is designed to operate 18 short takeoff *MiG-29K* fighters from a ramp with arrestor gear. It can host up to ten helicopters which would be configured to perform anti-submarine or search and rescue (SAR) missions.

Since the early 1990s, there has also been an intense debate in the naval and strategic community about the utility of aircraft carriers. The Indian navy's plans to acquire the Russian aircraft carrier, *Gorshkov,* has been the subject of controversy with regard to the cost, size and age of the vessel. Some have termed the proposed acquisition as an illogical purchase and have called it a white elephant.[13] The *Gorshkov* was offered for sale to the Indian navy in the early 1990s at a reported price of US$400 million. According to a revised deal, the vessel has been sold for free and is currently undergoing a major refit in a Russian yard that could cost as much as US$1 billion.[14] The upgrade involves improving radar systems and the installation of a 13-degree ramp providing for a six metres high takeoff.

Other than an aircraft carrier, the most advanced vessels in the Indian navy inventory are the indigenously built Delhi class guided missile destroyers. Three vessels have been built with the assistance of the Russian Severnoya Design Bureau and are the largest vessels ever built by Indian shipyards.

Designated as Project P15, they form the mainstay of the attacking force and are equipped with *KL Uran (SS-N-21)* anti-ship missiles with a range of 130 km and attached with a 145 kg warhead. These vessels have therefore enhanced the navy's stand-off capability. The surface to air missile package is equally impressive and can provide area defence up to 50 km. An important feature of these vessels is the capacity to host two helicopters that can be configured both for the anti-submarine role as well as the anti-shipping, thereby providing an extended range of attack out to 400 km.

With the ageing and subsequent decommissioning of the British designed *Leander* class frigates (*Nilgiri* class), the Indian navy has commissioned the *Brahmaputra* class of ships which is known as Project 16, follow-on to the *Godavari* class.[15] A total of three vessels are planned and the missile package is similar to the Delhi class destroyers. The important feature of this class of frigates is the indigenous surface-to-air missile suite, namely, the *Trishul*.[16] The *Trishul* is still being tested and will ultimately be fitted on all future missile vessels. In the meantime, plans are in an advanced stage to fit the Israeli *Barak* vertical launch surface-to-air missile system.[17] The Indian navy has also received from Russia three *Krivak* class frigates which are designed for multiple roles and incorporate advanced stealth features.[18]

During the 1990s, there has not been any appreciable change in the amphibious fleet. Instead, the number of such vessels has decreased. The Polish *Polnocny* class of ships constitute the bulk of the Indian navy's amphibious capability. Although the indigenously built *Magar* class and the Landing Craft Utility (LCU) vessels have augmented amphibious lift capacity, it is far from adequate.[19] The *Magar* class vessels are capable of hosting two helicopters and can land special marine commandoes in enemy areas. Since amphibious operations are equipment and logistic intensive, merchant vessels are used to augment amphibious lift capability. The Indian inventory of small craft is of at least three origins, Russian, Israeli and Indian. Among the combatants, a large number are equipped with surface-to-surface missiles.

Submarines are an important component of the Indian naval force structure. A 30-year submarine construction plan stretching to 2025 aims at acquiring an inventory of 24 submarines as well as boosting indigenous production.[20] The current inventory comprises a mix of boats of Russian and German origin. The bulk of the boats belong to the *Kilo* class and four *HDW Type 209/1500* boats (two built in India) of German origin. The Indian navy acquired 10 *Kilo* class (referred to as *Sindu* class in the Indian classification) submarines from Russia in the 1990s. The last vessel was delivered in 2000. These vessels have undergone modernisation and retrofitting of weapons and sensors. *Sindhuvir* was modernised at the Russian shipyards in Severodvinsk and fitted with modern sonar and advanced electronic warfare equipment with a capability to launch *3M-54 E (Klub)* cruise missiles. There are plans to modernise and retrofit the missile capabilities in the remaining submarines of this class.

The *Shishumar* class (*Type 209/1500*) of German origin were delivered between 1986 and 1994. The first two submarines of the series were built by HDW, Germany, and the remaining two were assembled at the Mazagaon Dockyard in Mumbai. There are plans to build conventional submarines in Indian shipyards. The Mazagaon Dockyard Limited is engaged in building conventional submarines under Project 75.[21] At least two redesigned versions of the *Shishumar* class are being built using existing submarine construction equipment.

Indian nuclear scientists, strategists and naval planners have carefully watched the development of nuclear submarines by several navies. By 1987, India began to negotiate with the Soviet Union for the lease of a nuclear submarine and in January 1988, a *670 A Skat* series (Charlie class by NATO classification) 4,800 ton nuclear submarine (fitted with eight *Ameist SS-N-7 Starbright* anti-ship missiles of 120 km range), capable of carrying nuclear warheads, was acquired by the Indian navy from the Soviet Union on lease and commissioned as the *Chakra*.[22] The submarine eventually became not only the training ground for the Indian naval personnel, but a design laboratory for developing and testing indigenous nuclear submarine technology.[23] On expiry of the lease period in 1991, *Chakra* was returned to Russia.

The indigenous nuclear submarine programme, designated as the Advance Technology Vessel (ATV), has been under way for almost two decades. It has made some progress, though unsatisfactory. The ATV submarine is expected to be of 4,000 ton displacement, and four to five such vessels are to be built.[24] According to the Russian Defence Ministry's official newspaper, *Krasnaya Zevezda*, Russia is assisting India in building a nuclear submarine.[25]

There are also other reports to indicate that India is planning to lease a Russian SSN to help bolster the development of the ATV. Reportedly, in October 2001, the Indian Ministry of Defence announced that New Delhi and Moscow had finalised a deal for India to lease a *Victor III (Schuka)* SSN for three years.[26] As regards the weapons, the ATV vessel is expected to host either the *Yahont* anti-ship cruise missile (designed by NPO Mashinostroyeniya) with a range of 300 km or the indigenous *Sagarika*.[27]

Paragraph 2.1 of the Indian Nuclear Doctrine (IND) notes, "India's strategic interests require effective credible nuclear deterrent and adequate retaliatory capability should deterrence fail". Further, the IND (paragraph 4.1 to 4.3) states that "credibility", "effectiveness" and "survivability" are the cardinal principles under which India's nuclear deterrent will function.[28] Therefore, any nuclear strike on India shall result in a retaliatory strike to inflict unacceptable damage on the attacker. In order to achieve the desired response, India must possess a credible and survivable nuclear deterrent. Given these specific conditions of "requirements and responses", nuclear submarines fit the bill. They possess inherent attributes of responsiveness, flexibility, survivability, endurance, and connectivity that offer national decision-makers the most credible and reliable nuclear deterrent in their arsenal.

The Indian naval air arm comprises of a variety of Russian, British and French aircraft and helicopters. There are also indigenously built helicopters (being produced by the Hindustan Aeronautics Limited) under license. These are fairly modern by regional standards and can provide effective air cover to the fleet for the aircraft carrier and for shore. The long-range maritime patrol aircraft are shore based and provide an effective surveillance to the fleet operating far from the shore. The navy has anti-submarine, early warning and missile capable helicopters that provide both defensive and offensive air capability to support fleet operations. The aircraft carrier can host up to eight *Sea Harrier* fighter jets and at least two-dozen helicopters (configured in anti-submarine and search and rescue roles). There are 16 naval air squadrons that operate a variety of aircraft: *Sea Harriers* and *Kiran* fighters, *Dornier*, *Tu-142*, and *IL-38* maritime patrol aircraft, and *Sea King* and *Chetak* helicopters.

Indian Navy: Roles and Missions

The Indian navy's roles and missions are closely linked to India's national interests. The *Strategic Defence Review* argues that India's maritime strength must "directly support national interests and not just the perceived threats". In broad terms, it classifies Indian navy's roles into four different categories: (1) sea based deterrence, (2) economic and energy security, (3) presence in areas of interests, and (4) multifaceted naval diplomacy.[29]

Deterrence lies at the core of the Indian navy's strategy.[30] The *Strategic Defence Review* notes that Indian navy should be able to deter any maritime challenge posed by littoral states individually or in concert with other regional states. It should safeguard territorial integrity and protect national interests. The naval capability should be such that it should raise the threshold of intervention or coercion by both littorals and extra regional forces. As regards strategic nuclear deterrence, the *Review* notes that sea based deterrence is critical to second strike capability. In the absence of naval nuclear capability and the possibility of nuclear threat, the Indian navy should be able to protect itself and take necessary precautions to clear nuclear contaminated areas.[31]

The Indian Maritime Doctrine stipulates the missions envisioned for the Indian navy. These are: (1) Military (2) Diplomatic (3) Constabulary and (4) Benign (or humanitarian as it is more commonly known).[32] Under the military component, the Indian navy is required to provide conventional and strategic nuclear deterrence against regional states, deter intervention by extra regional powers, and exercise sea control in designated areas of the Arabian Sea and the Bay of Bengal. The navy must also guard India's mercantile marine and sea-borne trade both during peace and war and provide security to India's coastline, island territories, and offshore assets from sea-borne threat. The navy should also be able to project power and land the army in the area of interest. The navy should also provide a second-strike nuclear capability in the event of a nuclear conflict.

Naval diplomacy is an important function of the Indian navy. It should act as the ambassador of goodwill and build maritime bridges with like-minded states and to achieve this aim, Indian naval ships have engaged in joint naval exercises. Joint exercises have helped promote closer cooperation and under-standing between the respective naval communities. Since 1995, the Indian Navy has hosted several navies from South Asia and Southeast Asia as part of "Milan", a bi-annual gathering of regional navies. More recently, the Indian Navy hosted the International Fleet Review (IFR), the first of its kind, since independence.[33]

The Indian navy has also been deployed for safeguarding the sovereignty of smaller nations and for preserving order at sea. For instance, in November 1988, a week before President Gayoom was to assume his third term in office, two Colombo-based dissident businessmen from the Maldives, along with about 80 Tamil mercenaries belonging to the left-wing People's Liberation Organisation of Tamil Eelam (PLOTE), attempted to overthrow the Gayoom regime.[34] The President sought urgent assistance from New Delhi over the phone. Some 1600 Indian troops including commandos reached Male by air and sea and ended the coup. The mercenaries were captured while fleeing with hostages.[35] The Indian navy participated in Operation Pawan in response to a request made by the Sri Lankan government to counter the Liberation Tigers of Tami Eelam (LTTE). The Indian navy was required to undertake maritime operations in the waters around Sri Lanka and particularly Palk Bay, north of Sri Lanka. Palk Bay was frequently used by the LTTE for carrying out strikes against the Sri Lankan naval forces and to keep the arms supply lines open at sea.

In the constabulary role, the Indian navy has also engaged in preserving order at sea. The capture of the hijacked *MV Alondra Rainbow*, a 7 000-tonne Panamanian registered vessel belonging to Japanese owners, by an Indian warship in November 1999 was a classical case of Indian efforts to maintain the safety of international sea lines of communication in the Indian Ocean.[36]

In the benign role, the Indian navy has been deployed for humanitarian relief and search and rescue missions. Recently, Indian naval ships, aircraft, helicopters, and personnel responded to the December 26, 2004 Tsunami in the Indian Ocean. The Indian navy deployed 32 naval ships, seven aircraft and 20 helicopters in support of five rescue, relief and reconstruction missions as part of *Operation Madad* (Andhra Pradesh and Tamil Nadu coast, India), *Operation Sea Waves* (Andaman & Nicobar Islands, India) *Operation Castor* (Maldives), Operation *Rainbow* (Sri Lanka) and *Operation Gambhir* (Indonesia). What is noteworthy is the fact that on 26 December 2004, the day that the Tsunami hit the subcontinent, the Indian Navy had deployed 19 ships, four aircraft, and 11 helicopters to the Maldives, Sri Lanka and Tamil Nadu, and the Andaman & Nicobar Islands. The quick response exemplified the efficiency and the operational readiness of the Indian Navy. India has therefore registered its presence in the tsunami-affected region as a sympathetic power capable of helping its neighbours even when its own shores are troubled. The Indian effort further exhibited its well-oiled disaster management machinery that was capable of assisting in any regional disaster or crisis.

Naval Coercion

The Indian experience with naval coercion presents a mix bag of successes and failures. On two different occasions in the past, the Indian navy was a victim of coercive diplomacy. During the India–Pakistan war in 1965, Indonesia had dispatched its submarines to Pakistan to deter India against Pakistan and threaten the opening of another war front in the Andaman and Nicobar islands.[37] The second event was the US Seventh Fleet, comprising the aircraft carrier *USS Enterprise* and its escorts, sailed through the Bay of Bengal to deter India against Pakistan during the 1971 India–Pakistan conflict. It is believed that the motive of this display of force was "to ensure the protection of US interests in the area". No Indian naval vessel encountered the US Seventh fleet.

During the 1999 Kargil conflict between India and Pakistan, the Indian Navy deployed both the Western and Eastern naval fleets in the Arabian Sea. This display of force was aimed at compelling Pakistan to vacate Indian territory in the Kargil sector in North India. The build up was also aimed at imposing a naval blockade of the Karachi port. The Indian fleet conducted offensive manoeuvres in the Arabian Sea which restricted the Pakistani naval fleet to operating very close to its coast. A Pakistani commentator interpreted this to mean that the Indian navy was preparing to enforce a "quarantine or blockade of the coastline" and prevent the supply of oil from the Persian Gulf. It is argued that this "was an important factor, which led to Pakistan's humiliating withdrawal from the heights of Kargil and the Indian navy played its part in convincing the Pakistani military leadership of the futility of prolonging the Kargil conflict".[38]

The Revolution in Military Affairs (RMA) in the Indian Navy

There has also been a constant desire among states to build forces to counter any threat posed by their respective rivals. Since most of the developing countries do not have the infrastructure to develop weapons, they have depended on external sourcing. The international arms industry has always remained eager to sell weaponry and also to transfer technology. This has led to a widespread diffusion of modern weapons among the developing countries.

During the last few decades, there has been a rapid rise in information and communication technologies. We now use net-based telephony, communication highways, satellites and terrestrial means of interacting using digital hardware and software for integrating complex networks have become common-place. The new architecture has allowed us to transport large volumes of information to the receiver at the other end.

Information technology is closely and inextricably linked to the concept of information warfare. In simple terms, information warfare is the means to deny, exploit, corrupt or destroy the information infrastructure (command, control and decision making apparatus and systems) of an adversary while protecting oneself.[39] Its application as a destructive force against enemy computers and networks that support infrastructures such as the government, military, power grid, communications, financial, and transportation systems is now a reality.

For the military, information technology plays an important role in the conduct of warfare. Military planners talk of information warfare as a prerequisite to the successful conduct of any operations, whether it be covert or overt.[40]

The aim is to attack enemy command and control structures to gain battle space superiority using information superiority and thus winning a war through asymmetry. In recent times, the Persian Gulf War (1991), the war in Bosnia (1992–1995) and the military action in Kosovo (1999) witnessed the dramatic application of information technologies to war.[41] During these wars, information technologies were used to support US-led coalition operations as well as to blind enemy forces to the extent that they were rendered incapable.

The Gulf War experience encouraged the Indian Navy to invest in information warfare and build a military with smart technologies. Importantly, the Gulf War showcased a new military strategy based on technology that came to represent a new era in strategy formulation. The technological inputs into this war had a far-reaching impact on the Indian naval understanding of the concept of future wars, and it began to reorient its tactical doctrines to deal with information-technology based tactics.

Economic reforms and a desire for self-sufficiency are two important parameters that have shaped the technological revolution in India. Since the 1980s, a liberalisation process has been underway to make Indian industry more competitive in the international market which has also helped the development of the domestic technological base. A series of initiatives have improved the performance of public sector and state-owned-enterprises, and the private sector has been provided with incentives to support the technological revolution.

The changes in Indian naval combat operations are primarily driven by technology in the form of long-range precision-guided munitions and intelligent/smart weapons. The naval leadership believes that these tools of warfare can effectively destroy fixed and moving targets at long distances across the globe. While the effectiveness of these weapons is not in question, the ability of Indian navy to obtain and integrate these systems onboard platforms and into tactical doctrines remains a challenge. These challenges have become critical for the Indian Navy. One also finds that the Indian navy is also upgrading low technology platforms with "smart" high technology systems that are capable of performing multiple functions.

According to *The Indian Naval Doctrine for Information Warfare,* the information age has offered both capabilities and challenges that were not available to maritime forces in the past.[42] Navies are currently engaged in drawing conclusions from recent conflicts in terms of the relevance of technology as a tool for information superiority. It notes:

> Commanders must have a precise idea of how information fits into operations
> and how it is to be handled and disseminated. Clear understanding of issues

related to complexities of information warfare would also enable them to seize the initiative from the adversary.[43]

The doctrine notes that information warfare is based on three key technologies: (a) information technology, (b) C4ISR (command, control, communication, computers, intelligence, surveillance, and reconnaissance) technologies, and (c) precision force technologies.[44] These technologies have to be supported by applications of information technology in the field of space, the electromagnetic spectrum, and micro-embedded technologies to penetrate enemy decision loops and weapon systems. The doctrine also notes that information superiority can be the winning tool in a war.[45] In order to protect against enemy attack, force posture must be based on the intensity of attack. Towards that end, the doctrine lists five postures that can be adopted.

Defensive Posture

The Defensive Posture is characterised by heavy dependence on information protection. It might prove advantageous in an environment where adversaries compete against a dominant power and pursue strategies to disrupt the equilibrium.

Offensive Posture

The Offensive Posture emphasises the denial of information. The posture might be adopted by organisations dissatisfied with their current standing and keen on engaging stronger adversaries.

Quantity Posture

The Quantity Posture emphasises the primacy of information transport capability. An organisation adopting this posture lays emphasis on the primacy of information transport capability. An organisation adopting this posture places its confidence in moving and using massive volumes of information. The posture may work well in organisations with less sensitive and widely distributed information assets.

Quality Posture

The main thrust of the Quality Posture is on efficient information management. Investments in IW are made intelligently and selectively to optimise priority areas. This posture is suitable for nations that cannot afford unrestrained investment without visible deliverables.

Sponge Posture

The Sponge Posture stresses the attainment of information dominance through innovative means and improvisation. Practitioners of the Sponge Posture may have to adopt a "follower strategy" and are quick to adopt proven methods and innovations.[46]

Kapil Kak argues that countries can achieve higher levels of military effectiveness if they exploit emerging technologies and transform their respective doctrines and organisational structures at the same time.[47] Such an adaptation would help bridge the asymmetry between the technologically advanced nations and developing nations. He argues that it would be crucial for political leaders, military establishments, civil services and defence research scientists to stay alert to emerging technologies and exploit their application so as to achieve a technological asymmetry that can be sustained against the competition and one's adversaries.[48]

It is true that the RMA would result in major changes in the naval doctrine, organisation and force structure of the Indian Navy, but can it change the mindset of its users? It is easy to import an idea, but to implement it is another challenge altogether. Implementing the RMA demands a change in thinking, creativity and innovations to exploit high technology. It calls for special training, education on the changing nature of warfare and a change in attitude towards the complexity of ongoing technology transformations. These new requirements will be added demands on naval leadership at all levels.

Revolution in Naval Affairs

As the process of information management becomes more complex, it challenges the conduct of classical naval operations. There are immense demands on tactical commanders to network with forces at sea and with shore authorities. The level and success of these networks directly impact on naval operations and missions and it has become imperative on the part of naval forces to undertake tactical, organisational and operational changes in their force structures and tactical doctrines to incorporate these networks.

The Indian navy is a technologically advanced force. It has begun to take note of the developments in information warfare and is focused on computer-aided signal intelligence, electronic intelligence, surveillance intelligence and computer intelligence. A number of programmes and projects have been underway to understand and exploit information technology.

Indian Naval Doctrine for Information Warfare spells out the Information Warfare (IW) strategy for the navy in the 21st century. The doctrine also notes that:

> Network centric warfare is the navy's adaptation of information technology. It aims for a total combat power involving seamless integration of all afloat, airborne and shore based threats so that decision making is knowledge based, on a near real-time basis navy-wide.[49]

Currently, some 350 units (ships, shore stations and logistic centres) have been connected to the Navy Enterprise Wide Network (NEWN).[50] Networks perform a variety of functions from operation directions to logistics and administrative support. The navy plans to use the NEWN to connect the above nodes by local area networks (within the establishment), metropolitan area network (within the metropolis) and wide area network among the naval units all over the country including island territories. The programme aims to create connectivity between any two-computer terminals. The navy also plans to connect the National Command Authority, Naval War Room at New Delhi, Maritime Operations Centres, Fleet Operation Centres and Command Shelters into a computer-aided networked web for decision and support activities.[51]

The Indian Navy's information warfare strategy involves development of networks "to integrate complex systems for naval applications such as sensors, weapons, decision support elements, communication/data link nodes, navigation aids, computer/processors, networking elements, and integrating/interfacing devices".[52] Since this complex network requires a high level of systems engineering, human skills, expertise and infrastructure, the Indian naval information warfare strategy aims to harness Commercial Off-the-Shelf Technology (COTS) and trained manpower available in the civilian domain. In its efforts towards "self-reliance through indigenisation", the navy has relied heavily on its in-house capability in system engineering and software development. It has also tapped the resources of the highly talented Indian IT industry. The Confederation of Indian Industry (CII) has acted as a catalyst to foster a long-term Navy–Industry partnership that forms the basis for a joint working and co-development of naval systems and applications. These initiatives have led to strategic alliances with leading IT houses in terms of technology transfer as well as resource sharing among personnel.[53]

The two important agencies that support Indian navy's information networking are the Directorate of Information Technology (DIT) and the Information Warfare (IW) cell. DIT is under the control of the Chief of Materials who looks after the implementation, operation and projection of the information based support infrastructure and is the central agency that procures hardware for the Navy.[54]

The IW cell is the executive agency for the conduct of information warfare and is managed under the Assistant Chief of Naval Staff (Information Warfare and Operations). Information Warfare Cells have also been constituted at the Command Headquarters to integrate information warfare as a part of naval plans. These cells coordinate all information and develop techniques relating to non-lethal operations. The IW cell at the Naval Headquarters addresses doctrine and policy issues relating to Information Warfare.[55] It also undertakes collection, processing and dissemination of information for decision making and implements measures to ensure security of information. As a nodal agency, it coordinates various information warfare tasks and provides administrative support to related agencies in terms of security of information and validation of doctrinal concepts.

Critical Deficiencies in RMA

Despite the advances made, there are still several critical deficiencies in Indian RMA capabilities and these include:

   (i) Obsolete naval hardware which is 10–20 years behind that of the West.
  (ii) Obsolete naval communications equipment that is only partially digitised and is at least two generations behind the West.
 (iii) The lack of real time photo-reconnaissance satellites.
  (iv) The lack of an airborne warning and control system (AWACS).
   (v) The lack of indigenous UAV technology which is currently still under development.
  (vi) Poor systems-integration skills, although maturing, are still behind western standards.
 (vii) The Indian Navy is still developing computer aided maintenance procedures and Integrated Logistics Systems (ILS) concepts are still to be used.
(viii) More progress needs to be made in the areas of command and control and cruise-missile technology.

(ix) The Indian Navy is still making concerted efforts to improve its ability to acquire and operate key elements of the RMA in an integrated, joint-force environment within the next decade.

Redefined Strategic Geography

Being a dominant power in South Asia, it is natural for India to consider the Indian Ocean as its own sphere of influence. In addition, New Delhi's strategic geography now extends far into the South China Sea in the east and to the Red Sea in the west. This is predicated on long-range naval operations and the exercising of influence around the strategic choke points of the Straits of Hormuz, the Straits of Malacca and the Sunda Straits.

As part of this strategy, the Indian navy has been undertaking distant operations as far as the South China Sea in the east,[56] the Straits of Hormuz in the west, and deep into the Indian Ocean towards the Cape of Good Hope in the south. India's Minister of Defence, George Fernandes, confirmed India's shifting strategic geography and its naval areas of interests in April 2000 at the launching of the Indian warship *Brahmaputra*.[57] The minister noted that India's "area of interest ... extends from the north of the Arabian Sea to the South China Sea".[58] Soon after, the Indian navy announced plans for naval exercises in the South China Sea.[59] The decision to conduct exercises was clearly aimed at extending the navy's reach into the South China Sea.[60] Recent acquisitions, particularly the *Delhi* class destroyers, *Krivak* class frigates and *TU-144* long range maritime patrol aircraft, point to the fact that the Indian navy has the capability to undertake distant operations.

Conclusion

The Indian navy has been engaged in major naval acquisition programmes in the late 1990s aimed at modernisation of the force. A variety of advanced platforms, missiles and electronic warfare equipment have been added to the naval inventory. The navy has the capability and capacity to safeguard India's maritime interests. However, it remains dependent on foreign sources for weapons and sensors. The current order of battle is impressive and the navy is concentrating its efforts to acquire a nuclear submarine.

The Indian navy has been actively engaged in building closer relations with several navies across the globe. It has participated in joint exercises and participated in international fleet reviews. It has also offered humanitarian assistance, carried out disaster relief activities, and conducted anti-piracy patrols aimed at building confidence and trust among regional countries. India believes that obtaining a secure maritime environment requires mutual understanding and the cooperation of all the countries in the region as well as in neighbouring regions. Despite differences in political, economic, social, cultural, language, national interests, military structures and threat perceptions, the Indian navy has cooperated on issues of common security concerns.

An examination of the Indian naval forces reveals that the implementation of the RMA is still in its infancy. Much of the ship-based missile systems and electronic warfare equipment is of Soviet/Russian origin. India has the capacity to build ships, but most of the weapons and sensors are imported. Advances have been made in missile development through indigenous programmes, but this cannot match the sophistication levels of the US and European models. Hybrid platforms have found a prominent place in the Indian naval inventory and the platforms host Russian, American, French, Dutch, Italian and British equipment, indigenous missiles and radars based on foreign designs and a variety of electronic warfare suites from several foreign sources. All this activity demonstrates the determination and capacity in the Indian navy to leapfrog capability development, challenge the status quo, and alter the relative balance of power to its favour.

Notes

1. Gwadar in Pakistan lies astride the sea-lane originating from the strategic choke point of Hormuz and is of strategic importance to China.
2. "Changing Tides in the Indian Ocean", *Jane's Navy International*, November 1997, p. 39.
3. Sanjay J. Singh, "India's Maritime Strategy for the 90s", *USI Journal*, July–September 1990, pp. 352–354.
4. Ibid.
5. Ibid.
6. *Strategic Defence Review: The Maritime Dimension, A Naval Vision* (New Delhi: Naval Headquarters, 1998), pp. 34–35.
7. Ibid.
8. *Indian Maritime Doctrine, INBR 8* (New Delhi: Integrated Headquarters, Ministry of Defence (Navy), 2004), pp. 50–51.
9. Ibid.
10. *Jane's Fighting Ships, 2001–2002*, p. 291.
11. Rear Admiral Satyindra Singh, *Blueprint to Bluewater: The Indian Navy 1951–1965* (New Delhi: Lancer International, 1992), p. 127. See also Rahul Roy-Chaudhury, *Sea Power and Indian Security* (London: Brassey's, 1995), p. 30.

12. Ibid.
13. Admiral J. G. Nadkarni, "The Indian Navy's White Elephant", *Rediff On Net*, 2 November 2001. Available at http://www.rediff.com/news/2001/nov/02nad.htm.
14. Admiral J. G. Nadkarni, "Does India Need to Invest Rs 9,000 Crores on a Russian Aircraft Carrier?", *Rediff On Net*, 13 July 2000. Available at http://www.rediff.com/news/2000/jul/13nad.htm.
15. *Jane's Fighting Ships, 2001–2002*, p. 299.
16. Ibid.
17. Ibid.
18. Ibid, p. 298.
19. Ibid, p. 305.
20. Admiral A. K. Chatterji, *Indian Navy's Submarine Arm* (New Delhi: Birla Institute, 1982), p. 62. See also Rahul Roy-Chaudhury, *India's Maritime Security* (New Delhi: Knowledge World, 2000), p. 134.
21. Ibid.
22. *Jane's Fighting Ships, 1988–1989*, p. 243. See also Rahul Roy-Chaudhury, *India's Maritime Security*, pp. 138–141.
23. "Need to Keep a High Priority on Indian Nuclear Submarine Project", *India Policy*, March 2000. Available at http://www.indiapolicy.org/lists/india-policy/2000/march/msg00013.html.
24. Ibid.
25. Igor Kudrik, "Russia Helps India Build Nuclear Submarine", Bellona Foundation: The Russian Northern Fleet, 17 September 1998. Available at http://www.bellona.no/en/international/russia/navy/northern_fleet/vessels/9518.html
26. C. J. Ihrig, "Indian Navy Gets its SSN at Last", *NAVINT Articles (NSL)*, 15 December 2001. Available at http://www.diodon349.com/Stories/Stories_SS/indian_navy_gets_its_ssn_at_last.htm. <Accessed on 29 September 2005>.
27. "Advanced Technology Vessel (ATV)", India Defence (The Online Edition), 29 September 2005. Available at http://www.india-defence.com/specifications/submarines/60. <Accessed on 29 September 2005>.
28. Vijay Sakhuja, "Sea Based Deterrence and Indian Security", *Strategic Analysis*, April 2001, p. 30.
29. *Strategic Defence Review*, pp. 34–35.
30. Ibid.
31. Ibid.
32. *Indian Maritime Doctrine*, pp. 100–103.
33. "PM Calls For Institutionalisation of Co-operation Between Navies", *Rediff On Net*, 18 February 2001. Available at http://rediff.com/news/2001/feb/18fleet.htm. Addressing the gathering of naval ships from 23 countries, the Indian Prime Minister noted that the Indian Navy "plays a crucial role in India's

co-operation with other countries, especially those that share its maritime borders. Active co-operation between navies is a must in [these] times of sea piracy, gun-running and drug menace, which are all part of international terrorism". He said, "by institutionalised arrangements, we can actually say that we have built bridges of friendship" which was the theme of the fleet review.

34. Ravinatha Aryasinha, "Maldives, Sri Lanka and the 'India Factor'", *Himal South Asia*, March–April 1997. Available at http://www.himalmag.com/97mar/cov-mal.htm.

35. Altogether 20 were killed in the coup attempt, and 68, including four Maldivians, were captured. Of them, 16, Maldivians included, received death sentences, which were later commuted to life imprisonment. Prime Minister Rajiv Gandhi told the Indian Parliament that he saw the event as having "provided an opportunity for India to assist a friendly country and frustrate an attempt to overthrow a democratically elected government". While the big powers, including the US, endorsed India's intervention, the world media interpreted the action as indicative of "the scale of its ambitions in South Asia", as *Time* magazine observed, a confirmation of India's growing role as a regional superpower cum policeman.

36. Vijay Sakhuja, "Maritime Order and Piracy", *Strategic Analysis*, August 2000, p. 2007.

37. Pakistan Navy Historical Section, *Story of Pakistan Navy, 1947–1972* (Islamabad: Elite Publishers, 1991), pp. 228–229. During the 1965 India–Pakistan war, President Soekarno of Indonesia noted that an attack on Pakistan was like an attack on Indonesia and agreed to provide whatever Pakistan needed for its war effort against India. The Indonesian Naval Chief was of the view that the Andaman and Nicobar islands were an extension of Sumatra and even enquired if Pakistan wanted Indonesia to take over the island. The Indonesian Navy began to patrol around the islands and also dispatched a submarine and missile boats to Pakistan. But these vessels arrived only after the cease-fire due to the long distance and later returned to Indonesia without participating in the conflict.

38. Gurmeet Kanwal, "Pakistan's Military Defeat", in Jasjit Singh (ed.), *Kargil 1999 — Pakistan's Fourth War for Kashmir* (New Delhi: Knowledge World, 1999), p. 220.

39. Akshay Joshi, *Information Age and India* (New Delhi: Knowledge World, 2001), p. 83.

40. Information Warfare Bulletin, *Infowar Navy*, (New Delhi: Indian Navy, Naval Headquarters, March 1998).

41. Akshay Joshi, pp. 98–114.

42. *Indian Naval Doctrine for Information Warfare* (New Delhi: Information Warfare Cell, Naval Headquarters, 2001), p. i.

43. Ibid.

44. Ibid.

45. Ibid, p. 2.

46. Ibid, pp. 4–5.
47. Kapil Kak, "Revolution in Military Affairs: An Appraisal", *Strategic Analysis*, April 2000, p. 5.
48. Ibid.
49. *Indian Naval Doctrine for Information Warfare*, p. 45.
50. Ibid, p. 48.
51. Ibid, pp. 45–49.
52. Ibid.
53. Ibid.
54. Ibid, pp. 55–59.
55. Ibid.
56. "Indian, Singapore navies begin exercise", *Indo-Asian News Service*, 24 February, 2005. Available at http://www.eians.com/stories/2005/02/24/24apa.shtml. The Indian and Singapore navies carried out their first exercise in the South China Sea to jointly train for anti-submarine warfare. This is the first time that SIMBEX, an annual exercise conducted by the two sides, is being held in the South China Sea. Previous exercises have been carried out in the Indian waters. The Indian navy fielded several powerful warships, including the indigenously built frigate *INS Gomati*, the destroyer *INS Ranvijay* and the corvette *INS Kora*. The Republic of Singapore Navy was represented in the exercise by the missile corvettes *RSS Valiant* and *RSS Vengeance,* the patrol vessel *RSS Dauntless*, the missile gunboat *RSS Sea Dragon* and the submarine RSS Chieftain. Singapore's military aircraft also took part in the exercise.
57. "India Challenges China in South China Sea", *Stratfor.com*, 26 April 2000. Available at http://www.stratfor.com/.
58. Ibid.
59. Ibid.
60. Indian naval ships have carried out exercises in Asia-Pacific waters in the past, but recent exercises involved the deployment of long range maritime patrol aircraft based in India.

Chapter 6

Japan's National Maritime Doctrines and Capabilities

VADM (Retd.) Hideaki Kaneda

Japan's Strategic Environment and the Characteristics of the Asia-Pacific Region

There are four basic characteristics of the Asia-Pacific region that serves as the backdrop and impacts on the maritime security doctrines and capabilities of Japan. The first characteristic is that the basic structure of strategic environment in the North East Asian region can be characterised by the remnants of the Cold War overshadowing the Korean Peninsula and Taiwan Strait, while South East Asia features extensive geopolitical diversification. The second characteristic is the change in the security framework, as the "apparent threats" of the Cold War era is replaced by more complex and diversified "potential threats" and "risk factors" of the post Cold War era, commonly spread throughout the region. As a result, the regional countries appear to be adopting risk aversion measures by multilateral cooperation and coordination. The third characteristic is that the emergence of asymmetric "new threats" is about to bring significant changes in the geopolitical strategic environment of the region, along with various factors of historic regional conflicts. Furthermore, the wars occurring outside the region with new types of threats have extensively affected the situation characteristic to the region. The fourth and last characteristic is that the region finds a strong move towards the pursuit of new maritime order. As the UN Convention on the Law of the Sea entered into force, regional countries on the coast have increased their reliance on, and expectation from, the oceans. Intensified competition over maritime resource acquisition and territorial disputes are likely to bring more factors of potential conflicts. Among those countries building stronger naval forces, China's trajectory, especially, causes anxieties in regional countries. The possibilities of maritime terrorist attacks and piracy are other factors that may cause instability in the region.

Fundamental Policy of Security and Way of Defence — New National Defence Program Guideline

To respond to the new strategic environment in the region, the Government of Japan revised the National Defence Program Guideline (former Outline) on 10 December 2004, with the approval of the Security Council and the Cabinet Meeting.[1] In addition, it set the Mid-Term Defence Program with a budget of 24 trillion yen for five years from 2005 to 2009.[2] In the new Guideline, Japan recognised the diminishing possibility of full-scale invasion to Japan, and the rising need to respond against "new threats and various situations", including the proliferation of weapons of mass destruction and ballistic missiles, as well as the activities of international terrorist organisations. It expressed concerns on the military developments in North Korea as the serious instability factor in the region surrounding Japan, and indicated the need to continue being on guard over China's moves toward military modernisation and maritime expansion.

Furthermore, as the basic policy of Japan's national security, the Guideline set the goal to focus on the prevention of direct threats as well as the improvement of the international security environment to mitigate any threats facing Japan. To achieve such a goal, it planned to build a "Multi-functional, Flexible, and Effective Force" through Japan's own efforts. By developing such a force, Japan would be able to participate actively in the international peace cooperation activities that would aim to improve the international security environment through the cooperation of the international community, and to effectively respond against new threats and various situations, while maintaining the "Basic Defence Force" concept described in the former National Defence Program Outline.

In any case, it is essential to have the Japan–US security alliance to ensure the security of Japan. The Guideline stressed how Japan would need to subjectively participate in a strategy dialogue with the US in the future to discuss the role sharing between Japan and US, and to cooperate with other relevant countries to make efforts in stabilising the region that extended from the Middle East to East Asia. As the definition of Japan's defence capability, the Guideline first of all indicated the effective response to "new threats and various situations", which might include ballistic missile attacks, attacks by guerrilla and the Special Forces, invasion of island area, violation of territorial airspace and wilful invasion by armed spy ships, and massive or special types of disasters.

Next, it pointed out the needs of appropriate reduction of defence assets and the securing of fundamental functions, as the concept of developing defence capability has shifted away from the conventional one that persisted since the Cold War era, which was to focus on the defence assets of anti-armoured forces, anti-submarines, and anti-air invasion as the "preparation to deal with full-scale invasions". This shift of the concept was due to the decreased possibility of such serious scenarios occurring in the first place.

Moreover, in order to subjectively and actively pursue the "improvement of the international security environment", the Guideline planned to develop educational and training systems, improve the readiness of forces, and transportation capability amongst others. These duties used to be classified as auxiliary duties of the Self-Defence Forces, but the Guideline requested to properly recognise them as the major duties of the Self-Defence Forces, so they could develop necessary systems.

New Posture and Issues of the Maritime Self-Defence Force

In order to implement a new posture for the entire Self-Defence Force, the new Guideline plans to do six things: (1) to improve quick response capability, mobility, flexibility, and multi-functioning structure; (2) to pursue sophisticated technological and information capabilities; (3) to conduct fundamental review and enhanced effectiveness of existing organisation and equipment; (4) to establish a new Joint Staff Office to assist Defence Minister; (5) to newly organise the core units of each Self-Defence Force; and (6) to build organisation and equipment conform to the securing of peace and stability of international community.

Traditionally, the posture of the Maritime Self-Defence Force was to develop defence capability focused on the response against submarines or Anti-Submarine Warfare (ASW), when it came to the scenario of a full-scale invasion during the Cold War era. However, in order to make the Maritime Self-Defence Force conform to the new system, the Guideline recommended the appropriate development of the Maritime Self-Defence Force's capability that would be qualitatively advanced to enable response against any change in situation. At the same time, it called for ensuring the most fundamental functions to maintain deterrence capability, while developing response capability against any unpredictable change in the future. For this purpose, the Guideline requested the revision of the conventional defence programs, and the appropriate reduction in major equipment, such as major surface combatants, and fixed-wing patrol aircrafts, so as to ensure that the Maritime Self-Defence Force would conform to the increased needs of developing suitable posture to enable effective response against new threats and various situations.

In addition to the reduced number of assets, the Guideline requested to build an efficient system that could develop sufficient responsiveness forever expanding long-term obligations. This would include the unification of management for the skill levels of surface and air units, the shift of surface units from fixed to flexible organisation, and the change of the readiness postures of the fixed-wing patrol aircraft to allow simultaneous responses to various contingencies. Here is an issue many Japanese defence experts have pointed out, that is the "change of the Maritime Force development concept focused on ASW" needs to be reviewed. As the aim of the new Guideline is to develop the Maritime Self-Defence Force that would have a well-balanced capability, including deterrence and response against new threats under various scenarios, ASW capability would be the one area that needs further reinforcement and not reduction, as recognising the unchangeable importance of ASW in the West Pacific ocean under the consideration of the rapid enhancement and modernisation of Chinese Naval force capability centred around submarines. If Japan is to venture into the "reduction of appropriate scale" in such capabilities despite the aforesaid facts, then it has no choice but to enter into epoch-making changes in the quality of systems.

New Duties and Roles of the Maritime
Self-Defence Force

How then would the new Guideline view the changes in duties and roles of the Maritime Self-Defence Force? First of all, the "effective response against new threats and various situations" that was the centre of focus in the new Guideline would require the development of defence capabilities to respond against new threats and various contingencies, such as attacks using weapons of mass destruction and ballistic missiles, terrorist attacks, attacks by guerrilla forces and special forces, invasion of island areas, cyber attacks, and various illegal activities conducted by spies and spy ships. Secondly, the "readiness against full-scale invasion" would involve the duties and roles associated with conventional symmetrical wars, including the conventional scenario of invasion. Unlike other two missions, the new Guideline did not specify the kind of conditions this mission would assume. During the Cold War era, the assumption of invasion situations viewed the Soviet Union as the most apparent subject of threats, and the duties and roles in the combined response of Japan and US were thought to be the basic defence posture of Japan.

Currently, however, the issue requiring immediate attention is the real time response against threats that include attacks by international terrorists and countries that harbour terrorists who could use weapons of mass destruction and ballistic missiles, in other words, they are the very issue of the "effective response to new threats and various situations" discussed in this report. Now, for "consideration for the situations of full-scale invasion", Japan must be prepared to respond against North Korea as a near or short term threat, China as the medium-term strategic competitor, and the long-term risk of power balance shifts in the North East Asian region, as well as their ripple effects of structural changes in the strategic environment of the Asian region as a whole.

Nevertheless, the ongoing reorganisation of US Forces' forward deployment will eventually bring changes in the Japan–US Security relationship. With Japan's attempts to become a permanent member of the UN Security Council, Japan is actively conducting the practical discussion on the revision of Japan's constitution and the changes in its interpretation to allow the exercise of the right of collective self-defence. The Japan–US Security relationship will likely strengthen its features of "public properties" in the international security beyond the defence range of Japan and Far East, and it may become necessary to enhance the relationship between Japan and US from the tactical and operational levels to the strategic level.

Along with the above efforts, the system will likely require more dual-directional duties, and a change in the conventional US–Japan role sharing of US Forces as the "sword" and Japan's Self-Defence Forces as the "shield". On the other hand, as US Forces advance in the Revolution in Military Affairs (RMA), both countries will need to ensure their interoperability. Furthermore, to secure the entire Sea Lines of Communications (SLOCs) encompassing the oil transportation routes extended to the Middle East, which is beyond the conventional 1,000-mile SLOCs interest declared by Japan, will continue to be the supreme duties and roles requested of the Maritime Self-Defence Force even under the new strategic environment. However, such duties and roles present difficulties that cannot be resolved through unilateral efforts of the Maritime Self-Defence Force, and it will be essential to have cooperation and close association with US Forces and relevant countries in the region.

Lastly, for "subjective and active participation in the activities for the peace and stability of the international community", the Guideline required a high level of readiness of the Self-Defence Forces to dispatch units immediately and continually for the activities of securing the peace and stability of the international community including Japan, such as the UN Peace Keeping Operation (PKO), cooperation with the international community for its efforts to combat international terrorism including maritime terrorism and piracy, international humanitarian restoration aids, prevention of the proliferation of weapons of mass destruction like the Proliferation Security Initiative (PSI),[3] and relief and rescue works for massive natural disasters. Also, the Guideline emphasised the importance of building cooperative relationships with relevant countries in many fields, and of addressing arms control and disarmament as well as confidence building measures.

Situation of Threats and Risks to Maritime Defence — Conventional and New Threats and Risks

Considering the situation of threats and risks to maritime defence in this new era, the threats from the Soviet Union during the Cold War certainly seem to be appeased, but there is a need to focus fresh attentions on the military near term threats from North Korea and mid-term risks of China, as well as the immediate threats from international terrorists as non-state actors. Here, let us compare the maritime threats of Soviet Union at the time of the Cold War, and those at present.

North Korea

First, let us examine North Korea. In view of the readiness of North Korean Military (Korean People's Army), North Korea is hardly ready to engage in "full-scale invasion" including the landing on Japanese main islands. However, in regard to other types of armed invasion, such as "military violation of islands, adjacent waters and airspaces", "destruction of key facilities by guerrilla attacks", "violation of territorial and neighbouring waters by spy ships", "violation of airspaces", and "ballistic missile attacks", their capability is sufficient to operate in all situations.[4] This is especially so with their capability of ballistic missile attacks using Nodong missiles. About 200 or more of these missiles are said to be deployed and ready for action, and this kind attack is not different from the "massive air attack situation", which used to be considered as a type of full-scale invasion during the Cold War. In a sense, these attacks can be described as a full-scale armed invasion without landing.

In order to conduct a forward area defence against ballistic missile attacks, Japan's Maritime Self-Defence Force (JMSDF) will contribute to the defence of the main islands by deploying several Aegis ships to the Sea of Japan. Since these Aegis ships have to be positioned to the Western side of the Sea of Japan for the effective execution of ballistic missile defence, they will inevitably be exposed to severe maritime and air attacks (including ballistic missile attacks) from North Korea.

In terms of situation in other types of attacks, North Korea has sufficient capability to instigate such an "armed invasion situation" any time, even if not a "full-scale armed invasion". From the viewpoint of maritime defence operation, the situation will assume North Korean threats using submarines, surface combatants, attack/bomber aircrafts, ballistic missiles, and Special Forces, which, in terms of operation, might not be as massive as a "full-scale armed invasion", yet not too far from it in terms of function.

China

Next, how should we view China? Considering the significant build-up of the Chinese military (People's Liberation Army) with a focus on the Navy and the Air Force, and their aggressive advancement to oceans, there is a wide spread support in Japan to recognise China as a future risk factor, even if it is not an immediate threat.[5] However, China's military power is, in quantity and quality, at the level far below that of the Soviet Union at the height of the Cold War, and the general opinion is that Japan at the moment does not need to prepare for the threat of a full-scale invasion from China.

In recent years, the Chinese Navy has been undergoing a rapid build-up and modernisation by introducing Kilo class submarines, Sovremenny class destroyers, and fighter/bomber aircrafts of Su-27 and/or Su-30 from Russia, while promoting the domestic production of modernised equipment, such as the 093 type nuclear submarines for attacks, Song-class submarines, and 052-type destroyers. However, the major part of their systems is outdated. Compared with the submarines, surface combatants, fighter/bomber aircrafts of Soviet Union's Navy and Air force during the Cold War, which was represented by Kiev class aircraft carriers, Kirov/Slava class cruisers, Sovremenny class destroyers, Oscar/Victor class attack nuclear submarines, Kilo-class submarines, and Backfire bomber aircrafts, the systems that the Chinese Navy have are far inferior in quality and quantity, and it is a general view that it will take China many more years to reach the level of the former Soviet Union.

In the first place, China is presently not in a position to pose threats as a clear enemy as the Soviet Union used to pose during the Cold War era. Therefore, one would argue that to introduce a concrete defence posture against China would be premature and unnecessary. However, such a view may be too optimistic. One must recognise that the Chinese Navy today and in the near future will be powerful enough and be comparable to the former Soviet Union's Navy by taking the utmost "advantage of geographical positioning", which will allow them to pose actual threats to Japan as well as the region more easily. Why?

During the Cold War, the former Soviet Union certainly posed threats to Japan's surrounding waters, mainly in the Sea of Japan and the Pacific Ocean, as well as through the SLOCs. However, the main forces of the Soviet Union's Pacific Fleet were located in their home port of Vladivostok, and thus had to face the Japanese archipelago across the Sea of Japan as the natural obstacle with openings only at the three narrow straits of Soya, Tsugaru, and Tsushima, in order to reach out to the Pacific Ocean. Because of these geographical constraints, the threat posed by Soviet Navy to Japan's surrounding waters and its SLOCs were limited.

During the later period of the Cold War, the Soviet Union was able to station some scale of forces in the Gulf of Cam-Ranh under the agreement with their ally at that time, North Viet Nam. Yet, the forces stationed there did not contain submarines or bomber aircrafts. Moreover, with powerful US Forces stationed at Subic Naval Base and Clark Air Force Base in the Philippines, watching the area, they could not pose significant threats to key SLOCs connecting the Middle East with North East Asia. In other words, the Soviet Navy used to be a full-scale threat at the Sea of Japan, but their deployment to the Western Pacific Ocean was limited even with the use of bases located on the Kamchatka Peninsula, and was negligible in the East China Sea and South China Sea.

China, on the other hand, one-sidedly proclaimed that their territorial water included the vast and long SLOCs extended from the east of the Strait of Malacca, through South China Sea, to the Taiwan Strait and Bashi Channel, while steadily advancing their practical control of islands in the South China Sea, which are under disputes with ASEAN countries. Since the Chinese Navy has three fleets along the coastline of Mainland China except near Taiwan, with strong intentions to proceed with rapid modernisation and build-up, they have strategically advanced geographical position, which will allow them to easily disturb the security of the entire SLOCs if needed. Moreover, China is boldly undertaking the advancement toward East China Sea in recent days, as seen in their activities over Japan's claim of the Senkaku Islands and the Japan–China mid-line in the East China Sea, bringing the extremely delicate situation in contention between Japan's maritime defence power and Chinese naval power.

In addition, the trend of China's aggressive oceanic advancement clearly demonstrates their strong interests in the coastal waters off the Sea of Japan, the three major Japanese straits, and the Pacific Ocean, as evidenced by Chinese Naval Intelligence ships cruising around Japanese waters. Chinese submarines have been observed to be operating submerged near Okinawa, violating Japan's territorial sovereignty in the process, and have also been observed on the surface near the Osumi Strait. Moreover, the movements of ocean surveillance ships and Naval Maritime Surveillance ships around the Ogasawara archipelago and Oki-No-Torishima clearly demonstrates that Chinese naval activity were a part of their military surveying activities in preparation for the operation of Chinese Navy submarines.

This implies that the Chinese Navy has already fortified their first-island defence line, which includes the Japanese archipelago, Nansei (Southwest) islands, and Taiwan, by the use of submarines, surface combatants, fighter/bombers aircrafts, and ballistic/cruise missiles (fully and repeatedly operable even if not modernised enough, since they are positioned near to major SLOCs along the Chinese coast line). Now China seems to be ready to extend the Naval activity footsteps to their so-called second island defence line, which is the national defence frontier of China, connecting Aleutians, the line of 150 degrees East Longitudinal, and New Guinea Island, embracing Ogasawara Islands and Oki-No-Torishima Island of Japan, and the Guam Island of the US. Such regions of waters would enclose the entire Exclusive Economic Zone (EEZ) of Japan.

The purpose of Chinese Navy advancing beyond the first island defence line to reach the second island defence line is clear. It is to check, as far advanced as possible, the actions of the US Navy, with which China will ultimately contest for hegemony over the West Pacific. In addition, it is to prevent the actions of US Naval fleets in case of any sort of crisis over Taiwan. For these purposes, the Chinese Navy intends to build forces including high performance strategic nuclear submarines that can endure long distance navigation and activities in these waters, as well as tactical submarines, surface combatants, air-refuelling bomber aircrafts, and ballistic missiles.

Furthermore, it is extremely important to recognise that the military confrontation between China and Taiwan will result in a direct defensive situation for Japan. This is because there is a possibility of far west end of Japanese Sakishima Islands such as Iriomote and Yonakuni Islands being dragged into the battleground. Moreover, once they resolve the Taiwan issue, China will earnestly advance toward the Senkaku Islands. If the US situation allows, China may resort to military actions on the Senkaku Islands even before resolving the Taiwan issue. In essence, Japan needs to realise the potential risks of Chinese Navy, which may, at least in the near future, resort to full-scale armed invasion: (1) at the long SLOCs or in the EEZ where Japanese interests lie, or (2) at islands, ports, straits, waterways, coastlines of waters surrounding Japan.

Threats Caused by International Terrorists as Non-State Entities

In terms of international terrorist attacks, we need to assume on-the-ground terrorism in or out of Japan, targeting the international community, and sometimes Japan or Japanese people, as well as non-discriminatory maritime terrorism at the Strait of Malacca and other converging points of key SLOCs.[6] Such threats are likely to include attacks using ships obtained in conspiracy with pirates, or procured independently, like container ships, small boats, and small submarines. The terrorists may conspire with countries of concern such as North Korea, and in such an eventuality, the situation will become more complex, uncertain and serious. Moreover, there will also be a need to exercise power to prevent the proliferation of weapons of mass destruction originating from North Korea and other countries through PSI activities.

Functions Required for the Maritime Self-Defence Force

The new Guideline does not elaborate on the functions that the Maritime Self-Defence Force must possess. However, enlarging on the basic concept of the Guideline, the JMSDF will likely maintain and enhance the following functions. The command, control, communication and computer functions and the functions for anti-air, anti-ship, anti-submarine, and electronic warfare are the basic functions of maritime units, and they must be maintained, modernised and enhanced in the future. The functions for ASW, anti-mine warfare, as well as surveillance, reconnaissance and intelligence functions are not only the basic functions of maritime operations but also strategic functions that continue to be most required by the Maritime Self-Defence Force under the Japan–US security relationship, and therefore needs constant and continual maintenance and enhancement. Besides these, other conventional functions of the Maritime Self Defence Forces need to be newly introduced and reinforced.

Anti-Ground Attack Function

Considering the ballistic missile defence from the start, the defence system will be complete only when there is capability in three areas. These are the "denial deterrence" posture that include the pre-launching in a pre-emptive move of ballistic missiles (offensive defence), the elimination and nullification of launched ballistic missile (active defence), and limitation of damages when hit (passive defence). Japan has already determined that the SM-3 be loaded on Aegis Ships and PAC-3 be used for "active defence", but has no choice but to rely wholly on the US for "offensive defence" at least, apart from "passive defence".

However, in view of the security environment that Japan is in there is potential for the sudden and unexpected realisation of threats of ballistic missiles in the future. Therefore, the Maritime Self-Defence Force along with the Air Self-Defence Force needs to possess a capability for conducting conventional precision anti-ground attacks using the cruise missiles or ship based fixed-wing attack aircraft in the future, as the "offensive defence" to defeat enemy's missile launchers and storage silos in a pre-emptive mode to prevent the launching of ballistic missiles by rogue countries.

For the integrated operation to recapture islands and occupied regions, on the other hand, the Maritime Self-Defence Force needs to be able to implement assault landing operation in addition to the prevention of enemy's supply and reinforcement, and the escorting and carrying of ground units to recapture territories. However, it has extremely limited capability for anti-ground attack, due to domestic political restriction. In order to enable the Self-Defence Forces to complete the integrated operation of territorial recovery without anticipating excessive dependence on US Forces, the Maritime Self-Defence Force and the Air–Self-Defence Force need to have functions to enable precision anti-ground attacks using conventional weapon systems in the future.

In relation to this, the Maritime Self-Defence Force must develop full C4ISR (Command, Control, Communications, Computers, Intelligence, Surveillance and Reconnaissance) functions of the Aegis ships and others in order to maintain appropriate C4ISR interoperability with other forces at the theatre level throughout the joint operation and for the ballistic missile defence.

*Complete Function of Surface Mobile Force Operation
(Tactical Aircraft Carriers for Fleet Defence)*

In the future, the surface mobile force is expected to operate beyond the air cover of US Forces or Air–Self-Defence Force. As the possibility of severe air-raid increases depending on the spectrum of battle and operation area, the need to have fixed-wing tactical aircrafts on carriers to defend entire surface mobile forces will rise, as even the Aegis ships are not fully functioned for thorough air defence of fleets. This implies the appropriateness and necessity to possess tactical (fleet defence) aircraft carriers, which can comprehensively operate in the various types of maritime battles, as a ship to hold full C4ISR function, and carry several types of fixed-wing and rotary-wing tactical air-crafts that are capable of anti-air warfare, anti-ship warfare, electronic warfare, anti-submarine warfare as well as early warning and control and patrolling capability. In addition, as mentioned in the above, tactical aircraft carriers can carry tactical aircrafts with the capability of ground attacks, if it becomes necessary for ballistic missile defence, and landing operation support for territorial defence.

The Government's view on the possession of aircraft carriers is based on the interpretation of the constitution that "would not allow the possession of offensive aircraft carriers equivalent to ICBM or long range strategic bombers",[7] and does not essentially impede the possession of tactical aircraft carriers for general maritime operations at sea.

Other Functions

In the future, as the duties of international peace cooperation expand, the Maritime Self-Defence Force will be required to have functions of air transportation-in-fleet, sea-based ship repair as well as a hospital ship. Moreover, it will need to perform functions of special operation or ground combat at landing operation (Marine Corps) for island defence through joint operation.

Future Vision of the Maritime Self-Defence Force

Major Surface Combatants

Major surface combatants are deployed to mobile surface forces and regional district forces today. While the new Guideline stated the decrease of seven combatants (−13%) from the current number of 54 ships, mostly from regional district units, the immediate and continuous responses to international peace cooperation activities and against new threats and other situations on the distant region of Middle East and Indian Ocean would actually in contrast require the increase of major surface combatants for a highly skilled and readied mobile surface forces.

In the future, therefore, it is inevitable to efficiently possess highly skilled forces by making clear distinction of responsibilities and authorities between the commanders controlling fleet operations (force users) and the commanders in charge of fleet training and skill management (force providers). However, there is still a limit. In order to secure the absolute quantity of highly skilled mobile surface forces, while warranting defence posture of regional district units, it will become necessary to maintain as many surface combatants in regional district units as possible to be equivalent to multi-purpose ships of mobile surface forces. In the future, bold change in concepts will be needed; so regional district forces can be congregated by newly introducing Littoral Combat Ships (LCS) that are light-footed, quick responsive and mission convertible (territorial defence patrol, anti-ship, anti-submarine, anti-mine or other local maritime operations with optimum use of Unmanned Air Vehicle/Unmanned Subsurface Vehicle (UAV/USV) and onboard helicopters which conform to the regional unique characteristics, be it coastal, strait, waterways, ports, or islands.

At the core of mobile surface forces, the Maritime Self-Defence Force will eventually need to have tactical aircraft carriers, helicopter carriers, Aegis ships with Ballistic Missile Defence (BMD) functions, and multi-purpose ships.

Submarines

Submarines are stealthy, highly offensive and have a long-time action capability. They provide an extremely effective capability to respond against invasions to Japan, and to move even in the area of enemy's influence. Therefore, it is the only asset Japan has that can attack the enemy, even when air and maritime superiority cannot be secured. Moreover, due to recent improvement in their functions, submarines can be a significant strategic deterrent. Currently the Maritime Self-Defence Force has 16 conventional type submarines, which effectively perform strict mission patrols, in addition to educational and training operations with several training submarines. While the Maritime Self-Defence Force will need to enhance the operational capability of the Air Independent Propulsion (AIP) type submarines and promote further noise reduction, it can maintain the current system for the moment, but should consider the introduction of high performance submarines, including nuclear propellant submarines, in the future.

Mine Warfare Combatants

Minesweepers are deployed to mobile minesweeper forces and regional district forces. For the moment, current assets (29 vessels including mine-sweeper tenders) should be maintained, while holding sufficient assets and posture to allow the possible dispatching of minesweepers to international waters in the future, as Japan did to the Persian Gulf in 1991.

Replenishment and Transportation Ships

To provide replenishment at sea to major surface combatants and other bigger ships, the Maritime Self-Defence Force has five replenishment ships. With the larger replenishment ships named "Mashu" and "Oumi" to enter service (and the retirement of two smaller ships), all five ships will hold larger sizes. So they are to maintain the current force for the moment, while responding to the duties of international peace cooperation activities. The Maritime Self-Defence Force also has three transportation ships that can respond to the duties of massive disaster assistance in Japan, or be dispatched to international peace cooperation and international emergency relief activities. To execute international activities expected in the future, however, it is preferable to reinforce the transportation capability of the Maritime Self-Defence Force by adding more ships. For the moment, it is likely to maintain the current force as other ships including minesweeper tenders can provide some transportation services. The Maritime Self-Defence Force also needs to review the creation of Special Operation Units and Ground Combat Units (Marine Corps) given the need to develop and maintain ground forces accustomed to the maritime environment, the growing requirements to build and hold sufficient responsiveness and flexibility to respond to any emergency situations, as well as the growing demands to practice joint operations for territorial recovery and international peace cooperation.

Fixed-Wing Tactical Aircraft

As to fixed-wing tactical aircrafts, the Maritime Self-Defence Force has fixed-wing patrol aircrafts (P3C) under the mobile maritime air forces, which implement constant patrol, surveillance, reconnaissance and intelligence operations, while being able to respond to any anti-submarine or anti-ship operation.

In future, the aircraft will develop functions that will provide them more flexibility, and multi-purpose and self-completing functions in both hardware and software. Moreover, there is a need to introduce new fixed-wing Maritime Patrol Aircrafts (MPA) that will be able to provide various missions, including international operations.

The new Guideline plans to decrease 15 aircrafts (−19%) from the current force of 80 aircrafts. For this, it will be necessary to start studying the introduction of sea-based fixed-wing tactical aircrafts on tactical aircraft carriers of mobile surface forces, with various missions including anti-air, anti-ship, anti-ground attack, electronic warfare, anti-submarine, and early warning and control.

Rotary-Wing Tactical Aircraft

As the rotary-wing tactical aircrafts, the Maritime Self-Defence Force has sea-based rotary-wing patrol aircrafts (SH-60J/K) at the mobile surface forces and ground-based rotary-wing patrol aircrafts (SH-60J) for regional district forces with 83 aircrafts in total. In the future, there will be an increasing need for every rotary-wing patrol aircraft to become a sea-based one, in order to respond to the increased duties of joint operations at island seas in the East China Sea or other areas. Moreover, the scheduled type change of mine-sweeping and transportation helicopters (MH-53E), currently 11 in total, to MCH-101 will require further development of air transportation-in-fleet functions using these new helicopters, so it becomes possible to respond to various duties. It will become necessary also to start studying the introduction of rotary-wing tactical aircrafts for the various operations on the tactical aircraft carriers.

Spiritual Foundation of Maritime Self-Defence Force Personnel (Neo-Military)

Besides hardware and software, heartware is also important. In the future, the officers and enlists of Maritime Self-Defence Force must be aware that they will be required to have not only the spiritual foundation of so-called "Classic (20th Century type) Military", which demands tough physical and mental abilities, strong moral of missions and dedication to teamwork, and highly advanced military skills, but also the consciousness of a "New (21st Century type) Military" with ability, knowledge and technologies required to perform the functions of the "representative of a nation", "diplomat", and "law executioner". This will require them to have thorough knowledge of relevant international and domestic laws, and Rules of Engagement (ROE), proficiency in foreign languages, manners and ethics, deep interests in media and public relations, and the training in policing skills.

Notes

1. Japan Defense Agency, *The National Defense Programme Guideline for FY 2005 and After* (Tokyo: Japan Defense Agency, 2004). Available at http://www.jda.go.jp/e/index_htm. < Accessed on 27 December 2005>.
2. Ibid.
3. Bureau of Nonproliferation, *The Proliferation Security Initiative* (Washington D.C.: U.S. Department of State, 28 July 2004). Available at http://www.state.gov/t/np/rls/other/34726.htm. <Accessed on 27 December 2005>.
4. "North Korea", in Japan Defence Agency, *Defence of Japan 2004* (Tokyo: Japan Defence Agency, 2004), pp. 39–47.
5. "China", in Japan Defence Agency, *Defence of Japan 2004* (Tokyo: Japan Defence Agency, 2004), pp. 49–60.
6. "Terrorism", in Japan Defence Agency, *Defence of Japan 2004* (Tokyo: Japan Defence Agency, 2004), pp. 64–65.
7. "Constitution and Self-defence Right", Japan Defence Agency, *Defence of Japan 2004* (Tokyo: Japan Defence Agency, 2004), p. 79.

Chapter 7

Security in the Pacific Rim: Evolving US Strategies, Doctrines, and Forces for Maritime Cooperation and Regional Collective Action

Captain Lynn D. Pullen, USN (Retd.)
and Scott C. Truver, PhD

Introduction

The US concept of maritime security has undergone broad and far-reaching changes from the height of the Cold War, through the fall of the Soviet Union, and in the aftermath of the terrorist attacks on 11 September 2001. This process has included changes in how it employs its sea services — the Navy, Marine Corps, and Coast Guard — how the sea services work together or separately, and how they are equipped. The process of change is still ongoing, with some predicting ultimately a merger of the Navy, in the Department of Defense (DoD), and the Coast Guard, in the Department of Homeland Security (DHS). Also continuing is an evolution in the way in which the US regards the Pacific Rim. After decades of focus on Europe and the Soviet Union, the realisation of the importance of the Asia-Pacific region has spread from the uppermost echelons of government throughout the country. The critical economic links between the Pacific Rim states and the US, and the transnational threats that have characterised the 21st Century thus far, are combining to force adjustments in maritime strategies and doctrines, the forces that support them, and the level of cooperation and collaboration which America seeks with its Asia-Pacific neighbours.

The Maritime Strategy

While the US licked its wounds from the Vietnam War, the administration of President Ronald Reagan vowed to never again commit forces to war unless vital national interests were clearly at stake, and when it did, it would do so with overwhelming force, rather than a limited force augmented incrementally.

John Lehman served as Reagan's Secretary of the Navy from 1981 to 1987. His "Maritime Strategy" was specifically designed to press home attacks against Soviet naval forces and homeland bases, and focused on development of a "600-ship Navy" with forward-deployed rotational forces, an offensive and overwhelming force, and 15 carrier battle groups (CVBGs) and 100 nuclear-powered attack submarines (SSNs) as its twin "pillars". The Maritime Strategy emphasised power projection, with a primary goal of taking a war to an enemy's naval forces, and quickly preventing any constraint upon the use of the seas by America and her allies.[1] The strategy envisioned the Navy conducting global attacks against Soviet and Warsaw Pact naval forces and subsequently taking the battle ashore, Marine Corps forces would "marry up" with pre-positioned material and attack the Soviet/Warsaw Pact flanks while strike aircraft from CVBGs would directly contribute to defeating enemy forces in the land campaign.

According to the Maritime Strategy, naval forces would help fill national security requirements by means of flexible forward positioning, early global deployment, and being able to seize the initiative if deterrence failed.[2] In reality, the 15 CVBG/100 SSN "600-ship Navy" envisioned by the strategy would have been hard-pressed to carry out such an ambitious plan; requirements analyses at the time indicated that a force of 22 CVBGs and some 140 SSNs would have been needed to conduct operations at "minimum risk".[3]

The collapse of the Soviet Union in 1989–91 left American strategists floundering for a new direction. However, the immediate post-Cold War years continued the determination to resist being drawn into conflict, but when unavoidable, that conflict was to be pursued with the same overwhelming force. In that light, the US Navy (USN) continued its emphasis on the large-decks carrier and carrier battle groups with standard Cold-War formulations and deployments. Integrated operations with Marine Corps forces were secondary and the US Coast Guard (USCG) an afterthought in maritime strategy.

As defence budgets and forces began to shrink in a chimerical search for "peace dividends," questions emerged from inside and outside the American military establishment about the necessity to persist with the same strategy and acquisitions, which had become the norm in the latter part of the Cold War. How many was enough, and what kinds of assets would be required in a world dominated by a single superpower?

Transition and Transformation: "... From the Sea"

The early 1990s marked an abrupt transition away from Lehman's Maritime Strategy. The 1992 joint Navy-Marine Corps strategic concept, "... From the Sea," heralded an increased focus on the world's littorals: power projection and employment of naval forces, with greater emphasis on joint Navy-Marine Corps operations, from the sea to influence events on the littoral brought an expeditionary emphasis and a growing recognition of the threats in the littorals, including passage of naval ships and protection of commercial vessels. The USCG meanwhile increased its role in drug interdiction and maritime law enforcement, but remained focused on traditional missions and tasks. Only a few Coast Guard visionaries[4] fully understood the role of the Coast Guard as a "unique instrument of national security" and championed a nascent concept of a "National Fleet" in which USN and USCG assets were commingled at home and abroad to defend US citizens, interests, and friends whenever and wherever they might be at risk.[5]

The next evolutionary step away from the US Cold War maritime strategy was framed by the concept document "Forward... from the Sea". In 1994, this new document reaffirmed and updated the expeditionary emphasis of its predecessor, the need for rotational forward-deployed forces, and also expanded the strategic concept to focus specifically on the unique contributions naval expeditionary forces could bring to peacetime operations, response to crises, and to regional conflicts.

"Forward... from the Sea" reflected the lessons learned in the first Gulf War, Operations Desert Shield and Desert Storm: the post-Cold War need for operational collaboration with allies and coalition partners, and the growing value of the law enforcement capabilities of the USCG in dealing with situations and issues outside the normal purview of the USN and Marine Corps. The mid to late 1990s were a time of strategic transition in American maritime thinking. In 1995, the Secretary of the Navy and the Secretary of Transportation (the cabinet-level department to which the Coast Guard had been assigned since 1967) signed a Memorandum of Agreement (MOA) that defined the relationship between the Coast Guard and the Navy. This MOA allowed the Coast Guard Commandant and the Chief of Naval Operations, under certain circumstances, to engage and to exchange resources, and authorised the Coast Guard to assist the Navy without further negotiations needed through the bureaucracy.[6] The Coast Guard was authorised to augment the Navy in[7]:

- *Maritime Interception Operations.* Such operations were conducted in the Arabian Gulf where cutters and law enforcement detachments have assisted the Navy's 5th Fleet.
- *Port Operations, Security and Defence.* Such operations where Coast Guard units protect the ports, combat logistics force, maritime pre-positioning ships, and sealift ships.
- *Military Environmental Response Operations.* Such operations include responding to intentional environmental disasters, such as the 1991 disaster created in the Kuwaiti oil fields by Iraqi forces.
- *Theatre Security Operations.* Such operations as those performed by USCG cutters throughout Latin America, and when required, in other regions around the globe to assist allies and friendly nations in conducting operations and building their own maritime security capabilities.
- *Coastal Sea Control Operations.* Such operations include operations offshore to provide for safe passage of strategic sealift to and from deepwater ports, harbours, and anchorages, including surveillance and reconnaissance of seaways, interdiction of enemy shipping as well as force protection of logistics forces, offshore structures such as oil platforms and sea-to-shore pipelines.

The National Fleet

In 1998, the USN and USCG took their relationship a step further, through the National Fleet Policy Statement, which committed the two services to a shared purpose and a common effort, and explicitly recognised the wide-ranging contributions of the Coast Guard to American maritime security. The term "National Fleet" referred to development of interoperable multi-mission surface warships and maritime security cutters, and to coordination of ship planning, integration of information systems, and research and development, as well as expanded joint concepts of operations, logistics, training, exercises and deployments.[8] The policy statement was initially signed by Chief of Naval Operations Admiral Jay Johnson and Coast Guard Commandant Jim Loy, reconfirmed by CNO Admiral Vern Clark, and then, in 2002, expanded and signed by Admiral Clark and the new Coast Guard Commandant Admiral Thomas Collins.

The USCG's vision publication, "Coast Guard 2020", also issued in 1998, reflected the evolution of the service's role by clearly defining its mission: "... to protect the public, the environment, and US economic interests — in the Nation's ports and waterways, along the coast, on international waters, or in any maritime region as required to support national security".[9] A prescient document, "Coast Guard 2020" foresaw a future in which "More than ever, America will call upon the Coast Guard to protect lives and serve the national interests on the high seas, along the nation's maritime borders and coasts, and in the inland waterways. Mindful of these responsibilities, the service has charted its course and embarked on an ambitious plan to renew assets and increase capabilities".[10] To that end, the USCG has embarked on an ambitious plan to recapitalise current platforms and systems, and to acquire more advanced ships, aircraft and technology — the Integrated Deepwater System.

The Coast Guard's contribution to the National Fleet includes its statutory authorities (including law enforcement), multi-mission cutters, boats aircraft, and Command, Control, Communications, Computers, Intelligence, Surveillance and Reconnaissance (C4ISR) missions. The Deepwater programme, with new cutters and associated boats, manned and unmanned aircraft, and systems for C4ISR and integrated logistics support, provides the means by which the Coast Guard will fulfil its commitment to the National Fleet in the coming years.

In addition to the establishment of MOUs between the Deepwater Programme Executive Officer (PEO) and the Navy's PEO Ships, National Fleet initiatives include Joint USCG/USN training of West Africa naval/coast guard assets, USCG support to USN Anti-Terrorism/Force Protection initiatives, and USCG support to ballistic missile submarine security missions.

Implications of 9/11 on US Geostrategic Perspectives

All of these previous incremental steps in changing American maritime strategy seem particularly prescient, when viewed through the prism of 11 September 2001 and the world thereafter. Suddenly, the American public was aware of its vulnerabilities at home and abroad, and of the risks facing US and allied interests. Previously insulated from the specifics of these realities, the population rapidly had to come to terms with the concepts of global transnational and asymmetric threats.

Overnight, interest was aroused in the threats from the proliferation of weapons and technology, and the real effects that proliferation had for the American homeland and for America's friends and allies. The benefit of an open society, global commerce, international travel, and instant telecommunications upon which the nation depends, was suddenly being used for lethal purposes by foreign elements.

"Homeland Security" became the new mantra in the US following 9/11, and the daunting complexity of trying to "secure the homeland" in a globalise world was realised by the US government. While some immediate reactions to 9/11 harked back to America's pioneer days of "Circle the wagons!" that would have "secured" the nation by isolating it, the unreality of this reaction led the US to recognise the need for *cooperative and collaborative international efforts* to contend with the threats posed by terrorism without strangling the commerce and interaction upon which the modern world depends. The nation has both initiated and joined a variety of international efforts to this end with particular emphasis on security in the maritime domain.

Sea Power 21

The strategies of America's sea services since 9/11 have recognised the urgent need for changes to contend with asymmetric and non-state threats. In October 2002, then Chief of Naval Operations, Admiral Vern Clark, promulgated the USN's dynamic strategy to respond to the realities of the 21st Century called *Sea Power 21*. The "Capability Pillars" of *Sea Power 21*, Sea Strike, Sea Shield, Sea Basing, and FORCEnet, are the foundations for the bridge to a transformed Navy. The following are short descriptions of each of the capability pillars.

- *Sea Strike*. An expanded power projection that employs networked sensors, combat systems, and warriors to amplify the offensive impact of sea-based forces.
- *Sea Shield*. A global defensive assurance produced by extended homeland defence, sustained access to littorals, and the projection of defensive power deep overland.
- *Sea Basing*. An enhanced operational independence and support for joint operations as well as forces provided by networked, mobile, and secure sovereign platforms operating in the maritime domain.
- *FORCEnet*. The operational construct and architectural framework for naval warfare in the information age that integrates warriors, sensors, networks, command and control, platforms, and weapons into a networked,

distributed combat force that is scalable across all levels of conflict from seabed to space and sea to land.

The Navy also determined that it needed to revise its deployment scheduling and to develop a surge capability to be better ready to deploy sea-based air and ground forces in the event of emergencies. In May 2003, the Navy unveiled the Fleet Response Plan, designed to provide more flexible deployment schedules and to ensure deployments were performed for well-defined missions, rather than just a traditional "presence" role. "Presence with a purpose" would mean that some traditional areas of post-World War II USN deployments, especially the Mediterranean and waters nearby the Soviet Union, might be seen as a lesser priority.

The "1,000-Ship" Cooperative Navy

Relieving Admiral Clark on 22 July 2005, Chief of Naval Operations Admiral Michael G. Mullen has endorsed the *Sea Power 21* and Fleet Response Plan concepts and continues to emphasise the need for greater international maritime cooperation and collaboration, although his understanding of *Sea Power 21* is that it is a framework for programmatic decisions rather than a strategic concept. In 31 August 2005 remarks at the US Naval War College, he announced: "I'm after that proverbial 1,000 ship Navy — a fleet-in-being, if you will — comprised of all freedom-loving nations, standing watch over the seas, standing watch over each other. Because I believe, with every fibre of my being, that we are all united by more than just fear".

Admiral Mullen's vision for the future of the USN focuses particularly on the importance of the littorals in the 21st Century, while not ignoring the "deep blue" of the open ocean. As this essay was completed, his staff was reviewing the Navy's shipbuilding plans to ensure that the platforms acquired, both the number and types of ships, are "Balanced to face the challenges of our age: Piracy, drug smuggling, transport of Weapons of Mass Destruction (WMD) over the high seas, exploitation of economic rights, organised crime, and yes, terrorism. As well as not taking our eye off the requirement for major combat operations".[11]

Current Force Structure Modernisation: Planning Capabilities to Match New Threats and Strategies

The US Department of Defense 2005 Quadrennial Defense Review (QDR), the latest in a series of congressionally mandated reviews of the status of

America's forces and capabilities, will be the first truly post-9/11 review.[12] The Pentagon's summer 2005 planning concept for the first time seemed to give fairly equal weight to requirements for "Homeland Defence" (a somewhat circumscribed concept that complements "Homeland Security"), the Global War on Terrorism, and to more traditional military campaigns. This signals a shift from the force planning philosophy that has predominated since the early 1990s, which emphasised a "two-war" formula, based on fighters, warships, armour, and other such traditional combat systems.

Although the 2005 QDR was still in process in December 2005, as this essay was completed, four challenge areas were seen as critically important. These four areas were: (1) building coalitions to defeat terrorism; (2) defending the US homeland; (3) countering the proliferation of WMD; and (4) shaping the choices of countries at a strategic crossroads.[13]

The Navy

Former CNO Admiral Vern Clark noted this shift as the 2005 QDR got under way: "... our Navy is not correctly balanced and optimised for the world, the future that we're facing. The Navy that we possess today must be reshaped to deal with the challenges that we have in the future".[14] The acquisition of new types of ships such as the Littoral Combat Ship (LCS), and their modular design will provide the Navy with a more flexible and adaptable force, which emphasises speed, agility and a commitment to joint and coalition interoperability.

CNO Admiral Mullen has taken this a step further, stating, "We cannot sit out in the deep blue, waiting for the enemy to come to us. He will not. We must go to him. We need a green water capability and a brown water capability and quite frankly, I want a more robust onshore capability".[15] Admiral Mullen's plans include a return to a riverine capability, with which to "operate and exercise and learn from many nations who do not need or desire a blue-water navy. We can be a better partner, and we can help extend the peace to every shore".[16] The Navy has formed a new Expeditionary Combat Command with headquarters in Norfolk, Virginia, and plans to create three riverine squadrons of 12 boats each by 2007 as an element of the new command.[17]

However, the capabilities and planning the Navy face budgetary constraints. President George W. Bush has committed to the rebuilding of the US Gulf of Mexico coast, devastated by hurricanes with at least $200 billion pledged. The US looks to be committed to landing people on the moon by 2018, a quest that will require more than $100 billion. Other "entitlement" programmes are costing billions of dollars, too. The US DoD is thus looking to carve more than $50 billion in near-term budgets. These and other demands for increasingly scarce resources will hamstring USN shipbuilding programmes, keeping the future fleet to an approximate size of 313 ships and presenting hard choices in acquisition programmes and operations.

The Coast Guard

The USCG's Integrated Deepwater System (IDS) acquisition programme faces similar financial hurdles. IDS is designed to give the USCG a new "Deepwater" system of cutters, aircraft, and C4ISR capabilities. The intent of IDS is to replace the USCG's aging and increasingly obsolescent fleet of high- and medium-endurance systems with 21st Century capabilities specifically tailored for demanding operations offshore, and will enhance operations with smaller Coast Guard units in coastal areas. Totally compatible with DoD architectures, IDS will result in a much more efficient and effective mix of Coast Guard assets. A total of approximately 90 medium- and high-endurance cutters are seen as complementing the resource-constrained USN, particularly in peacetime constabulary operations.

Although senior leadership talks continued between the Navy and the Coast Guard, in the late fall 2005 there was no indication that the "National Fleet" policy would formally be reaffirmed. The planned early November meeting between Admiral Mullen and Admiral Collins was cancelled, giving rise to concerns in Coast Guard Headquarters that "National Fleet" commitment was indeed waning.

Into the 21st Century: Evolving US Maritime Security Strategy

A New National Maritime Security Strategy

Recognising the vital importance of maritime security to the defence and prosperity of the country, on 20 September 2005, President Bush signed the US *National Strategy for Maritime Security* (NSMS). The NSMS is the result of an interagency effort between the Department of Homeland Security and the Department of Defense, among other US government participants, to align all Federal government maritime security programmes and initiatives into a comprehensive and cohesive national effort involving appropriate Federal, State, local, and private sector entities.

New initiatives are needed to ensure that all nations fulfil their responsibilities to prevent and respond to terrorist or criminal actions with timely and effective enforcement. More robust international mechanisms will ensure improved transparency in the registration of vessels and identification of ownership, cargoes, and crew of the world's multinational, multi-flag merchant marine.

National Strategy for Maritime Security, September 2005

The NSMS is augmented by eight supporting plans that address specific threats and challenges in the maritime domain. These plans will be updated periodically to respond to changes in the maritime threat, the world environment, and national security strategies and policies. The eight supporting plans are:

- National Plan to Achieve Domain Awareness.
- Global Maritime Intelligence Integration Plan.
- Interim Maritime Operational Threat Response Plan.
- International Outreach and Coordination Strategy.
- Maritime Infrastructure Recovery Plan.
- Maritime Transportation System Security Plan.
- Maritime Commerce Security Plan.
- Domestic Outreach Plan.

The NSMS is based on three overarching principles: freedom of the sea; uninterrupted flow of commerce; and, good border management, which is facilitating the movement of legitimate people and cargo, while screening out the dangerous. The NSMS also identifies five strategic actions necessary for maritime security. These five actions are: (1) Enhancement of international cooperation; (2) Maximisation of domain awareness; (3) Embedding of security into commercial practices; (4) Deployment of layered security; and (5) Assuring continuity of the marine transportation system. Importantly for the future in the Pacific Rim, "international cooperation" is the highest priority element of the five Strategic Actions.

Indeed, this new maritime strategy fully acknowledges the need for international cooperation in the pursuit of maritime security due to the ever-increasing integration of the economies of individual nations. The strategy also commits the US to pursue new initiatives diplomatically through international organisations such as the International Maritime Organisation, the World Customs Organisation, and the International Standards Organisation. Specifically, the September 2005 NSMS promises that the US will continue to promote development of cooperative mechanisms for coordinating regional measures against maritime threats that span national boundaries and jurisdictions. By reducing the potential for regional conflict, maritime security is enhanced worldwide. The US will also work closely with other governments and international and regional organisations to enhance the maritime security capabilities of other key nations by:

- Offering maritime and port security assistance, training, and consultation.
- Coordinating and prioritising maritime security assistance and liaison within regions.
- Allocating economic assistance to developing nations for maritime security to enhance security and prosperity.
- Promoting implementation of the Convention for the Suppression of Unlawful Acts against the Safety of Maritime Navigation and its amendments and other international agreements; and
- Expanding the International Port Security and Maritime Liaison Officer Programmes, and the number of agency attachés.[18]

A Transforming US Navy Strategy: Purpose, Flexibility, Speed, Agility, Missions...

Former CNO Admiral Clark observed that "predictability is a liability" and the US Navy's standard six-month "presence" deployments made it easy for adversaries to know where the Navy's forces would be at any given time and for how long. The Navy has restructured those deployments so that USN forces go somewhere for a purpose, whether it be partnering with allies for training or for exercises, that is "presence with a purpose", rather than just going to an area for six months as a "hangover" from a half-century of tradition.

The Fleet Response Plan supports *Sea Power 21*'s Global Concept of Operations and is an element of the Navy's "Transformation Roadmap". The "Global CONOPS" was introduced to support current and future forward-deterrent and rapid-response constructs such as the Carrier Strike Group (CSG) and the Expeditionary Strike Group (ESG) as key components of the global integrated naval force. The Global CONOPS recognises that organising naval deployments around ESGs and CSGs will increase the number of independently employable naval strike groups available to American Regional Combatant Commanders, and scaleable joint response options. Future forward naval operating forces may be organised into Expeditionary Strike Forces (ESF) of which elements will train together to meet a wide variety of contingencies. An ESF would comprise CSGs, ESGs, and Maritime Pre-positioning Groups (MPGs). An ESF could be augmented with forcible-entry-capable Marine Expeditionary Brigades, combined with in-theatre assets. The ESF could also complement, as needed, the Air Force's Air and Space Expeditionary Task Forces, the Army's Future Forces, and the Joint Command's Special Operations Forces for integrated joint operations at any level of conflict.

As the need for counter-terrorism actions has mounted, variants of previous operational concepts have become part of the tasking of American sea services. Extended Maritime Interdiction Operations (EMIO) is an integral part of the new flexibility of US maritime forces and a key component of the Global War on Terrorism. EMIO's purpose is to deter, delay, and disrupt the movement of terrorists and terrorist-related materials at sea.

The Fleet Response Plan has thus reinvigorated the USN through its more flexible deployment, maintenance, manning, and training processes. The Navy had also demonstrated a substantial capacity to stream its capabilities around the world through revised operating schedules and exercises such as "Summer Pulse 04". For almost two months, seven CSGs, several ESGs, and accompanying naval forces participated in simultaneous deployments, surge operations, joint and international exercises, and other advanced training and port visits in all US Regional Combatant Commanders' areas of operations. Summer Pulse 04 also stressed the shore establishment and logistics enterprises.

> The vision we seek is: Americans secure at home and abroad; sea and air lanes open and free for the peaceful, productive movement of international commerce; enduring national and international naval relationships that remain strong and true; steadily deepening cooperation among the maritime forces of emerging partner nations; and a combat-ready Navy — forward-deployed, rotational and surge capable — large enough, agile enough, and lethal enough to deter any threat and defeat any foe in support of the Joint Force.
>
> Admiral Michael Mullen
> "Meeting the Challenge of a New Era"
> CNO Guidance for 2006

While warfighting capabilities remain central to the USN's mission, CNO Admiral Mullen has observed that "while warfighting is certainly what we are about, it is not, and cannot be *all* we are about".[19] Maritime security in today's Navy lexicon has — and must continue to have — a broader meaning. America's sea services were all involved in Operation Unified Assistance (the response to the December 2004 tsunami), and found that the involvement was in fact a "pro-active defence" measure. Participation in humanitarian assistance and disaster relief operations gains friends and allies, replacing categorical distrust and even outright hostility.

Admiral Mullen noted that the actions of American sea services, acting with international partners in Operation Unified Assistance, "started changing some hearts and minds. We started showing a side of American to them that wasn't perceived as frightening, monolithic or arrogant. We showed them American power — American sea power — at its finest, and at its most noble".[20] Mullen underscored the importance with which he viewed this proactive defence, saying "Make no mistake about it, I view relief efforts like that — and any other number of engagement activities we do — as very much a part of winning the war on terror".

The CNO has exhorted the USN to take a slightly different look at "sea power", as a team effort, not just with the Marine Corps and Coast Guard, but also with international maritime relationships based upon "understanding and trust, enduring relationships that bloom into partnerships". Building on ideas like Theatre Security Cooperation,[21] the Proliferation Security Initiative, and the Regional Maritime Security Initiative, Admiral Mullen noted, "We find that every nation has a stake in security, and a distinct, unique capability — as well as a great desire — to contribute".[22] To that end, as noted above, the CNO is looking for something like a "1,000-ship navy, — a fleet-in-being if you will — comprised of all freedom-loving nations, standing watch over the seas, standing watch over each other".[23]

The Emerging US Coast Guard (USCG) Strategy: Acceptable Presence... Everywhere

The USCG is likewise evolving its strategy to better cope with the challenges of the 21st century. Since its beginnings in 1790 as the US Revenue Cutter Service, the Coast Guard has built a worldwide reputation as a highly-regarded agent of law enforcement, life-saving, and environmental protection both within US territorial waters and economic zones, and increasingly, in the international arena. The USCG has adopted the term "acceptable presence" to describe one of the key components of its operating principles.[24]

Foreign governments and non-state actors generally regard the USCG's forces as less threatening or objectionable than those of other US armed services which are seen as implementers of US national foreign policy rather than international legal concerns.

The "acceptability" of USCG operations makes it the ideal inter-actor with international organisations; foreign governments, navies and coast guards, and domestic and international *non*-governmental organisations on a wide range of defence and maritime related issues. Since the Coast Guard is accustomed to performing operations by cooperative effort, working with and coordinating efforts of a diverse set of governmental and non-governmental entities to achieve an objective, it has developed a well-deserved credibility as a partner with these entities, rather than as a dominant force.[25]

USCG Vice Commandant, Vice Admiral Terry Cross, addressing the more than 148 naval delegates from 75 countries at the 17th International Sea Power Symposium at the Naval War College, in September 2005, said ". . . the United States Coast Guard shares very similar missions with the Sea Services of other Maritime nations. The smaller your navy, the more likely that your mission set looks like ours. That provides an opportunity for us to collaborate, exchange best practices and learn from each other".

The Pacific Rim Strategy of the USCG's Pacific Command, still in development, seeks to provide an architecture and strategic framework for expanded use of Coast Guard assets — particularly its projected Deepwater National Security Cutters — in concert with US Pacific Command and regional navies/coast guards to contribute to regional maritime security and common interests.

> National coast guards for protecting national sovereignty in home waters are not new. The United States Coast Guard (USCG) in particular has a long history. What is new is that coast guards are being used more widely in the national interest, including as instruments of foreign policy in waters beyond the limits of national jurisdiction.
>
> Sam Bateman
> Coast Guards: New Forces for
> Regional Order and Security
> January 2003

Retired Australian Commodore Sam Bateman pointed out these advantages of Coast Guards being major components of maritime security regimes, in that Coast Guards may "overcome sensitivities that inhibit naval cooperation and provide a means of conducting law enforcement in areas where the use of naval vessels may aggravate the situation".[26]

Initiatives, Not Directives: International Cooperation and Collaboration

Since 9/11 the US has set in motion several initiatives, and has invited other governments to join in cooperative international action against transnational threats. Sole "superpower" or not, these initiatives constitute explicit recognition that international cooperation and collaboration are vital to the US and to the rest of the world against transnational threats. In January 2002, the US announced the Container Security Initiative (CSI), designed to protect the nearly 90% of all world cargo that moves by container. Through information exchange and the use of technology, the more than 20 countries currently participating are working together to thwart terrorist threats to maritime trade. The Proliferation Security Initiative (PSI), announced in May 2003, similarly responds to the challenge of the worldwide proliferation of WMD, as well as their delivery systems and related materials, and builds on other international cooperative efforts to prevent proliferation of these items.

Particularly important for its impact on Asia-Pacific maritime security — in addition to the Proliferation Security Initiative (PSI) and Container Security Initiative (CSI) mentioned earlier — is the Regional Maritime Security Initiative (RMSI). While the PSI and the CSI focused on global threats to specific trade items, the RMSI offered regional states what the US believed would be an ideal framework to deal with these and other transnational threats, particularly to the Asia-Pacific region.

The RMSI: Missteps and New Beginnings

The RMSI got off to a rocky start. In the March 2004 testimony to the US House of Representatives, Admiral Thomas Fargo, Commander US Pacific Command (USPACOM), described the RMSI as a means to combat piracy, terrorism, and trafficking in narcotics and people in the Asia-Pacific Region. His description indicated the RMSI would include not only intelligence sharing with the regional states, but could also include deployment of Marines and Special Forces on high-speed vessels to counter maritime threats, particularly those likely from terrorists. Admiral Fargo reiterated this description of RMSI in a speech that May in Vancouver.[27]

To its chagrin, the USPACOM discovered the extent of regional sensitivities regarding sovereignty over national and territorial waters. After the RMSI was announced by then Commander USPACOM, Admiral Thomas Fargo, in 2004, the negative Asia-Pacific reactions to the initiative reflected deep-seated regional concerns that the US was about to send in expeditionary forces to control the Malacca Strait and other regional waterways. These concerns were particularly strongly voiced by the littoral states of Malaysia and Indonesia.

Since that debacle, the US and the Pacific Command, in late 2005 led by Admiral William Fallon, have been determined to underscore that the intent of the RMSI is, in fact, to form a *partnership* with willing regional nations, one that *respects sovereignty* over national and territorial waters, to "work together to identify, monitor, and intercept transnational maritime threats under international and domestic law".[28]

The RMSI recognises the critical importance of secure maritime waterways to the peace and prosperity of the Asia-Pacific Region, and the threats to that peace and prosperity from transnational threats, like terrorism, maritime piracy, illegal trafficking in narcotics, human and other illicit cargo, as well as other criminal activities. The initiative particularly underscores the importance of information-sharing as a means to strengthen maritime security by creating an environment hostile to transnational threats. USPACOM is seeking a cooperative team approach and the leveraging of technology to enable all participants to build and share a clear picture of the maritime environment and thereby ensure maritime security. The RMSI identifies some of the common elements of maritime security as:

- Increased situational awareness and information sharing, fused information, shared among governments that will facilitate border security and cue effective responses to maritime threats.
- Responsive decision-making architectures, using standardised procedures, to support timely response and cooperation against emerging threats.
- Enhanced maritime interception capacity that will facilitate each nation taking effective action, as it deems appropriate.
- Agency, ministerial, and international cooperation, under international and domestic laws, that is essential to synchronise all elements of regional capability.[29]

At the June 2005 "Shangri-la Dialogue," Admiral Fallon indicated he supported the three-point maritime security framework that had been proposed by other speakers: (1) there are roles for both nations and non-governmental, international organisations; (2) littoral states should bear the primary responsibilities; and (3) sovereignty must be recognised. A collective maritime security effort, as envisioned by the RMSI, would empower each participating nation with the information and capabilities it needs to act against maritime threats in its own territorial seas. While responding to a maritime threat generally will require a cooperative effort, most frequently using maritime interdiction capabilities in the form of law enforcement or customs vessels, military forces might also be a resource to respond, particularly beyond territorial waters and economic zones or when other assets are not available.

In February 2005, for instance, the USS *Bonhomme Richard* (LHD-6), after delivering more than a million pounds of humanitarian supplies to Indonesian tsunami survivors, was performing maritime interdiction operations in the Persian Gulf when it responded to a distress call from Kuwaiti fishermen. One fishing dhow had been seized by pirates, and the rest of the dhows called for assistance in driving them off. The huge multipurpose amphibious assault ship made best speed in pursuit of the pirates, chasing them away. Captain Scott Jones, the skipper of the *Bonhomme Richard,* noted, "With 44,000 tons of combat power chasing after them, they got out of there in a hurry!"[30]

Implications of US Maritime Security Initiatives and the National Fleet for Maritime Balance and Relationships in the Pacific Rim

In late 2005 the US was wrestling with a combination of budget constraints and increased demands for homeland defence and other security measures against transnational threats. These challenges require that US military forces, such as the Navy, Marine Corps and Coast Guard, become better able to operate together, take on similar missions, and work cooperatively with the forces of other countries. This is combining with a growing awareness within the US that a new concept of "maritime" power, as opposed to "naval" power, is needed for maritime security operations short of war. Coast Guard Commandant Admiral Thomas Collins described this concept in an article in the *Naval War College Review* in 2004: "The world's oceans are global thoroughfares. A cooperative international approach involving partnerships of nations, navies, coast guards, law-enforcement agencies, and commercial shipping interests is essential — with all parties acting collaboratively to confront broadly defined threats to their common and interdependent maritime security".

Applying this strategy of "maritime power" in an integrated way among the world's navies and oceans is a powerful notion. We have within our grasp the opportunity to leverage new technologies and attain new capabilities that will enable coordinated, systematic, and fused intelligence that will, in turn, provide detailed, in-depth knowledge of the maritime domain".[31]

Global maritime security contributes to upholding national maritime sovereignty and regional peace. It does this by protecting maritime borders from intrusion, preserving global mobility for legitimate commerce and nation/state military forces, and protecting maritime-related infrastructures. All nations benefit from this collective security, and all government must share in the responsibility for it — not unlike all governments' responsibilities against *piracy jure gentium*.

While still maintaining the right to defend its interests unilaterally if all else fails, the US gradually seems to be understanding that its interests are generally best served through collective and cooperative action. The implementation of the various security initiatives has made this fairly clear. The initial negative reaction to Admiral Fargo's 2004 announcement of the RMSI re-emphasised to the US that many governments are justly highly sensitive about their own national territory and sovereignty, and that America needs to find its own place as an international partner, not always "sitting at the head of the table".

Collaboration and Cooperation: A Security Imperative for All Maritime Powers in the 21st Century

UN Security Council Resolution 1373 of 28 September 2001 was drafted in response to the 9/11 attacks, but holds valuable guidance for the world of the 21st Century and the maintenance of good order for the common good. By the text of the Resolution, "the Council called on all States to intensify and accelerate the exchange of information regarding terrorist actions or movements; forged or falsified documents; traffic in arms and sensitive material; use of communications and technologies by terrorist groups; and the threat posed by the possession of weapons of mass destruction".[32] States were also called on to exchange information and cooperate to prevent and suppress terrorist acts and to take action against the perpetrators of such acts. States should become parties to, and fully implement as soon as possible, the relevant international conventions and protocols to combat terrorism.

"The Council noted with concern the close connection between international terrorism and transnational organised crime, illicit drugs, money laundering and illegal movement of nuclear, chemical, biological and other deadly materials. In that regard, it emphasised the need to enhance the coordination of national, sub-regional, regional and international efforts to strengthen a global response to that threat to international security".

The Security Council further defined "Terrorism" in its Resolution 1566, adopted on 8 October 2004. This resolution calls on countries to prevent and punish "criminal acts, including against civilians, committed with the intent to cause death or serious bodily injury, or taking of hostages, with the purpose to provoke a state of terror in the general public or in a group of persons or particular persons, intimidate a population or compel a government or an international organisation to do or to abstain from doing any act". The acts "are under no circumstances justifiable by considerations of a political, philosophical, ideological, racial, ethnic, religious or other similar nature".[33] These UN resolutions have far-reaching implications. Nations must act together against the threats of terrorism or experience consequences to their national security and their economic prosperity.

Cooperation: A Critical Need for Asia-Pacific Maritime Security

The Asia-Pacific countries have been moving forward as concerns have grown about maritime security and the threats of terrorism and other criminal acts. They still have a variety of historical and territorial hurdles to overcome as they deal with the immense spectrum of problems that are encompassed by the term "maritime security". Sometimes the steps are tiny and frustratingly slow, but at other times, remarkable measures are taken.

A report on the overall costs of terrorism, particularly emphasising maritime terrorism, was produced in 2003 by the Australian Department of Foreign Affairs and Trade's Economic Analytical Unit. The report noted that while the costs of unchecked terrorism would be significant for all economies, the Asia-Pacific Economic Cooperation (APEC) nations' economies, trade and income growth would be disproportionately affected. The causes of this disproportionate effect were seen as[34]:

- Most developing APEC economies depend more heavily on trade flows, particularly with the US and OPEC economies;
- Many regional developing economies reply in receiving foreign direct investment, which would be at risk from an increase in terrorist activities; and
- Insurance premiums may be higher on cargoes and vessels travelling to and from developing countries because of uncertainty about the adequacy of local security procedures.

Thus, the protection of Asia-Pacific economies and trade from terrorist threats has become a major focus for APEC. APEC's leaders have reiterated their commitment to the organisation's shared vision of achieving stability, security, and prosperity for the people of the Asia-Pacific Region. Indeed, the APEC forum has been an important element in influencing greater regional cooperation on maritime security. APEC's Working Group on Maritime Security has focused on implementing the International Maritime Organisation's International Ship and Port Facility Security Code (ISPS) and aiding those members who faced challenges on compliance by the July 2004 deadline, and the APEC Counter-Terrorism Task Force (CTTF) has been helping member economies assess their counter-terrorism status and needs, and coordinate capacity building and programmes for technical assistance in counter-terrorism efforts.

> ...We have been asked why APEC, as a traditionally economic forum, has engaged in the mounting counter-terrorism dialogue. The response is simply that terrorism is one of the most destructive threats to the APEC goals of free trade and investment in the Asia-Pacific region. Terrorism not only destroys the lives and property of individuals, but also attacks the entire economies, undermining market confidence, inflating the cost of trade and reducing market activity.
>
> Ambassador Makarim Wibisono, Chair
> APEC Counter-Terrorism Task Force
> Bali, January 2004

APEC's Secure Trade in the APEC Region (STAR) initiative is a significant effort to evaluate and respond to the needs for trade security in the region. Counter-Terrorism Action Plans (CTAPs) filed by each member economy describe where they believe their strengths and weaknesses exist in counter-terrorism areas including maritime security.

APEC members have been cooperating to strengthen border security through enhanced supply security guidelines. The non-binding Private Sector Supply Chain Security Guidelines approved by APEC are business-friendly, and conducive to adoption by private sector participants in enhancing their supply chain security practices. Many APEC ports are also participating in the US Container Security Regime. This initiative assures the in-transit integrity of containers and provides electronic information on a container's contents to customs, port and shipping officials as early as possible in the supply chain. The battle against maritime piracy in the region has been further enhanced by the increased cooperation among APEC fora and organisations, such as the International Maritime Bureau's Piracy Reporting Centre in Kuala Lumpur.

STAR Initiative

A significant APEC action has been the STAR Initiative. STAR is intended to boost trade efficiency while simultaneously strengthening security against terrorist threats. The programme involves specific measures to protect cargo, ships, aviation, and people crossing borders. It also involves private-sector representatives working in partnership with APEC economies to implement necessary measures to secure trade. The STAR Initiative has also been help-ing to protect ships engaged in international voyages through capacity build-ing programmes to assist economies in adopting the International Maritime Organisation's international ship and port security codes that went into effect in July 2004, followed by the requirement for installation of automatic iden-tification systems on certain ships by December 2004. APEC also has been developing standards for detection equipment and other security technology.

Malacca Straits Security Initiative (MSSI)

Some remarkable regional efforts are underway to secure vulnerable waters in the Asia-Pacific region and offer great promise for improved maritime security. When Operation Malsindo kicked off on 20 July 2004, it marked a cooperative effort between ASEAN-states Malaysia, Singapore, and Indonesia to provide year-round anti-piracy and anti-terrorism protection in the Straits of Malacca. Each participating navy agreed to supply five to seven warships for the patrol, and a hotline has been established to provide for rapid communications, an important information-sharing link when a warship of one state is in hot pur-suit into waters of another partner.

At the June 2005 Shangri-la Dialogue, Malaysia's Deputy Prime Minister and Defence Minister, Najib Tun Razak, proposed multinational maritime air patrols over the Malacca Straits. That proposal, known as "Eyes in the Sky" or EiS, was greeted enthusiastically by the littoral states, as well as Thailand. The EiS has taken off rapidly, the first patrols were performed on 13 September with Thailand acting as an observer before becoming an active participant. The EiS participating states will each contribute two patrols per week, with permissions to fly above the waters of the EiS nations no closer than three nau-tical miles from land. The EiS aircraft will carry a Combined Maritime Patrol Team (CMPT) on board. The team will be composed of a military officer from each EiS state, and will broadcast any suspicious contacts to ground-based Monitoring and Action Agencies (MAA) in the participating countries.

The Malsindo and EiS patrols now form key elements of what has come to be known as the Malacca Straits Security Initiative (MSSI). The EiS patrols are aimed at providing maritime domain awareness, while the Malsindo naval patrols are intended to physically secure and defend the maritime domain. While the concepts are excellent, it will no doubt take time to iron out the details to make these cooperative efforts work smoothly. Phase 1, when

the littoral states are shouldering these responsibilities together, will provide
the opportunity to explore the pitfalls inherent in coordinating operations and
procedures between different nations.

This initial phase will also offer the opportunity for the original participants
to determine the best contributory roles for other states and stakeholders in
Phase 2. If it is determined that this substantial undertaking can be supported
by other stakeholders through maritime patrol craft or aircraft, or that technology to detect and conduct surveillance on offenders needs supplementa-
tion, these could be roles allocated to other interested parties, but within the
guidelines developed through experiences in Phase 1.

The nations of the Asia-Pacific region have undertaken several cooperative measures to ensure their maritime security. The Association of South
East Asian Nations (ASEAN), and its Regional Forum (ARF) are important
fora for exchange of ideas and recommendations on security in the region.
Both have contributed to the region's counter terrorism work, but efforts to
develop tools of preventive diplomacy and conflict management are still at an
early stage.

The Regional Cooperation Agreement on Anti-Piracy and Armed Robbery Against Ships in Asia (ReCAAP)

The Regional Cooperation Agreement on Anti-Piracy and Armed Robbery
against Ships in Asia (ReCAAP) is a November 2004 Japanese initiative to promote Asia-Pacific region anti-piracy cooperation. A key element of ReCAAP
is an Information Sharing Centre to be located in Singapore, designed to
facilitate communication and information exchanges between member countries, and to improve the quality of statistics and reports on piracy and armed
robbery in the region.[35] Japan, Singapore, Laos, and Cambodia have thus
far signed up. The goal is for all ASEAN members, plus Bangladesh, China,
India, Japan, South Korea, and Sri Lanka to ratify the agreement, which will
enter into force once a quorum of ten signatories is acquired.

The Batam Joint Statement

The Batam Joint Statement of the Littoral States on the Straits of Malacca and
Singapore in August 2005 reaffirmed the sovereignty and sovereign rights over
the Straits of Malacca and Singapore, and the responsibility of the Littoral
States for the safety of navigation, environmental protection and maritime
security in the Straits. However, the Ministers of Foreign Affairs of the Littoral

States also acknowledged in the Batam statement "the importance of engaging the states bordering the funnels leading to the Straits of Malacca and Singapore, and the major users of the straits".[36]

Joint War Committee of Lloyd's Marketing Association Declaration

Despite all measures taken thus far, however, the need to further coordinate regional maritime security in the Asia-Pacific was emphatically underscored in July 2005 when the Joint War Committee of Lloyd's Marketing Association declared the Strait of Malacca a "war risk area". This advisory committee to marine insurers felt strongly enough that the danger of war, strikes, terrorism and related perils including concerns about criminal actions perpetrated by pirates or, sea robbers exist in the Malacca Straits. This has had the immediate result of higher insurance costs, as well as raised the possibility that some insurers may refuse to completely insure shipping through the Strait.

Since the 900 km-long Strait is the transit route of 30% of world trade and 50% of global crude oil each year, perhaps the War Committee's declaration will, in the long run, be the factor that expedites needed cooperation. As the Secretary General of the International Maritime Organisation, Mr. Efthimios Mitropoulos, noted in Jakarta on 7 September 2005, "the need, in certain areas, for genuine progress to be made, and made without delay, carries a global imperative". Mr. Mitropoulos urged "making those using the Straits aware of the safety and security risks there through: sharing information on the moves and intention of criminals operating or planning to operate in the Straits; capacity-building; training personnel in the prevention and suppression of unlawful acts in the region; and enacting technical co-operation projects including on search and rescue and responding to marine pollution incidents".[37]

With the incidence of piracy within the Asia-Pacific region, and particularly the Strait of Malacca, still high, and the relative vulnerability of the 50,000 ships that pass through the Strait, and other waters in the region to terrorism and other acts of criminality, the international community remains concerned about maritime security. Security analysts indicate major concerns about the possibility of terrorist exploiting the piracy problem, by adopting similar tactics or teaming up with the criminals to board ships. Once seized, terrorists could either blow up a vessel, or even use it to ram into other shipping, ports, or other facilities.[38] The results could be devastating, both for commerce, and for the states concerned.

Cooperation and Collaboration for the Common Good: America's Evolving Asia-Pacific Maritime Security Strategy

The US concern for maritime security was sharply increased as a result of 9/11, and it has been making adjustments in its national strategies to cope with this heightened awareness. In truth, some of the evolutionary shifts of its military strategies began with the end of the Cold War, as it became ever more apparent that "joint" service capabilities would need to be emphasised. The Navy and Marine Corps began to cooperate and to stress "interoperability". This has gradually become an easier partnership for these two services.

Several years before 9/11, the need for the Navy to partner much more closely with the US Coast Guard was recognised by the agreement which gave birth to the National Fleet concept. As former CNO Admiral Clark noted several times, "In homeland security the Coast Guard is the supported command and the Navy the supporting command, while in homeland defence, the Coast Guard supports the Navy". The two sea services are still working out the differences and similarities in some of their roles and missions. It is a slow process, but holds promise for the maritime security of the US and other nations around the world, which recognise the vital part maritime security plays in the survival of their economies and their sovereign states.

The US Pacific Command

The US Pacific Command has sponsored the multilateral, biennial Rim of the Pacific (RIMPAC) power projection/sea control exercise since 1971. In recent years, it has added more RIMPAC exercise elements involving the USCG. In addition to exercises with Asia-Pacific region nations focused mainly on military warfighting objectives such as Ulchi Focus Lens in Korea, USPACOM also sponsors multinational exercises such as the Search and Rescue Exercises (SAREXs) held in May 2005 with Hong Kong's Civil Aviation Department (and elements of the People's Liberation Army–Navy).[39] USPACOM also is a rotational host to an annual trilateral Arctic SAREX between Canada, Russia, and the US as part of efforts to foster military-to-military contacts with the Russian Federation. In the most recent version of this event, approximately 230 participants from the US, Canada and Russia exercised their skills from 11–18 September 2005 during the Arctic SAREX in Alaska.

Demonstrating a clear understanding of intra-regional sensitivities, USPACOM also participates annually in a series of bilateral sea service exercises with various Southeast Asian Regions, under the umbrella title "CARAT," or Cooperation Afloat and Readiness Training.[40] CARAT has spun off the South East Asia Cooperation Against Terrorism (SEACAT) bilateral exercises, which give American, and regional navies and coast guards the opportunity to interact in maritime security scenarios.

The US Coast Guard (USCG)

The USCG has been an increasing presence in maritime security activities throughout the region — including exercises, agreements, and interoperation with Asia-Pacific region counterparts, and is fully engaged in USPACOM's Regional Maritime Security Cooperation (RMSC) activities. It also has an active programme of personnel exchanges, including hosting delegations from APR nations and high-level visits to regional nations, such as that of the Coast Guard Commandant to China in 2004 and the Vice Commandant to Southeast Asia in 2005.

The USCG was an active participant in relief operation for the catastrophic 26 December 2004 tsunami, delivering much-needed supplies and medical teams. The USCG works hand-in-glove with all Pacific Rim countries to implement the International Maritime Organisation's International Ship and Port Facility Security (ISPS) code for security of ships, cargo, crew, and port facilities. Its International Port and Ship Liaison Officers (IPSLOs), assigned to the regional USCG office in Tokyo perform "best practice" exchanges regarding port security. In 2005, these exchanges included Australia, Hong Kong, India, Indonesia, Japan, New Zealand, the Philippines, Russia, Singapore, South Korea, and Thailand.

The Coast Guard's Far East Activities (FEACT) has long been located in Japan. FEACT's primary missions include: commercial vessel inspections, marine casualty investigations, international engagement, and liaison to Commander, US Forces Japan. FEACT's personnel perform their missions throughout the Asia-Pacific region, including Korea, China, Hong Kong, Taiwan, Japan, Southeast Asia, Singapore, Indonesia, Malaysia, India, Diego Garcia, Philippines, Australia, and New Zealand.

The USCG's membership and participation in maritime security organisations and activities throughout the APR have gained it credibility as a valued regional team mate. It provides a growing number of international training teams to APR nations to assist in various areas of maritime skills and security. In addition to its membership in the International Maritime Organisation and other governmental and non-governmental organisations, USCG regional membership includes:

- *North Pacific Heads of Coast Guards Agencies (NPHCGA)*. The NPHCGA is an information-sharing network of coast guard services established in 2000. Members are Canada, the US, Japan, Russia, South Korea, and China.[41] The NPHCGA's "main focus is to safeguard international maritime commerce, enhance maritime domain awareness, deter human smuggling, prevent contraband trans-shipments, shield against maritime movement of weapons of mass destruction, fight piracy, and conserve living marine resources".[42] Through a series of bilateral agreements, member coast guards conduct joint law enforcement, and international security enforcement exercises with each other.
- *Asia Pacific Heads of Maritime Safety Agencies (APHMSA)*. APHMSA is an 18-member[43] nation forum whose representatives are primarily from maritime regulatory, safety, and environmental protection agencies. Nations represented include Australia, Canada, China, Indonesia, New Zealand, Singapore, South Korea, Thailand, USA.

The USCG participates in APR exercises, including RIMPAC, and the SEACAT portion of PACOM's CARAT exercise. SEACAT focuses on tracking a potential terrorist vessel, getting position reports and information about it, and then sending a ship to intercept the suspect vessel. In discussing USCG involvement in 2004s SEACAT, USN RADM Kevin Quinn, Commander of Logistics, Western Pacific, noted: "We have the Coast Guard involved, too, because in order to be effective, in many of these countries, once you get into the territorial waters, it is their version of the Coast Guard or the coastal police," who would perform interdiction.[44]

The USCG participates in a full range of other exercises, operations, and training with Asia-Pacific region counterparts, including:

- A sequential five-phase NPHCGA-sponsored international security enforcement exercise with Canada, Russia, Japan, South Korea, and China in spring and summer 2005.
- An annual China-sponsored, Hong Kong-led SAREX involving three to five countries.
- The biennial PACOM RIMPAC exercise which involves elements of all US military forces, and the ships and aircraft of six to eight Pacific Rim nations.
- Providing ship-riders with China on bilateral patrols for illegal drift-net fishing.

- Cooperative patrols for enforcement of the Maritime Boundary Line (MBL) between American and Russian waters in the Bering Sea.
- Cooperative enforcement with Canada, Russia, and China of illegal fishing activities in the North Pacific.
- Attendance by Russian Federal Border Service (FBS) officers at the USCG North Pacific Regional Fisheries Training Centre in Kodiak.
- USCG runs an International Maritime Officers Course in Virginia for foreign personnel from more than 84 countries.

There are clear elements of intersection and overlap of "Venn Diagrams" between the maritime security needs of Asia-Pacific regional nations and the maritime security strategy goals of the US. All of these regional nations have recognised the need for knowledge and awareness of the maritime domain, and the need for the protection of national security, economic growth, and stability. The region also functions best collaboratively when dealing with economic issues, rather than defence issues that raise the spectre of old, and current, disputes and conflicts.

The Way Ahead for the Pacific Rim and US Engagement?

The huge size of the Pacific Rim's maritime domain has led most regional states to scramble to meet the challenges of protecting ports and shipping against piracy, robbery, narcotics, human smuggling, and the activities of terrorists. These challenges lay, to a large degree, within the realm of law enforcement and constabulary operations, areas in which the Coast Guard has the needed expertise and assets. The USCG, as can be seen from descriptions of its activities with Asia-Pacific region nations, plays in all areas of interest in the Pacific Rim. It is, in fact, the "glue" that allows the US to be a player in many of the region's fora, and indeed, holds many of them together.

The US Pacific Command's exchanges, training and assistance programmes, multilateral and bilateral exercises are working well in building alliances with regional partners. However, it is important to recognise, from the negative reactions of some regional nations, that the use of distinctly military resources to assist in regional maritime security needs simply will not work. In those areas, in particular, the USCG is far more likely to be able to achieve American maritime security goals. Acceptance of that reality and the appropriate resourcing of the Coast Guard to take on the needed additional taskings are critical to securing the interests of the US in the Asia-Pacific Region.

Together, the sea services of America's National Fleet can contribute cooperatively to maritime security in the Asia-Pacific Region. The Coast Guard's Deepwater programme, combined with its well-deserved global credibility, can contribute to maritime security not just for the US, but also for other nations whom it can assist in areas of common interest, such as law enforcement, anti-smuggling, and counter-terrorism efforts. The Chief of Naval Operations has already made clear that he looks forward to cooperation with other nations on maritime security. He also has pointedly acknowledged that America's Navy understands that it has neither the mandate, nor the forces to take on all aspects of maritime security. In the 21 September 2005 remarks at the International Sea Power Symposium, Admiral Mullen noted:

> "... the United States Navy cannot, by itself, preserve the freedom and security of the entire maritime domain. It must count on assistance from likeminded nations interested in using the sea for lawful purposes and precluding its use for others that threaten national, regional, or global security. In this regard, the changed strategic landscape offers new opportunities for maritime forces to work together, sometimes with the US Navy, but often times, without. In fact, a greater number of today's emerging missions won't involve the US Navy and that's fine with me".

America has been making changes in its attitudes, strategies, and doctrines. Some of these may be slow and barely perceptible to the world at large, but the changes are happening. It has recognised the need for, and the advantages of, international cooperation against transnational threats. Issuance of strategy documents in support of that cooperation clears the way for needed funding and further changes for the future. America's sea services have also been making adjustments in their strategies, doctrines and planned forces to ensure that they are better able to interoperate with each other and with other international partners.

Notes

1. David Isenberg, *The Illusion of Power: Aircraft Carriers and U.S. Military Strategy* (Washington D.C.: Cato Policy Analysis No. 134, 8 June 1990).
2. Major Mark Gunzinger, USAF, *Power Projection: Making the Tough Choices* (Maxwell AFB, AL: USAF Air University Press, 1993).
3. Richard C. Allen, "Aircraft Carriers and Seabased Airpower", *Sea Power*, June 2001.

4. "The future will demand Coast Guard participation on a scale not heretofore seen. Tomorrow's challenges to America's national and maritime security are no longer focused strictly upon military threats, and 21st Century operations at sea will require the capabilities of not just the Navy and Marine Corps, but of the Coast Guard as well". See Vice Admiral James M. Loy, USCG, "Shaping *All* of America's Joint Maritime Forces: The U.S. Coast Guard in the 21st Century", *Joint Force Quarterly*, Fall 1997.

5. For an overview of the trends and developments in the U.S. Coast Guard during this period, see Captain Bruce B. Stubbs and Scott C. Truver, *Guardian of the Seas: Safeguarding U.S Maritime Safety and Security in the 21st Century* (Washington, D.C.: U.S. Coast Guard, February 2000).

6. *U.S. Coast Guard: America's Maritime Guardian* (Washington, D.C.: U.S Coast Guard, January 2002), pp. 12–13.

7. *Memorandum of Agreement on the Use of U.S. Coast Guard Capabilities and Resources in Support of the National Military Strategy* (Washington D.C.: U.S. Department of Defense, Department of Transportation, 3 October 1995), p. 1. This MOA remains in effect by the saving provisions of the 2002 Homeland Security Act which stipulate that all agreements remain in effect until superseded or cancelled by specific actions.

8. The National Fleet Policy Statement was further updated in 2002. For further information on the basis for cooperation between the U.S. Navy and the U.S. Coast Guard, see Thomas Fargo and Ernest Riutta, "A 'National Fleet' for America", *Naval Institute Proceedings No. 125*, April 1999, pp. 48–51.

9. *Coast Guard 2020* (Washington, D.C.: U.S. Coast Guard Headquarters, 1998), p. 2.

10. Ibid.

11. Admiral Michael Mullen, USN, Remarks at the Naval War College, Newport, RI, 31 August 2005.

12. The 2001 QDR was largely completed prior to 11 September 2001, and its publication in early 2002 could not truly reflect the impact of that event on the United States, and on its relationship with the rest of the world. As this essay was prepared, work on the 2005 QDR continued. Virtually all observers predicted that there would be far-reaching implications for future forces, force mixes, and budgets once it was released.

13. Jason Sherman, "The Two-War Strategy Begins to Fade Away", *Air Force Magazine*, September 2005.

14. Admiral Vern Clark, Edited Remarks by ADM Vern Clark to the Surface Navy Association, Arlington, Virginia, 11 January 2005. Available at http://www.chinfo.navy.mil/navpalib/cno/speeches/clark050111.txt.<Accessed on 28 December 2005>.

15. Admiral Michael Mullen, USN, Remarks at the Naval War College, Newport, RI, 31 August 2005.

16. Ibid.
17. Jim Hodges, "Admiral Clears Up Command: A New Boss for a New Navy Unit Brings Together Some Old Jobs in a New Way", *Hampton Roads & Newport News* [Virginia] *Daily Press*, 5 November 2005.
18. *The National Strategy for Maritime Security* (Washington D.C.: The White House, September 2005), Section IV.
19. Admiral Michael Mullen, USN, Remarks at the Naval War College, Newport, RI, 31 August 2005.
20. Mullen, Ibid., 31 August 2005.
21. Theatre Security Cooperation refers to programmes for exercises, visits, exchanges, training, humanitarian assistance, and civil affairs within the area of responsibility of each American Combatant Commander (such as USPACOM).
22. Ibid.
23. Ibid.
24. *U.S. Coast Guard: America's Maritime Guardian* (Washington, D.C.: U.S. Coast Guard, January 2002), p. 51.
25. Truver, Scott C., "The World is Our Coastline," *U.S. Naval Institute Proceedings*, June 1998.
26. Sam Bateman, "Coast Guards: New Forces for Regional Order and Security", *Asia-Pacific Issues: Analysis from the East West Center*, No. 65, January 2003, p. 2.
27. Adam Ward and James Hackett (eds.), "Dire Straits: Piracy and Maritime Terror in Southeast Asia," *Strategic Comments*, Vol. 10, Issue 6, July 2004.
28. "Regional Maritime Security Initiative, Overview", *U.S. PACOM Website*, 5 November 2004. Available at http://www.pacom.mil/rmsi/. <Accessed on 28 December 2005>.
29. Ibid.
30. Walter T. Ham, IV, "USS Bonhomme Richard Chases Pirates Away from Fishermen," *Navy Newsstand*, 22 February 2005. Available at http://www.news.navy.mil. <Accessed on 28 December 2005>.
31. Admiral Thomas Collins, USCG, "Change and Continuity: The U.S. Coast Guard Today," *U.S. Naval War College Review*, Newport, RI, Spring 2004, p. 19.
32. "Security Council Unanimously Adopts Wide-Ranging Anti-Terrorism Resolution; Calls for Suppressing Financing, Improving International Cooperation", Press Release SC/7158, UN Headquarters, New York, 28 September 2001.
33. Resolution 1566 (2004), UN Security Council, New York, 8 October 2004.
34. Aldo Borgu, Programme Director, Operations and Capability, Australian Strategic Policy Institute, Presentation to the Workshop on Maritime Counter-Terrorism of the Observer Research Foundation, New Delhi, November 2004.
35. "Regional Cooperation Agreement on Combating Piracy and Armed Robbery Against Ships in Asia", Ministry of Foreign Affairs Press Statement, Singapore, 28 April 2005.

36. "The Batam Joint Statement of the 4th Tripartite Ministerial Meeting of the Littoral States on the Straits of Malacca and Singapore," Batam, Indonesia, 1–2 August 2005.

37. Efthimios Mitropoulos, "Enhancing Safety, Security, and Environmental Protection", *Speech delivered at IMO Ad Hoc Meeting*, Jakarta, Indonesia, 7 September 2005.

38. Patrick Goodenough, "Maritime Terror Concerns Prompt New Initiatives in SE Asia", *CNSNEWS.com*, 2 March 2005.

39. The U.S. Coast Guard participated in this exercise in May 2005 with elements of the U.S. Air Force and Navy.

40. CARAT participants historically include Thailand, Singapore, Malaysia, Brunei, Indonesia and the Philippines.

41. Member agencies are the USCG, the Canadian Coast Guard, China Maritime Search and Rescue, Russian Federal Border Guard Service, Japan Coast Guard, and the South Korean National Maritime Police Agency.

42. CGC Jarvis, "Russia and United States Conduct Joint Protection Patrol", *U.S. Coast Guard Pacific Area News*, 6 July 2005.

43. Australia, Canada, China, Hong Kong, Indonesia, Japan, New Zealand, Singapore, South Korea, Thailand, USA.

44. Roxana Tiron, "Multinational Naval Exercises Welcome in Southeast Asia", *National Defense*, July 2004.

IV. *Nuclear Weapons and Missile Defences: The Maritime Dimension in the Asia-Pacific*

Chapter 8

China's Nuclear Doctrine, Its Strategic Naval Power and Anti-Missile Defence Initiatives

You Ji

Introduction

The end of the Cold War resulted in a complex global nuclear situation that poses an increased challenge to China's strategic security. Around its territories a number of new nuclear powers have emerged: North Korea, India, Pakistan and Japan, which may be on the edge of nuclearisation. Most importantly, the US *Nuclear Posture Review* promulgated in 2002 specifically identified the PRC as a potential target for a pre-emptive nuclear strike.[1] In response China has stepped up its nuclear weapons programs. In the last few years new generation nuclear missiles have been introduced to the Strategic Missile Force (SMF) of the People's Liberation Army (PLA). China has also achieved breakthroughs in the associated technologies such as satellite-based control and guidance systems for its intercontinental missiles. It seems that China has moved one step closer to real combat operations.[2] In PLA terminology, this means its nuclear units have set up full protocols to strike their designated targets, immediately after they receive orders from the Central Military Commission of the Party (CMC). In addition, the PLA Navy (PLAN) has acquired nine new prototype nuclear attack submarines, the 093, which are capable of firing nuclear tipped long-range cruise missiles. The 094 strategic nuclear submarines are also undergoing sea trials which have reached the final stages of development. With three multiple war heads in each of the 16 intercontinental ballistic missiles on board, China may soon truly have a triad capability.[3] This sharpening of the nuclear sword is reflected by the Chinese efforts in transforming its nuclear deterrence from a "hiding force" to a "fighting force".

Another factor driving China's slow but steady nuclear modernisation is external, namely, the development of the US missile defence system, either in the form of the National Missile Defence (NMD) or in the form of the Theatre Missile Defence (TMD). Although the Chinese are concerned about the US deployment of anti-missile capabilities in recent years, their worry is more political and diplomatic at the moment due to the tremendous difficulties inherent in the research and development (R&D) of both the NMD and TMD systems. They are fearful that that missile defence systems may provide a new mechanism for the US to forge closer military ties and develop alliances with regional countries as a way of deterring China. This is especially true if Taiwan is incorporated into the system. Moreover, because the PLA believes that technological progress may one day be such as to make the TMD work effectively, it sees the modernisation of its nuclear capability as a race against time. The TMD plans have generated a higher level of urgency for the PLA to achieve better readiness for action, develop new nuclear combat guidelines, deploy more launching units, and quicken the pace for deployment.

The Evolving Nuclear Strategy

The bulk of Chinese nuclear force is in the Strategic Missile Force (SMF), the smallest service in the PLA, with only 4.5% of its total manpower, and an allocation of about 5% of the country's defence budget.[4] Yet it assumes a disproportionate share of the burden of military deterrence through its capability to launch a second strike, nuclear or conventional, against the major powers. For a long time the Chinese nuclear strategy was based on the concept of *minimum deterrence*. It is defensive in nature and emphasises retaliation rather than pre-emption. The Chinese notion of deterrence is the belief that possessing a credible retaliatory capability will convince the enemy not to wage a war against China. The strategy is predicated upon China's ability to demonstrate that it can fight and not lose a nuclear war, and the high cost would convince the initiator that a nuclear exchange would be fruitless. Here the definition of victory is typical of the Chinese, as remarked by Major General Peng Guangqian, "In a nuclear war even if the US could destroy us 100 times we would be victorious if we could destroy it once".[5]

From Minimum Deterrence to Limited Deterrence

Nuclear deterrence is a part of China's overall defence posture, which consists of three tiers of forces — (1) passive civil defence, in keeping with the Clausewitizian notion that the social and political dimensions of war must be coordinated; (2) active defence to help minimise the potential damage; and (3) offensive forces able to take the war to the enemy.[6] China maintains only a minimum nuclear arsenal due to financial constraints, shortage of key materials and technological inadequacies. The posture is closely linked to China's no-first use policy, which was formulated in the 1960s under the understanding that an insufficient nuclear capability could invite a surgical strike by more advanced nuclear powers rather than assuring the Chinese of a desirable level of national security.

To the current PLA commanders, minimum deterrence is an awkward nuclear strategy: it is too defensive, and basically only a diplomatic statement. It is awkward also because it is not applicable to any foreseeable scenarios of a nuclear or conventional war. Considering China's strong conventional forces vis-à-vis her Asian neighbours, it is unnecessary to employ nuclear deterrence. The political price would be too high. Neither is this kind of deterrence effective enough against the superpower, given their overwhelming nuclear superiority. What then, is the use of the PLA nuclear force, which receives great resources? This doctrine of minimum deterrence has fatal flaws but it is an unavoidable transitional guideline for deterring an all-out war. When the strategy was first formulated, the main goal of Chinese nuclear weapons was to deter a massive land invasion inside its own territories, the most acute security threat against which the PLA had no other effective means to deal with.[7] In essence it is a strategy to "buy-time". Only when the enemy was deterred from invading China, would the PLA develop more nuclear weapons that could be used against the targets of the adversaries in their home land. By then the level of deterrence could be upgraded and the nature of deterrence changed.

As the demise of the USSR removed the last potential of a large land invasion of China, the concept of minimum deterrence has become ill-fitted to the PLA's nuclear strategy. At the same time the SMF has made great strides in improving both the quality and the quantity of its nuclear forces. The numbers of missiles have increased and their survivability, strike accuracy and mobility have also improved. The quantitative and qualitative improvements have allowed the PLA to contemplate a more offensive war-fighting doctrine as a guide for its transformation. As a result, the SMF has gradually focused on external targets for a second strike. More importantly, the retaliatory principle has also been gradually revised from that of a counter-force to one of counter-value, in tandem with Chinese technological achievements. In a way, the process of Chinese nuclear modernisation is one that is driven by technological progress rather than by a doctrinal concept. Certainly this is in line with the general trend of nuclear modernisation of any other country, that is, with improvements in the range and accuracy of missiles, targeting choices have become more abundant. The combat strategy and models have been consequently updated as a result.

For the PLA, technological progress has resulted in her updating its strategic thinking on the combat use of nuclear weapons. The outcome is the embrace of a new nuclear doctrine of limited deterrence.[8] In PLA terminology this is about a transition from "hide" to "fight" in war preparation, reflecting its changing attitudes toward nuclear weapons, from viewing them as an unusable means of mass destruction to recognising their practical use for battlefield conflict.[9] With the improvement of China's nuclear technology, particularly those that relate to accuracy, longer range and mobility, the PLA's confidence in its ability to successfully wage nuclear warfare has been enhanced. Indeed, younger PLA generals have gradually broken the psychological shackles imposed by the long-lasting strategy of minimum deterrence, which was the logical root-cause for the mentality of hiding. When designing "war game" plans, these younger generals are tempted to formulate scenarios in which they fire nuclear missiles in high-tech wars.[10]

What is interesting though is that Beijing's official policy is still minimum deterrence. Accelerated modernisation of nuclear arsenals by any country has become taboo in the post-Cold War world and is especially applicable to China who has proclaimed the goal of a peaceful rise. More importantly the Chinese effort to increase nuclear capability in terms of longer range and better accuracy at a time when the Soviet nuclear has diminished can easily be interpreted as targeting America and is diplomatically unwise. Therefore, limited deterrence does not appear in official vocabulary, and is basically a PLA conceptual discussion. However, whatever the official rhetoric, the fact is that the Chinese nuclear force is not, and it has never been, guided by minimum deterrence.

Contemplating Tactical Nuclear Warfare

Despite an element of offensiveness in the doctrine of limited deterrence, the overall posture of the Chinese nuclear force has remained defensive. This can be seen from the fact that the numbers of inter-continental ballistic missiles (ICBMs) have remained the same for several decades, although their quality has been continuously improved.[11] Furthermore, the number of PLAN's nuclear ballistic missile submarines will be small, probably ranging from six to eight. This may be due less to China's financial constraints on maintaining a large nuclear stock than to its concern of the US response. It is well within China's economic affordability to create a kind of mutually assured destruction (MAD) capability, which in the minds of China's strategists, is measured by about 200 ICBMs. The attainment of this MAD capability would only cost an incremental US$2 billion.[12] Yet, if Beijing embarks on this path, Washington would immediately view Beijing as a strategic competitor and the associated political and economic costs, that is, in terms of trade with the US would be very high. Unless the PRC is backed into a corner, that is to mean fighting a Taiwan war with US involvement, it would not choose this option. On the other hand, if Beijing feels that it is under an acute security threat, it will be relatively easy for the PLA to acquire a MAD capability, and this within a relatively short period of time. According to Johnston, at least a limited deterrence capability is within the reach of the PLA.[13]

Indeed the limited deterrence doctrine adds new dimensions to China's nuclear strategy: war game plans should be formulated on the premise of retaliation without being first hit by a nuclear bomb. Although Beijing is still politically bound by its pledge of non-first-use, the military has long explored scenarios of first use, as it believes that the lethality of new high-tech conventional weapons has matched that of tactical nuclear ones. If China is subjected to the Kosovo type of mass destruction, it may be left with no other choice but to contemplate using something dramatic as a counter-measure. After achieving a second strike capability some military planners are now tempted to contemplate the use of nuclear weapons in an escalation of conventional war, which they believe may place a nation's survival at stake just as much as nuclear attack.[14] PLA researchers often cite the example of the USSR's plan to initiate a nuclear attack against China to illustrate that the use of nuclear weapons is not inconceivable. They are particularly impressed by Russia's new national defence doctrine, which has deleted the provision of not employing nuclear weapons first in an all-out war.[15]

China's nuclear war-fighting preparation begins with its efforts to grasp the nature, process and consequences of a tactical nuclear war. According to the interpretation of PLA researchers, tactical nuclear war means attack on the opponents' military targets in general, and nuclear facilities in particular. Such an exchange is tactical because it is limited in nature, meaning there is still room for both sides to negotiate a cease-fire before it is escalated to engulf urban centres. In the last decade or so the PLA has accorded new emphasis to developing small-yield and highly accurate nuclear and conventional missiles for counter-force purpose only, in a hope that the Chinese population can be spared from nuclear disaster. In terms of doctrinal evolution the PLA has accepted the idea that even in an all-out war in the future, tactical nuclear weapons aimed at military facilities would be preferred to strategic ones aimed at urban centres. This has led PLA strategists to embrace the concept of a theatre nuclear war with missiles launched only against the intruding forces in a limited geographical area, although this area can be physically large. This is in sharp contrast to their old mentality that any nuclear fight was for mass destruction. They would argue that if a missile landed on the Bolshoi Theatre instead of the Kremlin, it would be equally effective and that, even if every missile had pinpoint accuracy, the limited number in the PRC's small arsenal could destroy only a small fraction of the enemy's silos, leaving China disarmed before the enemy's remaining missiles.[16]

PLA strategists now agree with their western colleagues that nuclear missiles would most likely be used at the theatre level and against defence assets. PLA war games are then played for achieving battlefield victory rather than the destruction of the world.[17] While ICBMs hold urban centres hostage at the strategic deterrence level, short-to-medium ranged, low-yield tactical nuclear weapons and land attack cruise missiles (LACMs) can be deployed to offer the second tier deterrence against the enemy's key defence sites. This is of particular value for a force inferior in conventional means. A weak navy, for instance, might be left with little choice but to use tactical nuclear means to deal with the superpower's nuclear aircraft carrier battle groups. In September 1988 when the PLA tested China's first neutron bomb, Western intelligence agencies discovered that China has possessed tactical nuclear weapons with a yield of below 30,000 tons from as early as the beginning of the 1970s.[18]

The fundamental reason for PLA planners to contemplate the use of tactical nuclear weapons is to fill a gap in China's nuclear deterrence strategy. As a weak nuclear power, China was long subject to nuclear blackmail by the superpowers, which could choose whether to wage a nuclear war, the kind of nuclear war to wage, and when to start such a war. China's deterrence can only be effective when it has the means to deal with all kinds of nuclear threats. By the PLA's assessment, if China were forced into a nuclear war, it is most likely a tactical one, such as a nuclear surgical strike. This would make it very difficult for the PLA to respond with strategic nuclear weapons that target only urban centres. So if China did not possess effective tactical nuclear weapons, it would be deprived of a crucial means for deterrence, both politically and militarily.[19] According to the PLA joint campaign guidelines, the function of tactical nuclear missiles parallels that of the Air Force and the Navy, although the use of missiles is under much tighter central control.[20] A maritime scenario has been postulated as one of a range of scenarios where the PLA might use nuclear weapons.[21]

Getting Ready to Fight

China's nuclear strategy designated a two-stage development process to attain readiness for a nuclear war. The first stage aimed to resolve the problem of survivability, or how to hide, under a PLA slogan of "force consolidation"; and the second, the problems of missile range and accuracy, or how to fight, under another PLA slogan of "practical operation".[22] The improvement of survivability, and of launching range and accuracy have been the primary objectives of the PLA SMF since the outset of its nuclear program. After 40 years of development, the SMF has accomplished these goals. Its ICBMs can target key American cities, and the technology of its sea-based missiles has gradually become mature. As a result, the PLA has now reached a relatively high level of nuclear readiness.

The emphasis of China's nuclear force had been placed on "force consolidation" which in actual terms means survivability. It is dependent on two crucial factors: (1) the survivability of launching sites, and (2) the mobility of the launching units. China's non-first use (NFU) policy puts great demands on the SMF, as it must be able to perform its mission after absorbing a nuclear strike. As the PLA had to rely exclusively on land-based ICBMs for a second strike before the 094 submarine becomes fully operational, the "consolidation" of the silos of DF-5 missiles is the key for China to hit back at a target 10,000 km away.[23] Long-range capabilities are regarded as another key factor of deterrence value. Without long-range missiles the PLA cannot target potential enemies beyond a certain distance, and without them China's deterrence is neither reliable nor credible. From the very beginning, goals for increasing the missile reach was set stage by stage, starting with the targeting of US bases in Japan and Korea, and then to the US bases in the Philippines, Guam, then Moscow, and finally, continental America. Currently, about 14% of China's strategic missiles can reach the US. In the long run, the PLA will proportionally augment this percentage as a key goal of force development. According to one PLA calculation, if this ratio can be raised to 70%, it will effectively strengthen China's national security. Therefore, a key task of adjusting the PLA nuclear force structure concerns the increase of ICBMs in comparison with short-range missiles.[24]

Mobility is about a strategy of nuclear "guerrilla warfare".[25] To this end, the PLA has tested various methods in the last two decades to improve the rapid response capabilities of its inter-continental (ICBMs) and intermediate range ballistic missiles (IRBMs). The launching units and facilities are put on the move all the time. Thousands of miles of roads have been constructed to link a great number of launching sites with the central command, control, communications, computerisation, intelligence, surveillance, and reconnaissance (C4ISR) networks. Every launching unit has several reusable launching sites. In each of these sites, launching data for fixed targets are continuously updated and different launching protocols are practised regularly. In war, the constant updating of data and the continuous training will save precious response time.

In order to raise survivability and mobility levels, the R&D of solid fuel propellants, miniaturised warheads, and the development of a sophisticated command, control, communications, and intelligence (C3I) systems are given top priorities. The solid fuels are of particular importance because most of China's mobile missiles (mainly the DF-3 IRBMs) are propelled by liquid fuel, which requires two hours to be prepared for launch, a time considered too long for the demands of a high-tech war.[26] Solid fuel is viewed as the key to improvements in response times and is especially crucial for the submarine-based missiles. Since 1985, when the PLA launched its first solid-fuelled mobile missile, China has invested heavily in its missile transportation vehicles and launching platforms.[27]

China's high-tech defence strategy has moved the PLA nuclear force from the stage of "force consolidation" to that of "practical operation". The PLA has since broken away from its traditional passive nuclear posture. In 1984, the CMC officially ordered the SMF to assume offensive retaliatory missions.[28] During the mid-1980s the SMF conducted 120 exercises. The majority of these were designed to assist the army's campaign operations at the divisional level or above.[29] By 1991, the SMF had acquired all-weather and all-situation operational capabilities. Every launching brigade has been put on strategic duty and is able to carry out combat missions assigned by the CMC. This meant that the SMF had transcended a historical developmental stage.[30]

Simulation and live ammunition launches in remote areas aim at specific targets and proceed in pre-determined circumstances of nuclear exchange. When China staged its "war games" in 1995 and 1996, group launch became the standard exercise. It is believed that group launches will be one of the chief means to affect a blockade of Taiwan's waterways. Since the Gulf War in 1991, the SMF has been trained to respond quickly in situations including retaliation after a nuclear surgical strike, bio-chemical warfare, and maritime warfare. Most of these are mobile launches. Reducing pre-launch time is one of the key aims in training. In addition to emergency launching plans, one indicator of the SMF's conceptual shift towards "how to fight" has been its troop redeployment and battle-field construction, mainly from the three "norths" (north China, northeast China and northwest China) to the east (the Taiwan Straits). It is part of the PLA's shift of security gravity: taking a strategically defensive posture in the north but preparing for an offensive posture in the east.[31]

New Modernisation Programmes

The modernisation of the SMF has speeded up in the last decade. One realistic but unpleasant prospect for the SMF is that the rapid high-tech advance of the US may translate the "Star Wars" initiative into reality. Once an effective missile defence system consisting of both strategic and theatre capabilities is established, the bulk of China's nuclear arsenal may be rendered impotent. The PLA has no other choice but to improve the penetrability and accuracy of its ICBMs. This sense of vulnerability underlies China's tenacious efforts to continue with nuclear testing in order to reduce the size of the DF-31 (ICBMs with a range of 8,000 km) and the JL-2 (6,000 km range) warheads (about 700 kg), so that they can be made multiple, independently targetable, re-entry vehicle (MIRV) capable and thus be able to better fit into mobile and submarine launching platforms. The weaker throw weight of their solid-propellant also highlights the need to lighten the warheads of DF-31 and JL-2. The DF-31 has become operational ahead of expectations and the JL-2 is near deployable status.[32] The first decade of this century will prove to be crucial for China's nuclear development.

At the same time, design and development is under way for an even more advanced second-generation nuclear weapon, the DF-41 mobile, three-stage solid-propellant ICBMs. With a range of 12,000 kilometres, it can reach almost any city in the world. As the largest missile in the SMF's inventory, this system will replace the DF-5A in the next five years.[33] Once deployed, the missile will represent a leap forward for China's war-fighting readiness. There have been reports that the Chinese are incorporating advanced Russian rocket technology into the design of the DF-41. For instance, China is learning how to improve cryogenic rocket engines from Russian technology associated with the Kosmos, Tsyklon, and heavy-lift Zenit rockets, and also learning indirectly from the technology associated with the SS-18/19 ICBMs.[34]

The Naval Nuclear Connection

All of China's inter-continental nuclear missiles are land-based, which means that they are vulnerable to an enemy first strike. Although these weapons are well hidden, the PLA is fully aware that advanced satellite technology will enable China's potential opponents to identify the whereabouts of the silos and mobile missiles by following the tracks of the vehicles that travel to and from those otherwise inaccessible areas. One counter-measure adopted by the PLA is to put up as many fake launching sites as possible. However, Western analysts quoted Admiral Liu Huaqing as saying that after a first strike, only about 10% of China's nuclear arsenal would survive.[35] By other PLA estimates, up to two thirds of the SMF's nuclear weapons might survive, leaving a sufficient number of warheads for a counter strike.[36] However, PLA leaders cannot be sure how many land-based nuclear weapons would actually survive a precision first strike and the numbers that will be available for subsequent attacks. Emulating the US approach to countering the USSR's nuclear threat, the Chinese has placed increasing importance on sea-based nuclear launching platforms, which were among China's three top R&D projects in the 1970s.[37] (The other two projects concerned inter-continental nuclear missiles and communications satellites.) Chinese strategists have studied and accepted the US's nuclear strategy, which relies on nuclear submarines as the basis for a second-strike capability. Admiral Liu summarised the new thinking in China's nuclear strategy as follows:

> "In the face of a large-scale nuclear attack, only less than 10% of the coastal launching silos will survive, whereas submarines armed with ballistic missiles can use the surface of the sea to protect and cover themselves, preserve the nuclear offensive force, and play a deterrent and containment role".[38]

Therefore, the top priority of China's nuclear modernisation has been to gradually move a significant proportion of its land-based nuclear capabilities onto submarines.[39]

In 2005 China has developed a relatively reliable nuclear submarine fleet. Nicknamed the 09 Unit and with a ranking equivalent to a group army in military bureaucratic ranking, the PLA Navy's nuclear submarine fleet is gradually expanding. In the next five to seven years it may comprise over a dozen nuclear-powered submarines. At the moment, however, most of these nuclear submarines consist of the *Han* class tactical attack boats, which have a displacement of 5,000 tons and a crew of 73. Numbering five or six, each of these tactical submarines can launch 12 C-802 cruise missiles with a range of about 50 kilometres. The C-802 is fairly accurate with terminal guidance measures. The missile is conventional but it can be equipped with a nuclear warhead. The only strategic missile submarine, *Xia* class SSBN, is more of an experimental boat. Manned by 104 officers and sailors, it is 120 metres in length, with a displacement of 8,000 tons. It is said to carry 12 HL-1 nuclear missiles, each propelled by solid fuel and deployed with a single two megaton nuclear warhead. Although its everyday running is the responsibility of the Navy, the control over the nuclear bottom is certainly not under the control of the Navy but higher up the chain of command. However, no detailed accounts are available for how the command, control and communications are channelled between the CMC, the Naval Headquarters, and the "09" Fleet.

The PLA high command is well aware that a single nuclear submarine will not make China's second strike capability robust. To achieve this goal, the PLA has undertaken two programs to simultaneously transform the navy. The first is to develop a new, much-improved nuclear attack submarine, nicknamed the 093, with technology similar to the Russia's Victor III SSN. Indeed, the PLA has reportedly received Russian help in coating the 093's hulls to improve noise insulation. It is said that at least two of them have entered service. The noise level of the 093 submarines may have reached about 115 decibels, similar to that of the US's in the early 1990s. This is a remarkable progress. The second program is the construction of a second but modified version of the *Xia* class submarine (094 type SSBN) in the Huludao Naval Ship Plant. This boat has an enlarged displacement of over 10,000 tons and carries the HL-2 nuclear missiles with multiple, independently targetable, re-entry vehicle nuclear warheads. With a much more sophisticated terminal guidance system and enlarged range of 8,000 kilometres, this new type of submarine will be of a greater deterrence to China's potential opponents. Despite this, Western analysts have raised their doubts regarding the technological sophistication of these new SSBNs, and funding difficulties have slowed down the development considerably.

Indeed the huge cost and complex technological requirements for developing new nuclear submarines have greatly slowed the realisation of the PLA plan to base its nuclear retaliatory capability in submarines. Rapid industrial development has compelled the civilian sectors to compete with the PLA for nuclear facilities that supply energy and other economic purposes. Moreover, the PLA has been confronted with serious accuracy problems of missiles launched from under water. Despite all the difficulties, the PLA will continue to give top priority to the development of submarine-based missile launching platforms that helped the Chinese to achieve breakthroughs in the late 1990s, as the first ship of 094 submarines was launched for sea trial. Its JL-2 missile, a sea-based version of the DF-31, is a huge improvement on the JL-1 with a range three times the latter (about 6,000 nm). Both the ship and its missiles were scheduled to enter service in 2003 and series production could follow. The significance of this new fleet lies in its MAD (mutually assured destruction) capabilities. If the PLAN constructs at least six of them, each with 16 launchers, and each missile with three multiple warheads, there will be a total of 288 strategic warheads that can reach North America. The deterrence equation will be significantly altered. Therefore, the completion of a strategic nuclear submarine fleet is well worth the money in the minds of top Chinese leaders despite its lengthy development process.

China's Effort to Break the US Missile Defence

As mentioned earlier, US missile defence systems, the ballistic missile defence (BMD), and the theatre missile defence (TMD) have constituted a driver for China's nuclear modernisation. For instance, Chinese military establishment is using BMD as a pretext to secure more funding for developing new missiles, such as manoeuvrable re-entry vehicles (MARVs), as a way to deal with BMD.[40] The National Missile Defence (NMD) of the US has set as a goal the interception of 20 ICBMs for the first phase of development. Logically, this clearly targets China's inventory of some 20 ICBMs.[41] Also, as the TMD gradually unfolds, the PLA is working out measures to counter its effect. The design of China's first generation of land attack cruise missiles (LACMs) has specifically configured into it an anti-TMD element.[42]

A New Arms Race in the Making?

Some Western security experts point out that US missile defence represents the security hazard that would cause an action-reaction arms race in the region.[43] Many Chinese strategists are eager to agree. To avoid a situation where China's limited ICBMs will be neutralised when NMD becomes operational, the PLA may have already augmented the effort to add more ICBMs to its arsenal. The US Department of Defence released a report asserting that the number of China's ICBMs could have more than doubled by the end of this decade.[44] What would be response of Japan or India? Certainly this not the concern of the Chinese who believe that maintaining a credible nuclear deterrence is crucial to make the US balk at intervening in a Taiwan war and that it is the US that has initiated the missile race in the first place.

This means that psychologically at least, the NMD/TMD initiatives may intensify the regional arms build-up. When missile defence widens the gap of military balance by one side, the other side will feel more threatened. Its impulsive reaction will be to increase its arsenal of attack missiles to overwhelm the system. A few rounds of this action/reaction race will pave the way for the qualitative improvement of missile technology. In fact the upgrading and enlarging of its missile inventory has become a strategic imperative for the PLA. Missiles are seen as one viable means to compensate China's inferior attack capabilities.[45] As the PLA's other punches are relatively weak and short, employment of missiles becomes one of its few asymmetrical measures in RMA warfare.[46]

Japanese military experts argue that because Japan has not had long-punch capabilities, it has to have a more sophisticated shield to cover itself from the enemy's attack.[47] But the PLA construes this as, "When one side in the conflict is safely protected by a shield, he would be emboldened to hit his enemy even with short punches".[48] Moreover, the missile defence technology can easily be used to augment the offensive systems capable of long punches. This is probably one of the reasons that Japan is participating in research involving the development of the missile defence system.

Regional Implications

In the foreseeable future, Chinese concerns about the missile defence system is less about its military value than its geo-political implications. The TMD program is behind the US's alliance-enhancing effort in the region and its real effect on China's military security is still debated in Beijing. Some analysts question the ability of the system in dealing with a saturated missile attack. The Patriot PAC-2 has a poor performance record, and the PAC-3 is not only too expensive for the user to fire in large numbers but also not fully reliable in combat.[49] For instance, normally three PAC-3 missiles would be launched to intercept one incoming ballistic missile. Now the PLA has deployed about 700 M-series missiles close to the Taiwan Straits. This requires over 2000 PAC-3s to achieve a successful destruction rate of 85%. In terms of the cost/effectiveness ratio, each M-missile is priced at about US$300,000 versus US$3 million for each PAC-3, a ratio of 10. For the defensive side, how would it plan a war of TMD? The interceptor of NMD can make only one manoeuvring move before its fuel runs out. More importantly, according to estimates by US scientists, for every dollar spent on developing attack missiles it has to be matched by seven in designing the defence system. This is the figure often cited by PLA specialists on missile defence. It is interesting to note that while China's IR generalists still insist on the driving effect of the missile defence for an arms race, the arms control experts have already disputed such a view and see the missile defence system as lacking real teeth.[50]

Yet politically, the TMD is seen as a major threat to China's security. Basically, it is a form of collective defence that connects the US and its allies more closely through an advanced technological network, that is, via an integrated command and control system. Taiwan, for instance, seeks to be part of the TMD exactly because it is in great need to be politically linked to such a network, even though from a military point of view, the TMD will not meet the requirements for the Island's air and missile defence needs.

Therefore, the TMD will, in the coming decade, be seen more as a US-centred regional defence system against China than an operational weapons system, given its current technological inadequacies. In this light TMD is an expression of US security commitment to its allies and signals a redefined power relationship in the Far East. An effective TMD cannot leave many geographic holes in its network and has to allow the participants to share top US C4ISR information and facilities. If Taiwan is brought into the system, it would embolden its leaders to pursue independence in a more forceful way, under the assumption that American assistance is guaranteed.[51] Therefore, the TMD works like a powerful magnet drawing the US and its allies together more closely.

Conclusion

China continues to press ahead with its nuclear modernisation as a way to obtain credible deterrence against any war scenario involving the US, and potentially Japan. To the PLA the need to enhance its nuclear forces stem from the concern over backward conventional capability. A reliable second-strike capability may provide it with a level of confidence that no other weapons can, although the PLA's nuclear arsenal is one generation behind the major powers. The development of nuclear weapons is also relatively cheap compared with the development of high-tech conventional arms in order to achieve the same level of deterrence.

In the last decade the world has witnessed the transition of the PLA Strategic Missile Force from a "hiding power" to a "fighting power", as both its hardware and software achieved qualitative progress. With a primitive retaliatory capability there is a sea-change in the mentality of PLA generals who are ready to discard the concept of *minimum deterrence*. In its place, a doctrine of *limited deterrence* is being developed to guide the preparation for future wars. Although still defensive in nature, the concept emphasises the adroit response to any nuclear threat confronting the Chinese. Diplomatically, Beijing may continue to stick to the non-first-use policy, which is a principal tenet of *minimum deterrence*. In military terms unpredictable combat situations may lead PLA commanders to contemplate the possibility of pre-emptive strikes. PLA Commanders have been alarmed by the US Nuclear Posture Review and renouncement of the non-first-use policy by Russia.

One important item of China's nuclear modernisation is the enhancement of its nuclear submarine force. With weak sea-based launching capabilities, China's nuclear triad exists only in theory. Under the acute threat of US precision strike, the survivability of China's land-based missiles is questionable. The PLA has no choice but to strengthen its nuclear submarine fleet. The end result of this effort would be a Chinese de facto MAD capability. Finally, the missile defence initiatives by the US have generated new impetus for the PLA to enlarge its nuclear arsenal. Although for the time being, neither the NMD nor the TMD poses a real threat to Chinese missile attack capability, the PLA has taken no chances, given that technological breakthroughs cannot be discounted, a phenomenon which China herself has benefited from over the last several decades. Working on the presumption that the missile defence may eventually work, the Chinese are devoting more resources in modernising its missile inventory by increasing the number of higher quality delivery vehicles in its force.

The Chinese nuclear force is looking visibly more mature than at any time in the last three decades, with a set of more practical combat doctrines from the strategic to the tactical levels, and more reliable second-strike capabilities. This development will certainly exert an enormous impact on the regional military balance in the years to come.

Notes

1. U.S. Department of Defence, *The Nuclear Posture Review 2002* (Washington D.C.: U.S. Department of Defence, 2003).
2. SMF has a nick name Dier Paobing (the Second Artillery), given by Zhou Enlai, China's first premier, in 1965. It was used then for the purpose of keeping China's nuclear forces in secret to both domestic and international watchers.
3. See western analysis on China's nuclear triad, Bradley Hahn, "China: Nuclear Capability — Small but Growing", *Pacific Defence Reporter*, May 1989, p. 42; and Chong-pin Lin, *China's Nuclear Weapons Strategy: Tradition within Evolution* (Massachusetts: Lexington Books, 1988). Although China was successful in developing a strategic nuclear submarine in the 1980s, only one was commissioned

as a test boat. The range of its missile is short, and the level of its combat readiness is low. Therefore, the much talked about triad capability of the PLA has been theoretical.

4. Alastair Iain Johnston, "The Prospects for Chinese Nuclear Force Modernisation: Limited Deterrence versus Multilateral Arms Control", *The China Quarterly*, No. 146, June 1996, pp. 548–576.

5. Peng's talk to *Across the Strait*, a current affairs program of CCTV, 25 June 2004.

6. Gerald Segal, "Nuclear Forces", in Gerald Segal and Bill Tow (eds.), *Chinese Defence Policy* (London: Macmillan, 1984), p. 104.

7. The initial proposal for the PLA to develop tactical nuclear weapons originated from the calculation of the PLA high command in the 1970s that they had no conventional weapons effective enough to hold back a large-scale Soviet tank invasion in the north and northeast China, where the land is flat and the distance between Beijing and Mongolia is only 600 kilometres. Against such an invasion no weapons other than neutron bombs or 105 mm nuclear shells would be more effective in putting up a desperate defence. Xu Guangyu, Yang Yufeng and Sang Zhonglin, "Zhanqiu He Zhanzheng De Kenenxin Jidui Wojun Zhanyi Zuo De Yingxiang (The possibility of theatre nuclear warfare and its impact on our army's campaign operations)", in Editor Group (eds.), *Toxiang Shengli De Tansuo (Exploration of the Path Toward Victory)* (Beijing: the PLA Publishing House, 1988), pp. 1086–1106.

8. Alastair I. Johnston, pp. 548–576.

9. Zhang Baotang, "Dui Xingshiqi Zhanlie Daodan Budui Zhanbei Jianshe Jige Wenti De Chutan (On a few questions concerning the development of the SMF in the new era)", in The PLA University of National Defence (ed.), *Jundui Xiandaihua Jianshe De Sikao* (Beijing: The PLA NDU Press, 1988), pp. 411–420.

10. Xu Jian, *Daguo Changjian (The Large Country and Long Sword: The Evolution of the SMF)* (Beijing: Zuojia Chubanshe, 1995).

11. There is not much change at all if we compare the figures presented in The International Institute for Strategic Studies' annual book on *Military Balance* between the mid-1980s and 2004.

12. Discussion with Shen Dingli in Beijing, November 2003. Also, Kori Urayama, "China Debates Missile Defence", *Survival*, Vol. 46, No. 2, 2004, p. 132. Also, discussions with Shen Dingli in January 2004, Beijing.

13. See the analysis of Alastair I. Johnston, pp. 562–564.

14. Xu Zhongde and He Lizhu, "Yuce Weilai Zhanzheng Buke Hushi Hewuqi De Weixie (The nuclear threat should not be ruled out in study of the future wars)", in the PLA Academy of Military Science (ed.) *Junshi Lilun Yu Guofangjianshe (Military Theory and Development of National Defence)* (Beijing: the PLA Academy of Military Science, 1988), p. 192.

15. In private conversations with a number of senior Chinese researchers immediately after the Gulf War, I asked them whether the PLA would consider the use of

nuclear weapons as the last resort if it were in the Iraqi's position and deemed that nothing could stop the enemy's advance. They agreed that it would probably be the only option left to the PLA. Some of them cited the Russian example to make the point.

16. Lewis, John Wilson, and Hua Di, "China's Ballistic Missile Programs: Technologies, Strategies, Goals", *International Security,* Vol. 17, No. 2, Fall 1992, p. 21.
17. Xu Guangyu, Yang Yufeng and Sang Zhonglin, pp. 1086–1106.
18. The U.S. Defence Intelligence Agency, *Soviet and People's Republic of China: Nuclear Weapons Employment Policy and Strategy,* Part II, March 1972, p. 25.
19. Xu Guanyu, Yang Yufeng and Sang Zhonglin, p. 1091.
20. Huang Bin, *Zhanqiu Yu Zhanqiuzhanyi (War Zones and War Zone Campaigns)* (Beijing: the PLA NDU Press, 1990), p. 158.
21. Editor group, "Zhanlie Daodan Budui Zhai Chengzhang (The development of the SMF)", in CCTV Press (ed.), *Junwei Jinxingqu (The Marching Song for the PLA)* (Beijing: China Centra Television Press, 1987), pp. 97–98.
22. Zhang Baotang, p. 412.
23. Zhang Jingxi and Zhang Mengliang, "Shilun Zhanliexing Zhanyi Heliliang De Yunyong He Zhujunbingzhong De Xietog (On the use of nuclear force in strategic campaigns and the coordination of the SMF with other services)", in Editor Group (eds.), *Tongxiang Shengli De Tansuo (Exploring the Ways Towards Victory)* (Beijing: the PLA Publishing House, 1987), p. 1018.
24. Quoted from "China's Nuclear Missile Strategy", *Independent (Russian),* 14 December 1995. However, China's focus on the Taiwan situation may have changed this plan.
25. Xu Jian, 1995, p. 378
26. Liu Zhongyi, "Taiyuan Weixing Fashe Zhongxin Ceji (The brief look at the Taiyuan satellite launching centre)", *Jingyang Wenyi,* No. 2, 1992, p. 26.
27. Yu Hao, *et al., Dangdai Zhongguo: Zhongguo Renmin Jiefajun* (Contemporary China: the PLA) (Beijing: Renmin Chubanshe, 1994), p. 528.
28. Ling Yu, "Zhingguo Daodan Yanxi He Dier Paobin (The Chinese missile exercises and the SMF)", *Guangjiaojing,* No. 8, 1995, p. 22.
29. Ling Yu, 1989, p. 69.
30. Wang Huangping and Xu Jian, "Ai, Zhuzao Daodan Bulou De Junhun (Love constitutes the soul of missile troops)", *Laiowang,* No. 25, 1993, p. 12.
31. Xu Fangting and Liu Hongji, "Xinshiqi Junshi Douzhan Zhunbei Juyao (Some Major Points on War Preparation in the New Era", *The Journal of the PLA National Defence University,* No. 10, 1995, p. 23.
32. "Chinese Nuclear Forces 1993", Supplement (8 November 1993) to *The Bulletin of the Atomic Scientists,* Vol. 49, No. 9, November 1993, p. 24. See also *Trends,* supplement to *Business Times (Singapore),* 27–28 November 1993.
33. John Wilson Lewis and Hua Di, 1992, p. 29.

34. IISS, *Strategic Survey 1997/1998* (London: Oxford University Press, 1998), p. 170.
35. John Downing, "China's Maritime Strategy", *Jane's Intelligence Review*, April 1996, p. 189.
36. Zhao Yunshan, "Zhonggong Hedaodan Zhanlie Sixiang De Guoqu, Xianzhai Yu Weilai (The past, present and future of the CCP's nuclear strategy)", *Zhonggong Yanqiu*, Vol. 31, No. 5, 1997, p. 95.
37. Yu Hao, *et al.*, p. 527.
38. *Liaowang*, No. 33, August 1984, cited from Mohan Malik, "Chinese Debate on Military Strategy", *Journal of Northeast Asian Studies*, Summer 1990, p. 18.
39. Bao Zhongxing, "Jianshe Tianjun Gguoxiang (The initial design for the creation of a space army)", in The PLA University of National Defence, *Jundui Xiandaihua Jianshe De Sikao* (Beijing: the PLA NDU Press, 1988), pp. 420–443.
40. Kori Urayama, p. 133.
41. The view of European participants at an IISS workshop on transatlantic dialogue on NMD in UK, 12–13 December 2000, *IISS Newsletter*, Spring, 2001, p. 11. Also Philip Gordon, "Bush, Missile Defence and the Atlantic Alliance", *Survival*, Vol. 43, No. 1, 2001, pp. 17–36.
42. This refers to the Hong Niao (Red Bird) LACM system consisting of four classes. HN-1 and HN-2 have become operational; the former with a range of 400–600 km and the latter 1500–2000 km. HN-3 with a range over 2500 km is still under development.
43. Desmond Ball's remark to the *15th Regional Security Roundtable*, Kuala Lumpur, 1 June 2000.
44. U.S. Department of Defense, *The DoD Annual Report on the PLA* (Washington D.C.: U.S. DoD, 2003), p. 31.
45. Dennis Gormley, "Dealing with the Threat of Cruise Missiles", *Adelphi Paper 339*, 2001, p. 51.
46. You Ji, "Learning and Catching Up: China's RMA Initiative", in Emily Goldman and Thomas Mahnken (eds.), *The Information Revolution in Asia* (New York: Palgrave Macmillan, 2004), pp. 97–124.
47. William Tow's speech to the conference *Strategic Update*, Canberra, 29 September 1999.
48. Yu Juliang, "A Review of U.S.-Japan Joint Security Communique One Year after its Announcement", *The Journal of the PLA National Defence University*, No. 6, 1997.
49. In the second Iraqi War some Iraq's Chinese-made HY-2 missiles came dangerously close to their targets before they were engaged by PAC-3, revealing the defects of the system. HY-2 is a primitive version of cruise missiles. Dennis Gormley, "Missile Defence Myopia: Lessons from the Iraq War", *Survival*, Vol. 45, No. 4, 2003/2004, p. 66.

50. When I presented the view that TMD/NMD may cause an arms race in a regional security conference jointly organised by Pugwash and Institute of Applied Physics and Computational Mathematics in Beijing in October 2003, a number of Chinese arms control specialists challenged me, saying the NMD/TMD initiatives would not lead to an arms race in the region.

51. Robert Manning and James Pryzstup, "Asia's Transition Diplomacy: Hedging against Futureshock", *Survival*, Vol. 41, No. 3, 1999, p. 59.

Chapter 9

Nuclear Weapons and Missile Defences: The Maritime Dimension in the Asia-Pacific

Arvind Kumar

Introduction

The global development, more particularly in the last one-decade and half especially after the demise of the Soviet Union and end of the cold war, has focused broadly in the context of emerging power centres in each and every region. The debate between unilateralism versus multilateralism has gained salience and the emergence of greater power concept has dominated the debate. It is generally believed that the global centre of gravity of political, economic, military activities and capabilities is shifting to Asia and to some extent a new strategic balance is emerging among existing powers in the Asian region. Under this existing milieu, South East Asia with its maritime dimension has lots to offer in terms of development in a holistic sense. The extra regional power, the US will continue to make its presence felt and enlarge its tentacles. The role of regional powers including China, India and Japan will keep growing as a result of their strategic security interests. Various studies have indicated that the US will remain the largest economy in the world and the three largest economies in purchasing power parity terms are China, India and Japan.

The presence of American, French, Russian and other navies in the Asia-Pacific region has also changed the scenario completely. It also seems that there is a rapid proliferation of non-conventional threats in the Strait and adjoining waters. The proliferation of threats like piracy, drug trafficking and human smuggling is of major concern. Many of these nations in Asia and more particularly in South East Asia are critically dependent on regional sea-lanes for trade. These sea-lanes are also the energy lifelines of many East Asian States and are very important for global trade. The Malacca and Singapore Straits are very significant and important. Hence, the maintenance of security of these Straits is a very significant and important role. There has been a constant fear since the 11th September event that terrorists might like to attack any of these sea-lanes. The 9/11 Commission wrote, "opportunities to do harm are as great, or greater, in maritime or surface transportation [compared to commercial aviation]. Initiatives to secure shipping containers have just begun".[1] Terrorists "may be deterred by a significant chance of failure".[2] It would be worthwhile to examine the role of nuclear weapons and ballistic missile defences in maritime context. How these have special role to play and how there will be an increase in the competition among the major powers of Asia-Pacific region?

Regional Security Environment with a Maritime Dimension: Indian Perspective

It is significant and relevant to understand the regional security environment before discussing the role of nuclear weapons and ballistic missile defences and implications for maritime security. India faces multiple and complex threats and challenges to its security from the land, sea and air. It is expected that the Indian Navy will have to play a critical role in keeping the sea-lanes free from the pirates who basically have been playing havoc with the merchantmen in the Straits of Malacca and the Straits of Singapore. This is mainly due to the proximity of the sea-lanes to India which thus impinges on her security and strategic interests. The narcotics trade is the main source of finance for illicit arms and which ultimately helps in breeding the terrorism. India and many other countries in the Asia-Pacific are the victims and have been seriously threatened by narco-terrorism. The other disturbing factor for India is that the bulk of the piracy at sea is concentrated in the Indian Ocean region. In fact, the major east–west sea-lanes, from the Indian Ocean pass through two choke points Straits of Malacca in the east, and the Gulf of Aden and Suez Canal in the west. It is, therefore, very important to highlight that the Indian Ocean is an area of considerable strategic importance both for powers external to the region as well as for the nations, which are littoral to it. India has definitely more concerns in the Indian Ocean region when compared to other littorals.

India has maritime boundaries with as many as seven countries. India also shares land boundaries with five South Asian neighbours who, between themselves do not share borders. The Task Force on Border Management set up by the Government of India as a follow up on the recommendations of the Kargil Review Committee came up with a shocking revelation that the 7,500 km long maritime borders of the country had not figured in the thinking of the nation's leadership, not once in more than 50 years of freedom.[3] In fact, "maritime borders have practically been unguarded", said the Report of the Task Force. For smugglers, poachers and more recently for terrorists, these "unguarded borders" have provided an open invitation to subvert India's security. The Andaman Islands, for instance, have been an open house to forces inimical to India.

The mercantile traffic transiting the Malacca Strait passes through India's maritime zone and any contingency in the Strait will be having security and environmental implications for India. Piracy and armed robberies of vessels is steadily spilling over to the Bay of Bengal. On the basis of existing statistics, Bangladesh and India are prone to such attacks after Indonesia.

India has taken a bold initiative in making a proposal for a satellite communication network of littoral states for effective monitoring of ships' passage across its maritime zone to contain hijacking, piracy and weapons of mass destruction (nuclear, chemical and biological) proliferation. India's Andaman and Nicobar Islands lie in the waters most frequented by drug traffickers that fuel secessionist movements and related terrorist activities.

India has a plan to initiate a joint naval exercise with Thailand to forge cooperation in curbing arms smuggling.[4] Thailand has already been doing joint patrolling with Indonesia in the Andaman Sea since 2002. In the existing milieu, a joint and combined action is required due to the trans-national nature of threats. The successful recovery of the pirated ship, MV Alondra Rainbow in 1999 by the Indian Navy with information from the Regional Piracy Reporting Centre (PRC) endorses the utility of such "joint-ness". It is a very good case in point to prove that bold initiatives are required to solve a common problem while dealing with the nature of transnational threats.

Extra regional initiatives required for securing the Malacca Strait has always been opposed by Indonesia and Malaysia in particular. It is a well-known fact that a major portion of the Straits lies within territorial limits of Indonesia, Malaysia and Singapore. Indonesia and Malaysia are averse to the idea of allowing extra regional powers to play a role because such act might encroach on the sovereign character and nature of State.

The proposal made by the US in April 2004 regarding its Regional Maritime Security Initiative (RMSI) was rejected by Indonesia and Malaysia whilst Singapore has supported this idea. It was seen an encroachment on the issue of sovereignty of the littorals. It was to a greater extent a reminder of 1992 event when Malaysia singularly had opposed the UK-led anti-piracy operations in the Strait.[5] During that period, the Royal Navy was prepared to escort ships in the Malacca/Singapore Straits and that point of time Malaysian Deputy PM made a strong objection and said that "UK had no right to initiate such action". Such actions will infringe on the sovereign character of the State.

It is, however, important to point out here that the continuing objection of Malaysia and Indonesia has led US to change its course of action and the US has restricted itself in terms of intelligence exchange, joint training and capacity enhancement. There is, however, no denying the fact that the laws of the sea have stipulated the right of transit passage through the Straits to all global shipping. The international law has conferred right upon all states to interdict any foreign vessel on the high seas suspected of being engaged in piracy or human smuggling. This again would be interpreted as an act of infringement of the flag state's sovereignty.[6]

Militarisation, Ballistic Missile and Nuclearisation in the Region

The many nations of ASEAN, in particular, and other nations of Asia-Pacific in general have seen considerable militarisation in the last three decades. At the conventional level, Singapore and Malaysia have acquired submarines. Almost every littoral has missile firing ships and craft. Pakistan has missiles, which can target many important Indian cities. China can target every Indian city through land as well as sea-based systems.

India has time and again expressed concern at the Chinese Navy's close interaction with countries in the region, particularly Pakistan and Myanmar. Of particular concern to India was Chinese assistance in developing Pakistan's Gwadar port and its aid in modernising Myanmar's naval bases that could support Chinese submarine operations. India has been closely monitoring the Chinese Navy's activities in the Straits of Malacca and Indian Ocean region. It is anticipated that the development of the Pakistani port could threaten important Indian shipping routes in the Persian Gulf.

It is generally believed among strategic community and official circles in India that the rapidly growing People's Liberation Army Navy (PLAN), bent on power projection beyond the Malacca and Singapore Straits into the Indian Ocean, could be India's main strategic challenge over the next 15 years. To counter "distant, developing threats", the Indian Navy has planned to strengthen its force levels and revise its operational doctrine to become the "best, largest and most efficient force in the Indian Ocean region" by 2015.[7] India plans to expand its navy through imports including an aircraft carrier, submarines and frigates.

Pakistan is also upgrading its navy. It seems that Pakistan has acquired three French Agosta 90-B diesel-electric-powered submarines, one of which has already been commissioned in 2000. Its six Type 21 frigates bought from the UK are also being upgraded and fitted with anti-ship missiles, while its three Lockheed Martin P-3C Orion maritime patrol aircraft (MPA) acquired from the USA in 1997 conduct regular patrols in the region.[8] It is a well-known fact that the Pakistan Navy has effectively pursued modernisation of naval ship building, particularly in the last decade.

It is obvious that many countries of the Asian continent in general, and the US in particular, has acquired many modern gadgets due to the rapid pace of change in technology. Hence, there seems to be a competition in the Asia-Pacific region. The asymmetric relationship and capability exists and there is a constant source of tension. Especially, when the question comes regarding controlling sea-routes or increasing influence in the region, the debate has always been conflicting.

The development made in the field of ballistic missiles and nuclear weapons have been phenomenal. The Asia-Pacific region, as a whole, possesses large standing armies, nuclear weapons, strike aircraft, and ballistic missiles. India and Pakistan going overtly nuclear in 1998, in particular, has changed the strategic landscape in the region.

Ballistic missiles present a combination of operational capabilities (range, survivability, lack of effective defence) and features (flexibility, cost) unmatched by aircraft. As nuclear delivery systems, they can provide a survivable deterrent force. As conventional delivery systems, the relatively low cost of missiles can enable a militarily weak state to counter its numerical inferiority in other areas. As a result, ballistic missiles have become an important part of the world's military arsenals with 34 countries possessing some type of ballistic missiles. Ballistic missiles play an increasing role in the political and security dynamics of the Asia-Pacific region. The presence of significant numbers of ballistic missiles concurrent with a crisis creates a security dilemma where the protagonists might opt for pre-emptive military action.[9]

The growth of ballistic missile forces in the Asia-Pacific region has resulted from an action–reaction cycle in which one side reacts to an act (or perception of an act) by another. India's concern about the ability of Chinese missiles to strike its territory is at the core of its threat analysis. Pakistan feels threatened by the development and capability of Indian missiles. China's transfer of ballistic missile technology to Pakistan, in response to India's development activities, alarms India. China's missile programme is the oldest and most advanced in Asia. Chinese leaders have articulated that a limited but long-range missile capability is a key component of national strength and prestige. China's nuclear weapons delivery systems are mainly land-based missiles, plus a few submarine launched systems of intermediate range.

Experts have debated whether the introduction of ballistic missiles in the Asia-Pacific contributes to or detract from an overall stability. Some argue that ballistic missiles promote stability and cite the Cold War to illustrate how they helped to ensure military restraint by maintaining nuclear deterrence.

It is obvious from the rapid advancement and the increasing competition among major powers in the Asia-Pacific region that there is an element of strategic uncertainty. Sino-Pakistan nexus and horizontal proliferation is a case in point. There are three overt and one covert nuclear weapon state in the Asia-Pacific region. Rationally speaking, nuclear weapons should not be allowed to play any role in the Indian Ocean region including east and west of the region. But the crucial situation is that as long as they exist they will continue to have a major impact on perceptions and reality in the ongoing era of tension. The current trend in the subcontinent suggests that nuclear weapons have assumed a significant relevance and it will stay that way for the foreseeable future.[10]

Pakistan believes that it has finally acquired parity with India through nuclear weapons. This is perhaps the reason why Pakistan keeps promoting and provoking India. Hence, the current milieu has forced India to grow its naval power, increase the activities of the Indian Navy and acquire sea-based assets. It is most likely that India pursues on a priority basis the development and deployment of nuclear weapons. India will certainly maintain a credible minimum nuclear deterrent. The reality of this nuclear deterrent is that India has kept everything in ready posture only. As of now, there is a lack of integration between nuclear warheads and delivery systems. Hence, the current posture allows for the fabrication of warheads and other components of nuclear weapons only.[11]

India has adopted a formal nuclear doctrine. One of the components of the doctrine states that India should develop nuclear forces based on a triad of aircraft, mobile land-based missiles and sea-based assets. A triad for India is required because aircraft and land-based missiles can be vulnerable to a first strike. To complement India's no-first use policy and maintain an effective second-strike capability, sea-based assets are an essential component of India's proposed force structure. Currently, India has a programme to develop indigenous sea-based assets at a much faster pace than in the past. The work on acquiring sea-based assets is very much in progress. India is also likely to continue conducting missile tests to validate delivery systems for its nuclear deterrence while exercising strategic restraint.

The Government of Pakistan has not released any formal nuclear doctrine. However, one might reasonably infer from the statements of senior military figures that they, too, endorse a massive response to Indian strikes against sensitive targets or crossing of Pakistani "red lines".[12]

It is important to note here that neither India nor Pakistan has deployed nuclear weapons in Indian Ocean.[13] If one argues a hypothetical situation then one might say that the geo-strategic environment of the subcontinent and the Asia-Pacific region including Indian Ocean might prompt or provoke India to deploy sea-based or air deliverable nuclear weapons that will directly utilise space as opposed to those occurring in the broader Indian Ocean region that could encompass as many as 51 separate nations.[14] In this context, many nations in Asia-Pacific region might follow suit.

The main factors that will influence India's decision making regarding the possible deployment of nuclear weapons are also in the context of the potential strengthening of its air-based nuclear deterrent vis-à-vis China. China is not an Indian Ocean littoral, but it has extensive interests in the region. There is no doubt in saying that if geo-strategic environment in the Asia-Pacific region was already bad then it could only get worse with the proliferation of nuclear weapons more widely around the region. There seems to be a lack of genuine and serious commitment on the part of the NPT nuclear weapon states to attain a global nuclear disarmament. Other nuclear weapon states, including Russia and the US have placed their nuclear deterrence at sea. Nuclear weapons at sea provide the most significant and substantial mode of assured deterrence with a viable second-strike capability. Deployments of nuclear powered submarines with nuclear tipped ballistic and cruise missiles have a formidable role in posturing and nuclear signalling.

The other important reason for India taking such extreme position of deploying nuclear weapons broadly in the Indian Ocean would be the increasing interests of the US. India does not want to play a greater power role but would like to have a certain degree of strategic autonomy, which is the hallmark of India's nuclear doctrine. It is a well-known fact that the US has engaged itself in a big way in the Indian Ocean region. From the coast of East Africa to Djibouti, Yemen, Oman, Pakistan, India, Sri Lanka, and Diego Garcia, and on to the Strait of Malacca and Singapore, the US has been increasing its security presence in this broad region.[15]

It can be said that India's determination to keep its nuclear weapons until global nuclear disarmament has little to do with Pakistan but much to do with China, and everything to do with the US. Unless the US takes an active and concrete interest in attaining the nuclear weapons free world, nuclear weapons will be a feature of the future security environment of the Indian Ocean region in general and Straits of Malacca in particular. The nuclear posture review of the US is a pointer in this direction where the US has a plan to integrate both non-nuclear and nuclear assets. It also talks about acquiring earth-penetrating devices and for this to be achieved, it will be mandatory for the US to break the moratorium on its nuclear tests. The US in particular has shown its intentions to establish a robust seamless joint forces posture meant to enhance the US autonomy of operations in the maritime realm. The current trend of development suggests that the US would develop maritime-based capabilities and that these capabilities would be able to support both offensive and defensive operations at sea.

Implications of Ballistic Missile Defences: Indian Perspective

Reactions to US ballistic missile defence programs differ among Asia-Pacific nations depending not only on the system to be deployed — that is either the Theatre Missile Defence (TMD) or the National Missile Defence (NMD) — but also depending on their relationship with the US, their specific security situation, and their perceptions of how missile defences will change the balance of power in the region.[16]

Indian perspectives on US ballistic missile defence initiatives are varied and fluid. In an interview on 24 July 2000, Jaswant Singh stated, "We have consistently held a view that opposes the militarisation of space. The NMD will adversely influence the larger movement towards disarmament of which India is a staunch advocate. We believe that technological superiority will result in a reaction in other parts of the world, thus reviving the possibility of yet another, and newer arms race. We cannot support this development".[17]

The tone of this statement was quite different from the Ministry of External Affairs (MEA) press release within 24 hr of President Bush's address at the National Defence University on 1 May 2001. The press release stated, "India, particularly, welcomes the announcement of unilateral reductions by the US of nuclear forces, as an example. We also welcome moving away from the hair-trigger alerts associated with prevailing nuclear orthodoxies. India believes there is a strategic and technological inevitability in stepping away from a world that is held hostage by the doctrine of mutual-assured destruction to a cooperative, defensive transition that is underpinned by further cuts and a de-alert of nuclear forces".[18] However, if one goes through the MEA press release carefully, it is obvious that India had not supported US intentions to deploy ballistic missile defences. Media accounts have drawn the erroneous conclusion that India has supported and welcomed BMD because the press release does not specifically criticise it.

However, there has been a perceptible change in the thinking process of both India and the US. A major development has been an Indo–US agreement signed in September 2004 formally on the matters related to the implementation of the Next Step in Strategic Partnership (NSSP). It has provided ample means to have cooperation in the spheres of missile defence in addition to a number of other important sectors. There is a greater likelihood that India and US might collaborate in the missile defence venture in the foreseeable future. However, such collaboration will change the strategic calculus in the region. India's acquisition of a TMD system will complicate Pakistan's nuclear strategy and dent its ability to indulge in nuclear blackmail.[19]

India at the same time believes that the US would deploy a technically feasible NMD, taking into account its national security requirements, despite global reactions to it in general and from Russia and China in particular. There is a fear that the US would threaten the whole architecture of nuclear disarmament and non-proliferation by deploying missile defences which may result in an action–reaction cycle in the Asia-Pacific region.

China would start questioning its deterrent posture vis-à-vis the US once Washington deploys a technically feasible NMD, as its second-strike capability could be rendered obsolete. US NMD deployment could cause China to increase its number of inter-continental ballistic missiles. China might also try to acquire or refine technologies to evade limited NMD. An increase in the number of Chinese missiles in response to US NMD would likely have at least a limited effect on India's force structure. The deployment of Navy Theatre Wide missile defences is also a major concern for a number of littoral countries and would certainly permeate competition among major powers of the Asia-Pacific region.

Conclusion

The sea will always remain a theatre of domination between countries. The importance of the Sea in the existing environment is growing day by day. In this current century, it is anticipated that the Indian Ocean would provide the most important sea lanes for the transport of merchandise. It would emerge as a pivot for the economic security of the Asia-Pacific region. However, the fears from terrorist attacks in the maritime domain still exist despite measures that have been taken to mitigate such threats.

Unlike land and air power, sea power allows a country to make its capability visible well beyond its own shores. India's interest might be served in the Indian Ocean region including Straits of Malacca and Singapore Straits by becoming a credible sea power in the coming decades. Nuclear weapons are going to stay and the US might like to deploy its ballistic missile defences including the Navy Theatre Wide Missile Defences. The other littorals of the Indian Ocean will have to live with this harsh reality. Equilibrium in Asia in general and the Indian Ocean in particular will require a balanced relationship among the major countries of the region, that is, Russia, China, Japan, India and the US, together with cooperative engagement with ASEAN and other sub-regional groupings.

Notes

1. U.S. National Commission on Terrorist Attacks upon the United States, *The 9/11 Commission Report* (New York: Norton, 2004), p. 391.
2. Ibid.
3. George Fernandes, "Maritime Dimensions of India's Security", *Indian Defence Review* (New Delhi), Vol. 15, No. 4, pp. 53–54.
4. Bangkok Post, 27 May 2003.
5. Sam Bateman, "Confidence and Security Building" in Jasjit Singh (ed.), *Maritime Security* (New Delhi: Institute for Defence Studies & Analyses, August 1993), p. 114.
6. UNCLOS, Article 110; Permitted by Protocol of UN Convention Against Transnational Organised Crime, 25 September 2003 and finally entered into force since 28 January 2004.
7. The former Chief of Indian Navy, Admiral Madhavendra Singh, made this statement in an interview with Jane's Defence Weekly and which was later covered by Indo-Asian News Service on 21 May 2003.

8. "Back on Course", *Jane's Defence Weekly*, 24 January 2001, p. 24.
9. Michael D. Swaine and Loren H. Runyon, "Ballistic Missiles and Missile Defence in Asia", *NBR Analysis*, Vol. 13, No. 3, June 2002, p. 72.
10. See for detailed analysis, Donald L. Berlin, "The Indian Ocean and the Second Nuclear Age". Available at http://disramament.un.org/rcpd/pdf%20ROK/Berlin.pdf where he has quoted the works of Paul Bracken *Fire in the East: The Rise of Asian Military Power and the Second Nuclear Age* (New York: Harper Collins, 1990); Colin S. Gray, *The Second Nuclear Age* (Boulder, Colorado: Lynne Reinner Publishers, 1999); Keith B. Payne, *Deterrence in the Second Nuclear Age* (Lexington: University Press of Kentucky, 1996) and Paul Bracken, "The Second Nuclear Age", *Foreign Affairs*, January–February 2000, pp. 146–156.
11. This is what was described as "Recessed Deterrence" by Jasjit Singh, India.
12. Michael Krepon, *The Stability-Instability Paradox, Misperception, and Escalation Control in South Asia* (Washington, D. C.: The Henry L. Stimson Center, May 2003).
13. "Deployment" means a nuclear weapon system: (1) is not in developmental testing; (2) exists in significant numbers; (3) is assigned to the military; and (4) is ready for use with short preparation.
14. Donald L. Berlin.
15. Ibid.
16. Michael J. Green and Toby F. Dalton, "Asian Reactions to US Missile Defence," *NBR Analysis*, Vol. 11, No. 3, November 2000. Available at http://www.nbr.org/publications/analysis/vol11no3/index.html. <Accessed on 15 February 2005>.
17. Interview with *Times of India* (New Delhi), 24 July 2000. Also quoted in Indian weekly *Outlook*, May 2001.
18. Ministry of External Affairs Press Release, 2 May 2001. Also see, Arvind Kumar, "Missile Defense and Strategic Modernisation in Southern Asia" in Michael Krepon and Chris Gagne (eds.), *The Impact of US Ballistic Missile Defenses on Southern Asia*, The Henry L. Stimson Center, Report No. 46, July 2002.
19. C. Raja Mohan, "Next Steps in Missile Defence", *New Indian Express* (Bangalore), 22 February 2005.

Chapter 10

Transforming Old Idealism into New Realism: A New Dimension in Japan's Strategy for Non-Proliferation and Counter-Proliferation and its Implications for Security Cooperation in the Asia-Pacific

Katsuhisa Furukawa

Living with Uncertainties

In the current years, global security faces two major challenges: how to deal with the emerging new global threats as represented by terrorism, proliferation of the weapons of mass destruction (WMD), or newly emerging infectious diseases; and how to build constructive security relationships between major land powers whose future still remain uncertain (most notably, China, India, and Russia) and other major powers, namely, the US, EU, and their allies and friendly countries.[1] These challenges are most evident in Asia where the geopolitical landscape has been in transition and remain unstable. Indeed, Asia is the very nexus of these global security threats and geopolitical uncertainty. At the core of this nexus are key security problems which have global implications, including the threats of North Korea's nuclear weapons program, Islamic fundamentalist movements in Southeast Asia, nuclear weapons proliferation by Pakistan, and the uncertain future of the land powers, namely, Russia, China, and India, all of which possess nuclear weapons.

On the other hand, while there have been several modest developments in multilateralism in Asia, as represented by East Asia Summit or ASEAN Plus Three, the development of institutional tools available for addressing these problems still remains immature in this region. Regional efforts need to intensify in order to build effective regional mechanisms to deal with these threats and uncertainties. Countries in this region sporadically rely upon a combination of their independent capabilities, bilateral and multilateral security relationship with other countries, especially, the US and the United Nations (UN) as a primary tool to assure their safety. In the post-Cold War era, Asia presents one of the most pressing needs for stability and predictability that are essential for constructing a benign global security environment.

The intelligence tools to deal with these new security threats are also limited in their effectiveness. The US intelligence community has so far invested a significant amount of resources in strengthening its capabilities, including imagery intelligence, radiation and environmental sensors, communications intelligence, signals intelligence and human intelligence. Even so, there are limits as to what the US can know about other countries, especially when it comes to the issues related to proliferation of WMD or radical Islamic terrorism.

Take, for example, the cases of "alleged" WMD programs of Iraq and confirmed nuclear development programs of Iran and Libya, all of which highlighted the difficulties in dealing with the proliferation of WMD. In the case of Iraq, both the US and UK intelligence communities are blamed for having "hyped" the threats of Iraq's WMD.[2] In January 2004, David Kay, who led the weapon hunt efforts of the US Iraq Survey Group, testified that he did not find "large stockpile of newly produced weapons of mass destruction" and that "we were almost all wrong".[3] He pointed the cause of the inability to find illegal WMD in Iraq to a major intelligence failure.

In the cases of Iran and Libya, however, the international community was surprised again, but this time, by the fact that their nuclear development programs were even more advanced than their previous assessments. Nobody had correctly estimated the extensiveness of Iran's uranium enrichment facilities until an Iranian exile group leaked inside information about these facilities, verified by the subsequent International Atomic Energy Agency (IAEA) inspections since 2003. Also, Libya had clandestinely acquired and set up more advanced centrifuges that were identical with "second-generation" Pakistani designs through the black market, although it had not assembled them into a large-scale cascade for producing highly enriched uranium.[4] As David Albright, former IAEA inspector, stated, "The fact that Libya could go out and buy an entire centrifuge plant without anyone detecting it is startling".[5]

The situation is more complicated by the fact that many technologies, materials, devices, and facilities to produce WMD have dual use applications, which essentially blurs the boundary between the production of legitimate material for civilian use and the one for WMD. Also, these technologies have widely diffused on a global scale, making the distance between the "intention" to produce WMD and the "capability" to do so shorter than ever before.

The issue of how to redress or improve intelligence capability has become, and will remain to be, a subject of heated discussion. Sooner or later, various measures will be adopted to improve such capability. Improved intelligence would probably enable to narrow down the scope and size of the potential errors in the information and analyses about suspected or determined WMD proliferators, but it would still remain extremely difficult for the international community to construct sufficiently credible intelligence information and analyses, especially without the presence of credible human intelligence assets that could penetrate into the top leadership of the subject countries or networks. In short, it is very difficult for us to know precisely what we do not know. All in all, intelligence can and will never be perfect. As Richard Pearle, former Chairman of the Defence Policy Board of the US, said, "Intelligence is not an audit... It's the best information you can get in circumstances of uncertainty".[6] Indeed, as one senior US official of the Central Intelligence Agency (CIA) recalled, "Intelligence analysis was in part about placing the best bets possible"[7] by sorting out and analysing credible information out of available ones.

Still, however, both horizontal and vertical proliferation of the WMD, poses one of the gravest challenges to international security. And this is the reality we have to live with in the 21st century. Intelligence information about the WMD proliferation might not be entirely reliable for years to come. However, ambiguity or imperfection of intelligence alone should not constitute an excuse for inaction. We have to shape our policy-based upon information that is available but may have at least some level of uncertainty.

In order to meet the new security threats of the WMD proliferation under the above constraint, intense international cooperation and consultation are essential and such collaboration needs to be regularised and institutionalised. This is particularly true in Asia where the challenge of proliferation has been steadily growing while the countries in this region have invested relatively limited resources to curb the problems associated with the WMD proliferation.

Under this circumstance, the US has functioned as the linchpin of Asian security and stability. The US has approached security relations in Asia as a hub-and-spoke arrangement — with the US at the centre of bilateral alliances and security relationships among nations that, in turn, have limited bilateral, if any, military interactions and security arrangements with each other.[8] US bilateral treaties and security partnerships, backed by capable, forward-stationed and forward-deployed armed forces, remain the indispensable framework for deterring aggression and promoting peace and stability in the region. Especially, the US security relationship with the allies has been an essential factor that has ensured the regional stability. Among the allies, Australia, Japan, Singapore, and South Korea stand as a key partner for the US in the Asia-Pacific region.

With this context in mind, this paper aims to explain the salience of Japan's role in enhancing the multilateral security cooperation in dealing with major security challenges in Asia in the post-Cold War era, especially, those associated with both vertical and horizontal proliferation of nuclear weapons and missiles. Particularly, this paper focuses upon Japan's perspectives and endeavours to strengthen a wide range of non-proliferation and counter-proliferation measures, including diplomatic, military, and law enforcement measures, as represented by the missile defence, the Proliferation Security Initiative (PSI), and other multilateral export control systems, since these measures can serve as a primary driving force to institutionalise bilateral or multilateral security cooperation in this region.

A New Direction for Japan's National Security Policy

Over the past decade, Japan has demonstrated unique assertiveness in leading regional and international efforts to address security problems. Contrary to predictions by the realists, Japan became assertive in its external policy only after its relative power began to decline in the 1990s. In fact, since the late 1990s, there have been considerable changes in Japan's diplomacy, national security policy, and strategic culture. Japan has come to demonstrate a heightened sensitivity toward regional threats, particularly in terms of balance of power vis-à-vis China and North Korea, global threats of radical Islamic terrorism, and the WMD proliferation. Those changes have significantly affected Japan's national security strategy that has gradually but remarkably changed over the past years, in tandem with the Bush administration's pursuit of a rigorous national security strategy to strengthen the Japan–US alliance.

In the area of arms control and non-proliferation, Japan traditionally regarded its policy primarily as a means to achieve Japan's idealistic goal of an eventual elimination of nuclear weapons on a global scale. In the past, however, up until the late 1990s, there was a relative lack of recognition in Japan that this policy should be meant as a means to deal with more imminent security threats of the WMD proliferation to Japan's homeland defence. Japan's position to address the problems of the WMD proliferation was characterised by its tendency to resort to an idealistic pacifist posture which was evident in its efforts to pursue a global disarmament of nuclear weapon principally through international negotiation, although, in fact, Japan has been protected by the US nuclear umbrella. Japan primarily focused on continuing to negotiate new treaties on international arms control and non-proliferation with an expectation that member countries may eventually develop a common global norm against all types of nuclear weapons in the future. However, Japan placed relatively limited emphasis on the necessity to actually enforce the existing international agreements, and, not to mention, evidently lacked a determination to enforce such agreements even by resorting to coercive measures. In addition, up until 1998 when North Korea launched the Taepodong missile over the head of Japan, Japan had placed few serious emphases on the importance of counter-proliferation. In short, in the area of non-proliferation and arms control, Japan's strategic culture in the past was principally characterised by idealism and pacifism with few component of realism.

Since the mid-1990s, however, Japan's optimistic posture gradually began to change. Japan has started to incorporate more elements of realism into its diplomacy and national security policy, and has grown out of its traditional pacifist posture. Japan attempts to establish a comprehensive national security strategy from a pragmatic perspective by employing various considerable measures, including diplomatic, economic, political, and military means, and no longer hesitate to adopt even coercive measures when inevitable. This characteristic can be seen clearly in the October 2004 report of the Japanese government's Council on Security and Defence Capabilities which clearly identified the necessity for Japan to adopt an integrated security strategy,[9] which was subsequently reflected in the *New Defence Program Guideline for Fiscal Year 2005 and After*.[10] In a sense, Japan has been steadily learning how to pursue its traditional, ideational objective of a stable global peace in a more pragmatic manner, by employing new measures that are increasingly characterised by realism. Japan has been transforming its posture from old idealism into new realism.

These changes have been most evidently observed since 2001 under the US administration of President George W. Bush who prioritises Japan–US alliance as one of the core pillar of its global security system. External events significantly prompted these changes, especially the terrorist attacks in the US on 11 September 2001, the resumption of another round of North Korean nuclear crisis in December 2002, and the sustained China's efforts of military modernisation. These events have significantly altered the Japanese government's view of its security environment and have enlarged Japan's operational theatre from its surrounding areas in Northeast Asia to global areas.

As a result, Japan has been strengthening its overall defence capabilities and has taken a number of substantial steps to set in place various new legal, diplomatic, and military frameworks to protect Japan's homeland and to enforce international agreements related to national security affairs, as represented by the enactment of the Three Laws Regarding Response to Armed Attacks in 2003, the decision to deploy missile defence systems to be completed by FY 2011, and the multiple diplomatic initiatives for non-proliferation, including Asian Senior-level Talks on Non-Proliferation (ASTOP), Asian Export Control Seminars, and Japan–ASEAN Non-Proliferation Cooperation Mission. Through these various initiatives, Japan has been building capacity for its national security strategy in an integrated manner, both internally and externally, by employing pragmatic measures with realistic objectives.

An emergence of Japan's new posture on national security has substantive implications for global and regional security; it intends to complement and strengthen the existing international regimes as well as the bilateral, regional, and multilateral security networks with the US at the core. Also, Japan's assertiveness in the areas of international security has the potential of contributing to building and institutionalising an Asian security network through the steady strengthening of the Japan–US alliance.

Given the reality of the imperfectness of intelligence capability of any country, it has become even more imperative for the entire international community to jointly shape a collaborative framework for an effective regional and global security in order to slow down and eventually roll-back the threats as well as to remove uncertainties. Japan has become one of the assertive countries in the Asia-Pacific region that intend to lead such international efforts to combat the threats.

Traditionally, Japan relied principally upon *assurance* and *dissuasion* when dealing with threats: namely, the Japan–US alliance and international institutions represented by the UN. Now, however, Japan has been increasingly attentive to the need to develop a more comprehensive strategy covering a wide range of areas including assurance, dissuasion, deterrence, denial, offensive defence measures, active defence measures, and damage confinement. The primary driving factor behind this change has been North Korea's deployment of the Nodong missiles, which has placed Japan within the range of a direct attack from the Korean Peninsula for the first time in the history; the increasing power projection capabilities of Chinese military forces as well as China's unilateral activities that relatively disregard Japan's sovereignty over its territorial waters; and the expanding trend of the global radical Islamic jihadists' movement that shows increasing interest in acquiring WMD for future terrorist attack, even extending their reach to Japan's homeland, all of which present clear dangers. Thus, Japan has responded by diversifying its "national security portfolio" to adopt a more balanced posture in a comprehensive manner. The following sections examine the advancement in each function of Japan's integrated national security strategy, particularly in association with the areas of non-proliferation and counter-proliferation, and their implications for enhancing multilateral security cooperation in the Asia-Pacific.

Shaping a New Integrated National Security Strategy

Assurance and Deterrence: Strengthening the Japan–US Alliance

Japan has been steadily strengthening its deterrence capability, as defined by the *National Defence Program Guideline (NDPG) for FY 2005 and After*.[11] The new NDPG emphasises Japan's capability to respond effectively to new threats, including terrorism and WMD proliferation, and diverse contingencies, as well as Japan's active engagement to improve the international security environment and the importance of the Japan–US alliance.

Japan's national security policy has always evolved dramatically every time when there was a crisis on the Korean Peninsula. After the North Korean crisis in 1993–94, Japan decided to redefine its roles and missions within the Japan–US security alliance, announced the Japan–US Joint Security Declaration in 1996, and created the new Japan–US defence-guidelines in 1998. When North Korea launched the Taepodong missile over Japan, Japan decided to embark upon the joint research of missile defence with the US. As North Korea escalates the nuclear problem since it expelled IAEA inspectors in December 2002, in conjunction with the rapid increase in the perceived threat of terrorism after 11 September 2001, Japan has strengthened its alliance with the US by demonstrating its support for US military operations in Afghanistan and for reconstruction of post-war Iraq.

In addition, for the first time in the history in this bilateral alliance, the Japanese and US governments issued a joint statement on 19 February 2004 which specified their common strategic objectives.[12] In this statement, the two governments clearly stated that newly emerging threats, such as international terrorism and WMD proliferation and their means of delivery, have surfaced as their common challenges, and that these persistent challenges continue to create unpredictability and uncertainty in the Asia-Pacific region, together with the continuous modernisation of the military capabilities in this region, particularly the one of China.

Also, as a central component of the US broad defence transformation effort, the US has been reorienting and strengthening its global defence posture to provide it with appropriate, strategy-driven capabilities to meet with an uncertain security environment, which has triggered realignment of US force structures in Japan and continuous examination of the roles, missions, and capabilities of Japan's Self Defence Forces (SDF) and the US military forces. The two militaries strive to enhance interoperability mutually in order to ensure and strengthen effective security and defence cooperation to be able to respond swiftly to diverse challenges in a well-coordinated manner. The two governments' agreement in this regard has been published in *Transformation and Realignment for the Future*, a document of the Japan–US Security Consultative Committee on 29 October 2005, and its implementation plan is to be finalised by the end of March 2006.[13]

Apparently, China has been gravely concerned with these changes in Japan's national security posture and with the strengthening of the Japan–US alliance. Ironically, North Korea has almost always contributed to escalating China's sense of insecurity regarding Japan's expanding national security posture which has been triggered by the North's "rogue" behaviour. Another provocative behaviour by the North will surely prompt Japan to adopt a more advanced security posture for stronger defence and stronger alliance with the US. Both Japan and the US intend to address China's security concern by initiating strategic dialogues with China as well as by adopting various measures to secure transparency and to build mutual confidence. There are views within Japan that such strategic dialogues can be conducted not only bilaterally but also trilaterally.

The strengthening of Japan–US alliance has been conducted in correlation with the US Global Posture Review. As noted before, the US intends to forge an alliance network in the Asia-Pacific that consists of multiple bilateral alliance systems in a mutually coordinated manner with the US at the core. Multilateral joint exercises among the allies and friendly countries of the US have been conducted, including the 2004 PITCH BLACK exercise led by Australia, the 2005 Cobra Gold exercise for disaster relief operation in Thailand where 23 countries participated, and the 2005 Western Pacific Naval Symposium in Singapore where nine countries participated.

Japan's participation in these joint exercises have been somewhat constrained due to its constitutional constraint to prohibit Japan to exercise the right of collective self-defence. As such, although it is difficult for Japan to be engaged in a combined command and control system with other countries in these exercises, Japan and other countries have been building experience to jointly operate under coordinated command and control systems. The process of strengthening Japan–US alliance will provide Japan with opportunities to engage itself with bilateral coordinated joint operations with the US constantly.

In addition, as a measure of assurance, Japan has been engaged in, and led, a number of multilateral security dialogues over the past decade, including ASEAN Regional Forum, Tokyo Defence Forum, and the Asia-Pacific Chiefs of Defence Conference. These assurance measures constitute another pillar of regional security in tandem with efforts to construct the alliance network in the region.

The strengthened Japan–US alliance supplemented by multilateral security dialogues is expected to constitute an indispensable basis for constructing a dense web of alliance network in the Asia-Pacific that can function under a coordinated command and control. Such alliance network is essential for joint operations to curb down the WMD proliferation, as represented by the PSI exercises. Moreover, it can also serve as an essential tool to build confidence among the Asia-Pacific nations, to enhance the credibility of deterrence, and even to enable adoption of coercive measures against hostile countries or WMD proliferators. The strengthened alliance is an essential requirement for ensuring assurance and deterrence both in peace time and during any contingency.

Dissuasion and Offensive Defence Measures

Strengthening multilateral institutions and treaties have traditionally served as Japan's primary measures for dissuading proliferators from obtaining the WMD and for encouraging states to adopt effective measures to curb down the WMD proliferation. Japan has been leading international efforts to press negotiation on arms control and non-proliferation, including the Comprehensive Test Ban Treaty and the Fissile Material Cut-Off Treaty.

In addition to promoting *negotiation* of treaties, Japan has come to place more emphasis than before on the importance of *enforcement* of the existing treaties and of *compliance* with these treaties by the signatory states since early 21st century. Particularly, in the realm of non-proliferation, Japan has come to regard *compliance* as a key element of non-proliferation, given the difficulty of detecting any WMD stockpile with an ample amount of time before its threat materialises. The reality is, however, that most countries lack a systematic review of treaty obligations by other states, which is one of the primary problems that Japan intends to redress.

Additionally, although the Bush administration's concept of *pre-emption* has sparked an intense controversy, there seems to be a reasonable ground for discussing the possibility to apply some sort of pre-emptive or preventive measure, especially as a law enforcement tool. A legal framework based upon prosecution rather than prevention may no longer be sufficient in curbing WMD proliferation.

With a view to advancing regional and global efforts for non-proliferation, Japan has been also leading efforts together with other countries in the Asia-Pacific region, most notably, Singapore and Australia, to establish stringent multilateral export control systems in Asia, in close coordination with the US government. Together with Singapore and Australia, Japan has been trying to prompt other Asian countries to forge a common understanding about the necessity to prevent further WMD proliferation and to drive Asian countries to implement tangible measures to achieve the goal of non-proliferation.

With the increasing importance of compliance and enforcement as key elements of non-proliferation, there is an emerging view among the Japanese and US non-proliferation community that Asian countries need to establish a new principle of treaty compliance and enforcement. On of such attempts was materialised in the multilateral agreement on the Basic Principles Regarding the Export Control Policy in Asia which was agreed at the Asian Export Control Dialogue on 18 October 2004 with a purpose to strengthen the Asian countries' export control systems.[14]

Originally, Japan's focus to forge such a regional network for non-proliferation has been driven by the necessity to stop outflow of the WMD and related materials to North Korea. In the 1990s, when Japan realised that North Korea used China as a transit point for their secret imports from Japan of commodities and materials for the WMD production, Japan began to enforce more stringent export control upon its exports toward China. Subsequently, however, North Korea began diversifying the transit point to Southeast Asian countries. In order to stop these outflows of commodities and materials into North Korea, Japan has been assisting other Asian countries to adopt a stringent export control system and to forge an Asian network for non-proliferation, especially focusing on Southeast Asian countries, many of whom have fairly loose export control systems. Japan has taken a number of steps to enhance bilateral, regional, and global cooperation for non-proliferation, including the ones below:

- Japan has been arranging export control seminars for Asian countries since 1993, with a view to enhancing Asian countries' awareness of the importance of export control. Furthermore, since 1999, Japan has organised training seminars for relevant Asian officials to provide them with professional and technical expertise of export control.[15]
- Japan has initiated new multilateral initiatives for non-proliferation in 2003, including the Asian Senior-Level Talks on Non-proliferation (ASTOP), arranged by the Japanese Ministry of Foreign Affairs, and the Asian Export Control Dialogue, arranged by the Ministry of Economy, Trade, and Industry. As noted above, at the second Asian Export Control Dialogue on 18 October 2004, the Japanese government has led efforts, under close coordination with the US government, to obtain a consensus from the participating countries (Australia, China, Hong Kong, Singapore, Thailand, South Korea, the US and Japan) on basic principles for Asian export control policy and modalities for cooperation toward implementation of effective export control.[16] This principle is expected to set a new standard of export control for other countries in Asia. Japan intends to ask other Asian countries that have lax measures for non-proliferation, to adhere to this principle, in the near future.[17]
- Japan has also launched a new initiative to provide training seminars for ASEAN countries to provide practical expertise on how to interdict and inspect suspected cargo ships and airplanes at the seaport or airport.
- As for bilateral initiatives, Japan signed with Singapore an agreement for export control cooperation, in late April 2004. A similar bilateral agreement has been also concluded between Japan and Hong Kong in May 2004. The bilateral agreements include a plan to set up liaison offices in these countries and the region, and monitoring suspicious exports.[18] In the medium- to long-term, Japan intends to construct a network of export control cooperative agreements centring on Japan.[19] Japan has also held export control dialogue with the People's Republic of China, bilaterally.

- Starting in fiscal year 2004, the Japanese government has linked the contents of official development assistance to developing Asian nations to the strictness of their export control policies.
- Building upon the above initiatives for regional cooperation for non-proliferation, Japan organised Japan–ASEAN Non-Proliferation Cooperation Mission in February 2004, and Asia Non-Proliferation Seminar focusing on Maritime Cooperation in May 2004.
- In close coordination with the US, Japan has been trying to promote understanding of the PSI among other Asian countries, through bilateral meetings and dialogues. Japan paid significant effort to persuade the US to allow the participation of France and Germany into the PSI. The PSI's multilateral maritime exercise, *Team Samurai 04*, was conducted off the coast of Sagami Bay and within Yokosuka Port in Japan in October 2004, which was led primarily by Japan SDFs and Japan Coast Guard.

These multilateral efforts indicate clearly that Japan realises that it has a major stake in developing stringent measures for non-proliferation and arms control in order to constrain North Korea's capability to develop further arsenal and infrastructure associated with nuclear weapons and missiles. Various initiatives as shown above are intended to attain a certain level of function of dissuasion and offensive defence, as represented by the PSI. Together with the strengthened alliance system and multilateral security dialogues, these initiatives for dissuasion and offensive defence are also expected to contribute to forging regional security cooperation.

Japan's Nuclear Option?[20]

Despite the above developments in Japan's national security posture, however, there have been concerns consistently in Asia and in the US that Japan might decide to possess its own nuclear weapons as a part of its counter-proliferation strategy, given North Korea's development of nuclear weapon programs. In Japan, however, it has rarely been a subject of serious examination although a small number of experts and opinion leaders have certainly made argument in support of such an option.

Japan's nuclear option was speculated among foreign countries occasionally in the past, for example, during the North Korean nuclear crisis in 1993–94 and at the time of the international negotiation over the indefinite expansion of the Non-Proliferation Treaty in 1994–95. In 2003, an open debate about whether or not to acquire nuclear weapons emerged in Japan. The question is whether this is a manifestation of a new trend in Japan, diverging from a general preference for defensive realism, or simply a temporary phenomenon in emotional reaction to the escalation of North Korea's provocative behaviours, which might fade away as time goes by. In order to answer this question, one must analyse the *content, direction, and outcome* of this debate. It would be simply premature to reach any conclusion about Japan's intention to go nuclear, only by observing the mere *existence* of an open debate on this subject in Japan.

So far, the debate on nuclear option in Japan was a temporary phenomenon, as evident in the rapid decrease of such debate in Japan since 2005. There is an increasing recognition among serious Japanese experts and officials that all of the four conditions below would be essential before Japan should make a decision to develop nuclear weapons: (1) a perceived lack of credibility regarding US extended deterrence; (2) virtual collapse of international regimes for arms control and non-proliferation; (3) a significant increase in perceived threats from neighbouring countries; and, most importantly, (4) the US government's approval for Japan to go nuclear.[21] The following sections explains why Japan considers that the option to remain non-nuclear still far outweigh arguments for it to go nuclear, at least for the foreseeable future.

New Trends in Japan's Debate on Its Nuclear Option

By analysing the contents of the debates in Japan, several characteristics can be highlighted about contemporary discussions on Japan's nuclear posture.[22] Firstly, there still remain — as there always have been — a handful of die-hard, older right-wing politicians who harbour visions of a fully remilitarised Japan. However, such perspectives have been fairly marginalised. Secondly, it still remains very difficult and controversial for a majority of Japanese politicians to advocate nuclear weapons. Careless comments by Cabinet members on this matter can trigger a huge controversy and almost turn out to be an act of "political suicide".

Thirdly, a majority of the Japanese public, except for Japanese officials and experts, do not yet perceive neighbouring countries' nuclear weapons to be a grave threat. For example, even after North Korea's revelation of its nuclear weapons program in 2002, the Japanese public simply kept blaming North Korea primarily for the abduction of the Japanese citizens, while paying little attention to North Korea's WMD.[23] In fact, the presence of nuclear weapons on the neighbouring continent is nothing new to Japan. Over the past 50 years, Japan has "peacefully" co-existed with Chinese nuclear weapons even when

China repeatedly conducted nuclear testing. While a general sense of insecurity has been mounting among the Japanese public since the mid-1990s, a majority of them still tend to view the problems of nuclear proliferation as a matter to be handled principally by the US. In a sense, this may be a reflection of the public's tacit confidence in the credibility of the extended deterrence provided by the US.

Fourthly, however, while it is still inappropriate to advocate nuclear weapons for Japan, it is no longer taboo to discuss nuclear strategy and the *hypothetical* possibility that Japan could require such weapons some day. Although a nuclear option is still unacceptable to the general public, an increasing recognition has emerged that such an option should at least be thought through. In short, pragmatic debate on the nuclear option has emerged in Japan. All in all, today's Japanese experts no longer care about openly discussing the hypothetical possibility of Japan possessing nuclear weapons. However, the fact of the matter is that only a small number of experts and provocative advocates argue for Japan's nuclear weapons with the purpose of maximising Japan's relative power vis-à-vis China, irrespective of any costs associated with such a nuclear option. In contrast, a majority is not determined to possess nuclear weapons at all, but rather interested in simply examining whether Japan's possession of indigenous nuclear weapons would contribute to strengthening deterrence against any hostile country if any serious change should take place in Japan's security environment, and whether Japan would actually be able to develop nuclear weapons if it should decide to do so.

Younger politicians and experts are more conversant and comfortable with nuclear strategic issues. Indeed, many second-generation politicians and experts are graduates of international studies programs in the US. They are not looking to change Japan's basic nuclear stance, but to understand concepts like mutually assured destruction, and are conversant with the logic of nuclear deterrence. Some even openly argue that Japan would be able to influence international debates on nuclear issues more effectively if Japan retained the capabilities necessary to develop nuclear weapons but decides not to do so.[24] Having said that, a nuclear Japan is still far beyond imagination for a majority of the Japanese public, although discussion of Japan's nuclear option has been evolving somewhat among a limited number of audiences.

Lastly, among the pragmatic thinkers who support examining (though not necessarily pursuing) Japan's nuclear option, many of them favour a strong Japan–US alliance and focus on the long-term threats of Chinese military modernisation rather than the imminent threats of North Korea nuclear weapons. These pragmatists believe that North Korea can be deterred relatively effectively by the US nuclear umbrella, conventional military capabilities, including pre-emptive attack capability and missile defence systems, as long as the international community remains united and firm to persuade North Korea to disarm its nuclear arsenal. The uncertainty over China's future, especially its nuclear modernisation, has been at the top of their agenda. Former Japanese Ambassador to Thailand, Hisahiko Okazaki, one of Japan's most prominent strategic thinkers, argues that while recognising that Japan's nuclear armament under the US extended nuclear deterrence could be rather *redundant* from a military perspective, it could have the benefit of complicating China's strategic calculation on the use of nuclear weapons, as French nuclear arms did with regard to the Soviet Union during the Cold War.[25]

Strategic Analyses of the Utility of Japan's Nuclear Armament

From a technical perspective, experts have argued that Japan has sufficient capabilities to produce crude nuclear weapons. Japan has nuclear fuel-cycle programs that produce weapons-grade plutonium, although in the form of mixed-oxide, for civilian purposes. Japan also has the M-V rocket, which has potential intercontinental ballistic missile capabilities, operating with solid fuel and capable of placing a 1.8 tonne payload into orbit.

However, as even the proponents of nuclear armament acknowledge, Japan does not have the guidance or warhead technology necessary for operational missiles. In addition, Japan does not have the basic infrastructure that would be essential for nuclear weaponry, including a nuclear doctrine, a stringent legal framework to protect classified information, a unified C4I system, nor a unified intelligence system. Moreover, Japan's use of any nuclear material has been strictly regulated by bilateral and international treaties. It is simply impossible for Japan to use its plutonium without the consent of its treaty counterparts, unless Japan should dare follow the brinksmanship strategy of North Korea. Even the proponents of Japan's nuclear armament acknowledge that Japan would not be able to develop nuclear weapons without US approval and cooperation.

From a strategic perspective, the Japanese government in the past has quietly re-examined the nuclear option at times of fundamental strategic shifts in the international system.[26] The results of these strategic calculations are noteworthy. All such examinations have reached the same conclusion: Japan's possession of its own nuclear arsenal had little, if any strategic merit. The key points in the calculations that led to this conclusion are as follows:

- Japan's possession of nuclear weapons would undermine Japan's national security by triggering an arms race in Northeast Asia, prompting the two Koreas and Taiwan to accelerate their nuclear development programs or to go nuclear as well — ultimately undermining regional and global security.
- Nuclear armament would not be appropriate for Japan because this country is inherently vulnerable to a nuclear attack, considering the fact that it is an island country where a large part of its population lives in a limited number of densely populated areas and thus lacks strategic depth.[27]
- Japan is surrounded by seas and does not have sufficient ground for the use of tactical nuclear weapons;[28] and
- The threat of Russian and Chinese nuclear weapons can be deterred by US extended deterrence as long as it remains effective.[29]

In conclusion, it was analysed that Japan's nuclear option could motivate a number of other countries to pursue nuclear proliferation while only bringing minimal military benefit to Japan.[30] Dr. Shinichi Ogawa of the JDA's National Institute of Defence Studies, a prominent Japanese scholar on arms control and strategic affairs, points to a flaw in the logic behind the argument that Japan may become a nuclear weapon state in response to North Korea's possession of nuclear weapons.[31] Suppose that one day Japan might conclude that US nuclear deterrence could no longer deter North Korea's nuclear threat, and hence decide to possess nuclear weapons. Yet, however hard Japan might try, Japan's nuclear weapons would surely be far smaller in number than, and far inferior in quality to, US nuclear weapons. How could Japan's own nuclear weapons deter North Korea if US nuclear weapons could not even deter the North? In fact, foreign observers who believe that Japan may go nuclear anytime soon seem to assume unilaterally that Japan is so paranoid about North Korea's nuclear threats that Japan is incapable of making a rational judgment. More importantly, their assumption that Japan simply has fairly fragile confidence in the credibility of US extended deterrence needs thorough scrutiny. Rather, Japan's confidence in the US extended deterrence has been reaffirmed through the process of strengthening the Japan–US alliance. From the Japanese perspective, Japan's suspicion about the credibility of US extended deterrence was far higher during the Cold War than it is today.

Professor Matake Kamiya of Japan's National Defence Academy also argues that Japan's decision to go nuclear would only weaken Japan's political power internationally and the reputation it has built over past decades. As evident in the vigorous bid of the G4 states (Brazil, India, Japan, and Germany) for permanent seats on the UN Security Council (UNSC) in 2004, it has been a top priority issue for Japan to acquire a permanent seat on the UNSC. So far, Japan has won the respect of other nations for its decision not to go nuclear despite its latent nuclear capability. Many countries that have expressed their support for Japan's bid for a permanent seat on the UNSC have listed Japan's non-nuclear status as one of the primary reasons for their support. Japan's nuclear option will destroy almost all the political resources Japan has pooled over many decades. Because Japan is already the second largest economic power in the world, Japan, unlike India, does not need to acquire nuclear weapons to assert its power and prestige.[32]

Furthermore, in contrast to most other countries, Japan believes that the credibility of the international non-proliferation regimes is still sufficiently intact, although these regimes face serious challenges to their legitimacy, especially in the face of nuclear problems of North Korea and Iran. Japan has, as a result, intensified its efforts to strengthen these regimes by complimenting them with various national, bilateral, and multilateral measures, as explained in the previous section. Japan assesses that the relative costs associated with non-compliance with the treaties outweigh, and should continue to outweigh relative costs associated with observing the regimes.

Although detailed examinations of Japan's nuclear option have concluded that Japan's nuclear option would not bring any strategic benefit to Japan, these conclusions are based on the assumption that US extended deterrence will remain credible and that international regimes on arms control, disarmament, and non-proliferation will remain sufficiently effective. After all, the outcome of Japan's debate on adopting the nuclear option is contingent upon Japan's perception about the effectiveness of US extended deterrence and the international regimes for arms control and non-proliferation.

Japan's Perceptions of the Credibility of US Extended Deterrence

As noted, constraints on Japan's nuclear option derive not only from various legal and policy instruments but also from a more fundamental constraint, and that is the fact that the US extends its own nuclear deterrent to Japan. Japan considers its reliance on US extended deterrence, which Japan explains as a short-to-mid-term objective, as compatible with Japan's long-term policy to promote global nuclear disarmament, although such postures are often criticised as a double-standard by other countries. Thus, while the "nuclear allergy" and government regulations explain why Japan does not have nuclear weapons, it is ultimately the alliance with the US that makes nuclear weapons unnecessary, which means that these ideational and institutional constraints do not have to be tested. Indeed, US extended deterrence is like oxygen for Japan: one will never notice it when it exists, but one will never be able to survive without it. And because the US is an independent actor, Japan has been careful to make certain that the extended nuclear deterrent remains credible.

Historically, there has almost always been at least some degree of persistent anxiety in Japan about the credibility of US extended deterrence. There are always experts who argue that US extended deterrence has never been, and will never be, credible. They argue that if North Korea or China could retain a sufficient capability to strike the US homeland, the US would not be willing to sacrifice its security for the sake of its allies' security. Indeed, even among Japanese government officials, there remains a fear of abandonment, and Japan has, in the past, adamantly rejected any US move that could undermine the credibility of US extended deterrence.

Under the Bush administration, however, the credibility of US extended deterrence has been strongly reaffirmed to a greater extent than under the Clinton administration in the eyes of Japan's alliance managers. Factors that have significantly contributed to the strengthening of this bilateral alliance include close personal relationships between Japanese Prime Minister Koizumi and US President George W. Bush as well as close-knit relationships between senior officials of Japanese and the US governments. The bilateral alliance was further strengthened through Japan's cooperation with US military operations in both Afghanistan and Iraq. In addition, Japanese alliance managers perceived US extended deterrence as being strongly reaffirmed through the process of strengthening of Japan–US alliance, as evident in the February 2005 Japan–US joint security declaration and the agreement of Japan–US Security Consultative Committee on 29 October 2005.

Again, however, there still remain concerns in Japan about the continuity of the US commitment to the defence of Japan, especially when US administration changes in the future. Partly due to fears of abandonment, Japan was motivated to start working on institutionalising US-centred alliance networks quickly, which prompted Japan to conduct bilateral and multilateral security cooperation with other US allies and friendly countries, including Singapore, Australia, and Thailand, as explained previously.

All in all, however, as Shinichi Ogawa observes, Japan's fear of abandonment was far greater during the Cold War than in the post-Cold War period. But, even during these days, Japan has continued to choose the path of strengthening Japan–US alliance without adhering to the nuclear option.

As one American security expert has argued, even when the PRC succeeded in nuclear testing in the 1960s, Japan responded to China's nuclear armament by establishing the Three-Non Nuclear Principles as a core pillar of Japan's nuclear policy.[33] Japan generally adhered to these principles even during the massive build-up of Soviet nuclear weapons. Finally, in 2003, as tensions mounted with North Korea over its nuclear weapon programs, the Panel to Assess Japanese Foreign Policy, the Japanese Foreign Minister's advisory board, recommended the relaxation of one of the principles, namely, the principle that prohibits any entrance of foreign nuclear weapons into Japanese territory in order to permit US naval assets carrying nuclear weapons to visit Japanese ports. The panel argued that if North Korea seriously developed nuclear weapons, it would be a critical issue for Japan to determine the level of deterrence necessary for defending Japan's homeland. The panel also argued that given the fact that the Japanese government has for a long time tacitly permitted the entry of US naval assets with nuclear weapons into Japan, the Three-Non-nuclear Principles have been in fact "the Two-and-a-Half-Non-nuclear Principles".[34]

It is worth noting that even the measures recommended by the Japanese experts who advocate a nuclear option would also contribute to institutionalising and strengthening the Japan–US alliance, as opposed to the expectation that such measures would establish more independent defence capabilities of Japan. For example, Terumasa Nakanishi, one of the leading proponents of a nuclear option, argues that before becoming a nuclear weapon state, Japan must advance strategies and capabilities for national security, including: enacting an anti-espionage law; establishing a comprehensive intelligence organisation; deploying missile defence; shifting from the traditional doctrine of exclusive defence; establishing a special operations force and amphibious capabilities; and enabling the exercise of collective self-defence.[35] Ironically, however, all of these measures are regarded as essential components for institutionalising the Japan–US alliance. On contrary to his expectation, in particular, Japan–US cooperation for missile defence will advance the jointness of command and control between the two militaries. Nakanishi's proposal would, rather, end up strengthening the bilateral alliance and therefore reaffirm Japan's perception of a credible US extended deterrence.

As outlined above, Japan has made every effort to ensure that US extended deterrence will remain credible, and will continue to do so in the future. Japan will be continuously prompted to engage in the steady process to institutionalise its bilateral alliance with the US and to link the bilateral alliance with a broader multilateral security network in the Asia-Pacific.

Pre-Emption

While the mainstream perspective in Japan is that the option to remain non-nuclear still far outweigh arguments for it to go nuclear, there is an increasing attention within the Japanese government to develop ability to conduct a pre-emptive strike against North Korea, desirably under cooperation with the US. In fact, Japan has begun a preliminary, internal examination of a hypothetical option to develop Japan's denial capability against North Korea's medium-range missiles, that is, capability to conduct a pre-emptive strike against the launching platform of North Korea's missiles in the event where Japanese government might judge that there were no other option to protect the homeland other than by eliminating the source of the threat before it materialised. The newly released Mid-Term Defence Capability Development Plan (*chuki boueiryoku seibi keikaku*) for FY 2005–2010 authorises budget for those studies that could potentially be applied to developing Japan's pre-emptive capabilities, reportedly.[36] These include studies on a precision guided missile with a range of several hundred kilometres and on development of an electronic counter-measure device to be deployed by Japan's Air Self-Defence Force. Whether these measures may be actually developed and deployed by the Japanese SDFs in the future may most likely depend upon how Japan's threat perception may change in the future, most notably, with regard to the pace of Chinese military modernisation and North Korea's development of nuclear weapons and its delivery systems. Such measures will have to be carefully employed, even when decision has been made to do so, in order to avoid triggering a *security dilemma* in East Asia.

Damage Confinement

Japan's initial efforts to develop substantive and detailed plans for damage confinement has materialised in the legislation on the protection of Japanese national (*Kokumin Hogo Hou*) enacted in June 2004 and a summary of its operational guideline announced on 14 December 2004. This summary of the guideline, called as "Major Points of a Basic Guideline Regarding Protection of Japanese Nationals (*kokumin hogo ni kansuru kihon shishin no youshi*)," assumes four types of contingencies: (1) guerrilla warfare and foreign special force's operation in Japan's territories; (2) invasion of Japan's homeland by foreign force; (3) attack by ballistic missiles using WMD; and (4) attack on Japan's territories by foreign military aircraft.[37] This summary of the guideline offers a basic posture regarding the measures to be employed to protect and rescue Japanese nationals and regarding the framework for cooperation between local and central governments in the event of such contingencies. After reviewing this summary with local governments and other relevant organisations, the Japanese Cabinet has determined the Basic Guideline in March 2005. Based on this Guideline, each relevant ministry/agency of the national government has established a respective plan to protect Japanese nationals, all of which were endorsed by the Japanese Cabinet on 28 October 2005.[38] All local governments are also obliged to establish detailed operational plans to meet with each of these contingencies. In parallel with these legal developments, a number of exercises and trainings have been conducted jointly involving relevant national and local government organisations. Concrete planning for damage limitation and confinement has been steadily evolving in Japan, which constitutes another pillar of Japan's integrated national security strategy that contributes to strengthening Japan's overall deterrence capability. These initiatives may develop into another new subject for multilateral security cooperation to share expertise in the area of homeland security, in the near future.

Active Defence Measure: Missile Defence

Lastly, as another pillar of an integrated national security strategy, Japan prioritises to develop and deploy missile defence systems as an active defence measure. Although Japan's initiative on ballistic missile defence (BMD) started in 1995, Japan was relatively slow in deepening its commitment in the development of missile defence systems until around the end of 2002 when North Korea expelled the IAEA inspectors from its nuclear facilities. Japan has finally determined in December 2003 to deploy a two-tiered integrated missile defence system that consists of sea-based systems to be deployed on the Aegis destroyers and a land-based Patriot system,[39] starting with the introduction of the first fire unit (FU) of the Patriot PAC-3 system by the end of FY 2006. The final architecture of Japan's missile defence system is to be completed by FY 2011 that consists of four Aegis destroyers equipped with BMD function, 16 FUs of the Patriot PAC-3 system, four FPS-XX radars, and seven improved FPS-3 radars, all of which will be connected by an integrated command and communication system.[40] The Japanese government has also constructed a legal framework for missile defence by revising its Law Regarding the Self-Defence Forces (*Jieitai Hou*), which defined legal procedures to enable emergency launch of interceptors in case a hostile country may launch a ballistic missile.

In addition, Japanese and the US governments conducted joint research on the next-generation sea-based mid-course interceptor. Specifically, Japan has been responsible for researching on the nosecone, infrared ray seeker, kinetic warhead, and second-stage rocket motor, while the US takes care of remaining components of the interceptor. This joint research was completed by the end of March 2005, and the bilateral cooperation will advance into the next phase of joint development in FY 2006. So far, this joint development will be the first example of co-development between the US and its allies. In order to enable such co-development, Japan has decided to exempt this joint cooperation from the subject of Japan's Three Principles on Arms Exports which have traditionally limited Japan's arms export strictly. While Japan is increasing its interest in deepening technological cooperation with the US, the US Congress have enacted legislation that is unfriendly to deepening such bilateral technological cooperation, which remains to be at least some level of concern for the two governments in promoting bilateral cooperation for missile defence.

In Japan–US Security Consultative Committee Document released on 29 October 2005, the two governments emphasised the critical importance of constant information gathering and sharing, as well as maintaining high readiness and interoperability in light of the minimal time available to respond to a ballistic missile threat.[41] According to this document, Japan–US bilateral and joint operations coordination centre will be created at Yokota Air Base in Japan in order to ensure constant connectivity, coordination, and interoperability among the SDFs and US forces in Japan. Additionally, Japan's Air Defense Command and relevant units will be collocated with the headquarters of the US 5th Air Force at the same Yokota base in order to strengthen the coordination between air and missile defence command and control elements, and to share relevant sensor data through the bilateral and joint operations coordination centre. The two militaries intend to enable timely information sharing through the new US X-Band radar system to be established in Japan.

As of the beginning of January 2006, however, it is unclear to what extent Japanese and the US government's command and control systems will be mutually combined when deploying these missile defence systems, and in what modality the interoperability between the two militaries can be secured. There are views among the Japanese experts that a legal constraint that prohibits Japan from engaging in act of collective self-defence may eventually stall bilateral discussion of possible cooperation in the operation of the BMD systems. For example, Yuki Tatsumi of the Henry L. Stimson Center questions the degree of the Japanese systems' autonomy given these systems extremely close information linkage with US systems.[42] Certainly, the former Japanese Chief Cabinet Secretary Yasuo Fukuda stated clearly in 2003 that these missile defence systems are specifically intended to defend Japan and that Japan will operate them autonomously based on its own decision.[43]

However, recent news reports indicate renewed deliberation within the Japanese government to shoot down even those missiles that will fly over Japan toward the US.[44] Among the Japanese alliance managers, many take the view that it would be unrealistic not to fire interceptors against ballistic missiles flying toward the US from Northeast Asia, and that there is some legal leeway to make that happen even without changing the constitution.[45] In addition, there is also an increasing prospect for constitutional amendment in the relatively near future that may enable Japan to exercise the right of collective self-defence. Japan is still in the process to adjust its domestic legal constraint to the changing new security requirements.

While it is necessary for Japan to handle its own legal problems in order to secure interoperability with the US military forces and possibly with other US allies, Japan is also required to hedge against potential US unilateral requirements drift in the future when the US administration may change. In the 1990s, Japan already experienced US unilateral cancellation of bilateral cooperation for defence-related technological development, such as over-the-horizon radar system. In order to advance the bilateral cooperation for missile defence further, both Japanese and the US governments are required to institutionalise their cooperation at the operational level, and to reaffirm their common long-term objectives constantly.

Although Australia and India have already decided to join a network for missile defence with the US at the core, Japan has not yet expressed its interest to extend the missile defence cooperation from bilateral to multilateral forms. Whether missile defence system may serve as a vehicle for multilateral cooperation in the future may depend upon various factors, including the technological maturity, operational requirement, and depth of political commitment of the participating countries to the joint architecture of the missile defence.

Efforts to Forge Regional Security Networks

Over the past years, there have been increasing efforts among the Asia-Pacific countries to embark upon new multilateral security initiatives with a view to constructing regional security networks, particularly with a view to curbing down the WMD proliferation. Most notably, Australia, Japan, Singapore have played a key role in this regard, under close coordination with the US, in initiating and promoting these new initiatives, including the PSI, the ASTOP, and the Asian Export Control Dialogue, as described previously. In addition, these countries have also led multilateral cooperation to combat other types of threats, including crimes, terrorism, and natural disaster, in the Asia-Pacific region. In addition to providing seminars to other Asian countries on counter-terrorism, Japan has been an active supporter of multilateral initiatives, such as the Illegal Activity Initiative (IAI) and the Container Security Initiative (CSI). Japan was engaged actively in counter-terrorism operations in Indian Ocean since 2001, humanitarian relief operations in Iraq since 2003, and emergency assistance operations in Indonesia and in Thailand after the 2004 Indian Ocean earthquake and tsunami, as well as the establishment of a tsunami monitoring centre in this region, all of which provided opportunities to deepen multilateral security cooperation, especially, in the realm of maritime security cooperation among the Asia-Pacific countries.

The next challenge for Asia is whether these efforts can be more widely shared and implemented sufficiently by as many countries as possible in this region. Asian countries face diverse challenges to integrate these new initiatives into more regularised and institutionalised mechanisms and to form a dense web of regional security networks to meet with the changing nature of modern complex threats that are becoming ever more diverse and transnational. Particularly, the US and its allies in this region must strive to establish a broader regularised structure of multilateral security cooperation. The endeavours of the regional governments should also not stop at their borders, but instead, they have to be expanded to reach out to other Asian countries. All of them need to work together to varying degree of intensity depending on the circumstance and the nature of the threats. In order to do so, all relevant countries must be able to share mutual understanding about the respective capabilities, approaches and modality to deal with the threats as well as policy objectives and priorities. The cooperation between the US and its allies should function as a driving force to prompt similar efforts by other Asian countries. With this view in mind, the initiative to form a new East Asian Community (EAC) should avoid excluding the US and pursue the path of open regionalism in accordance with the spirit of the 14 December 2005 Kuala Lumpur Declaration on the East Asia Summit.

Traditionally, the promotion of regional organisations or initiatives in Asia has been conducted under a "normative" "approach" which prioritises the nurturing of a common norm and identities among the member states. This approach contrasts with the "functional approach" adopted by the EU, which focus on finding pragmatic solution to practical problems. While the normative approach has the merit to enable a certain level of sustained flexibility in its institutional management, and to provide a vehicle for confidence-building among the member states by avoiding the direct tackling of issues of potential confrontation, it has traditionally avoided to define specific objectives to be addressed and rarely attempted to find solution to specific problems, allowing only for an incremental progress for multilateral security cooperation to address the diverse threats.

In order for Asian countries to better address the various challenges for regional and global security, an approach that emphasises functional, global perspective should be integrated into the traditional "Asian way" of regional multilateralism that emphasises a normative, regional approach. Any initiative for Asian multilateral cooperation should be intended to address security problems in a substantive manner, rather than simply serving as a vehicle to reaffirm the "Asian identity," if any.

This paper has examined Japan's new approach of integrated national security strategy and the strengthening of Japan–US alliance as well as their implications for constructing a framework for closer regional cooperation to combat these threats. The changes in Japan's national security posture may continue to influence the future course of regional dynamics for multilateral security cooperation in the Asia-Pacific region as well as its potential to transform the alliance systems in this region into an integrated regional security mechanism.

Multilateral security cooperation in the present context needs to be constructed in a wide range of areas, including intelligence, law enforcement, customs, export control, diplomacy, and military. Such cooperation has become highly important because of the increasing importance of detecting the transportation of or smuggling of WMD and related materials as well as finding and detaining terrorists and criminals when they move across borders, as demonstrated by the utilities of international cooperation in the PSI, CSI, and IAI.

In order to meet with diverse threats, such multilateral cooperation has to be structured carefully among the relevant countries in a comprehensive manner connecting all relevant functions of the government so that it will serve as a vehicle not only for multilateral cooperation but also for intense inter-agency coordination amongst all relevant entities in each country.

Notes

1. A similar point was made in author's conversation with a senior U.S. official in Tokyo, November 2004.
2. To be fair, right after the second Gulf War was over in March 2003, not only the Bush administration, but also other governments which had been engaged in

224 The Evolving Maritime Balance of Power in the Asia-Pacific

intelligence activities in Iraq were also puzzled by the fact that the U.S. was unable to find the WMD.

3. Testimony of Dr. David Kay before the U.S. Senate Armed Service Committee, 28 January 2004.

4. Douglas Frantz and Maura Reynolds, "Individuals Supplying Nuclear Trade, Officials Say", *The Los Angels Times*, 29 January 2004.

5. Joby Warrick and Peter Slevin, "Probe of Libya Funds Nuclear Black Market", *The Washington Post*, 24 January 2004.

6. Glenn Kessler, "Arms Issue Seen as Hurting U.S. Credibility Abroad", *The Washington Post*, 19 January 2004.

7. Bob Woodward, *Bush at War* (New York: Simon & Schuster, 2002), p. 126.

8. Dennis C. Blair and John T. Hanley Jr., "From Wheels to Webs: Reconstructing Asia-Pacific Security Arrangements", *The Washington Quarterly*, Vol. 24(1), Winter 2001, p. 7.

9. Council on Security and Defence Capabilities, "Japan's Vision for Future Security and Defence Capabilities", October 2004.

10. Japan Defense Agency, *The National Defense Programme Guideline for FY 2005 and After* (Tokyo: Japan Defense Agency, 2004). Available at http://www.jda.go.jp/e/index_.htm. <Accessed on 7 December 2005>.

11. Ibid.

12. Joint Statement, Japan–U.S. Security Consultative Committee, Washington D.C., 19 February 2005.

13. "U.S.–Japan Alliance: Transformation and Realignment for the Future", Japan–U.S. Security Consultative Committee, Washington D.C., 20 October 2005.

14. Japanese Ministry of Economy, Trade, and Industry, "Regarding the Basic Principles of Export Control Policy in Asia", 18 October 2004.

15. "*Kyacchi O-ru Kisei no Unyou to Kokusai Renkei no Kyouka nitsuite* (A Document regarding the METI's Efforts to Strengthen Enforcement of the Catch-All Regulatory System and Relevant International Cooperation)", Security Trade Division of the METI, 28 January 2004, pp. 22–23.

16. A Japanese text of this principle is available at http://www.meti.go.jp/policy/anpo/kanri/topics/041018Export%20Control%20dialogue/041018AsiaExportControlDialogueSummary.doc. <Accessed on 7 December 2005>.

17. A METI's senior official's comment in a meeting in Tokyo, Japan, 6 November 2003.

18. "Japan, Hong Kong, Singapore to Curb Indirect Export of Products Convertible into Weapons", *The Daily Yomiuri*, 7 January 2004.

19. Masahiko Hosokawa (Director of the Chubu Bureau of Economy, Trade, and Industry), "Asian Export Control Initiative", *Gaiko Forum*, October 2003, pp. 47–49. (Translated in the Global News Wire, 1 September 2003).

20. For a thorough examination of this issue, see, Katsuhisa Furukawa, "Making Sense of Japan's Nuclear Policy: Arms Control, Extended Deterrence, and the Nuclear

Option", in Benjamin Self (ed.), *Japan's Nuclear Option: Security, Politics, and Policy in the 21st Century* (Washington D.C.: The Henry L. Stimson Center, 2003), pp. 95–147.

21. Ibid.

22. Ibid.

23. On 29 October 2002, during the Japan–North Korea Normalisation Talks, the DPRK threatened to break the missile moratorium, which was almost completely ignored by the Japanese media who kept focusing on the abduction issues. Frustrated by this, North Korea repeated the same threat on the following day, which was again ignored by the Japanese media. Japanese MOFA officials lamented the public's lack of attention to the threat of North Korea's missiles.

24. Kazuya Sakamoto, "Imaha Hitsuyouneikeredo ... (Although Nuclear Option is Not Necessary Now ...)", *Shokun!* August 2003, p. 82.

25. Hisahiko Okazaki, "Mazu Gijutsutekina Men wo Tsumeyo (First, We Needs to Examine the Technical Feasibility of Nuclear Option)", *Shokun!* August 2003, p. 58.

26. Matake Kamiya, "Nuclear Japan: Oxymoron or Coming Soon?", *The Washington Quarterly*, Winter 2002–2003, p. 68.

27. Ibid.

28. Goro Hashimoto, "Mazuha Kuge Kokka kara Dakkyaku wo (First, Japan Should Become More Realistic)", *Shokun!* August 2003, p. 78.

29. Ibid.

30. Ibid.

31. Shinichi Ogawa, "*Seinen shiteiru Nihon no Kakubusou wo meguru Giron ni tsuite* (A Perspective on A Revival of US Debate on Japan's Nuclear Armament)", National Institute of Defence Studies, 9 May 2003.

32. Matake Kamiya.

33. A comment by a participant at a conference on Japan's national security strategy hosted by The Henry L. Stimson Center in Washington, D.C. on 27 August 2003.

34. "*Kaku Tousai Kan no Ichiji Kikou Younin wo, Gaishou no Shimon Kikan* (Foreign Minister's Advisory Board Recommended to Permit the Temporary Visits of US Nuclear Ships to Japanese Ports)", *Kyodo News*, 18 September 2003.

35. Terumasa Nakanishi, "*Nihonkoku Kakubushou heno Ketsudan* (Decision to Arm Japan with Nuclear Weapons)", *Shokun!*, August 2003, pp. 35–37.

36. "*Jikibou, Taichi Choukyori Misairu no Kenkyu Chakushu Morikomu* (The Mid-Term Defence Capability Development Plan Included Study on A Ground-to-Ground Long-Range Missile)", *Yomiuri Shimbun*, 3 December 2004.

37. "Buryoku Kougeki, 4 Jitai Soutei Kokumin Hogo Kihon Shishin (The Basic Guideline to Protect Japanese Nationals Assumes 4 Situations of Military Attack)", *Sankei Shimbun*, 14 December 2005.

38. A website of the Cabinet Secretariat on the protection of the Japanese nationals. Available at http://www.kokuminhogo.go.jp/index.html. <Accessed on 13 January 2005>.

39. *Kanbou Choukan Danwa* (Remarks by the Chief Cabinet Secretary) on 19 December 2003.

40. Japan Defence Agency, *Heisei 17 Nen Ban Bouei Haskusho* (Defence White Paper for FY 2005), p. 149.

41. "U.S.-Japan Alliance: Transformation and Realignment for the Future", Japan–U.S. Security Consultative Committee, Washington D.C., 20 October 2005.

42. Yuki Tatsumi, "The Future of the U.S.–Japan Alliance", *CSIS Japan Watch*, 23 February 2005.

43. *Kanbou Choukan Danwa*.

44. "*Misairu Bouei de Shin Kaishaku Kentou Nihon Joukuu Tsuuka nara Geigeki* (Japan Examines A New Interpretation of Its Constitution to Shoot Down Any Missile That Flies Over Japan)", *Sankei Shimbun*, 14 January 2005.

45. Author's discussion with officials of the Japanese Ministry of Foreign Affairs and Self-Defence Forces, Tokyo, 19 December 2005.

Chapter 11

Nuclear Weapons and Missile Defences in the Asia-Pacific: A Maritime Perspective

Donald L. Berlin

Introduction

The Asia-Pacific region will likely be characterised by a gradual increase in the number of nuclear weapons states and in the size and quality of those states' weapons inventories. Moreover, more of Asia's nuclear weapons eventually will have a maritime dimension, either because they will be sea-based or because the battlespace in which they could be employed will be in the maritime domain to a significant extent. These developments will have a significant effect on the maritime balance of power in the Asia-Pacific. This is also true of missile defence, but it is too early to have any clear sense of the implications of such defences for the Asia-Pacific balance of power.

More Nuclear Weapons States

Currently, the Asia-Pacific nations equipped with nuclear weapons are the US, China, Russia, India, Pakistan, North Korea and, to construe "Asia" broadly, Israel. Asia-Pacific states that could decide to develop and deploy nuclear weapons in the future include Japan, the Republic of Korea, Taiwan and Iran, among others. While the latter states could decide to forego the nuclear option, this is unlikely over the long term. Moreover, while some nuclear weapons states in other regions of the world have given up their nuclear arms, this is improbable in the Asia-Pacific security environment in the foreseeable future.

More Nuclear Weapons with a Maritime Dimension

The Asia-Pacific nuclear weapons environment will be characterised by so-called vertical, as well as horizontal proliferation. In other words, not only will the region include more nations possessing nuclear weapons but the quality of these forces, particularly the relevant delivery systems, will also increase with time. The advent of more Asian nations equipped with nuclear weapons is an aspect of the general "rise of Asia" that is one of the most significant global phenomena of the 20th and 21st centuries. This trend, of course, will have a profound effect on the maritime balance of power in the Asia-Pacific.

Of particular significance for our purposes is the likelihood, eventually, that more of Asia's nuclear weapons will have a maritime dimension. This will occur because more weapons will be sea-based (on submarines or surface ships) eventually and because the battlespace in which Asia-Pacific nuclear weapons could be employed will be the region's seas and oceans to a significant extent.

Currently, the only Asia-Pacific states deploying nuclear weapons at sea in submarines are the US, Russia, China (barely) and, probably, Israel. Before very long, India and, some years thereafter, Pakistan, will likely do so as well. Over a longer time horizon, Japan and the Republic of Korea, should they opt to develop nuclear weapons, could well deploy some of these weapons on sea-based platforms, either on submarines or surface ships.

That Israel likely is a nuclear weapons state relevant to the maritime balance of power in the Asia-Pacific is not a matter that has received much attention from scholars or journalists. Nonetheless, Israel has strong strategic connections to the Indian Ocean region, highlighted by Israel's bilateral relationships with India and Singapore among other states. At the same time, Israel has been moving for some years toward a security footprint encompassing a part of the Indian Ocean region, a posture consistent with Israel's historic emphasis on power projection, and especially with Prime Minister Sharon's strategic vision of defending Israel from as far from its borders as possible. Tel Aviv's land-based missiles, air power, and developing sea-based deterrent all appear to be part of this quest.

Israel's missile force, by virtue of an upgraded version of the multistage Jericho missile, with a reported range of up to 2,800 miles, has become capable of reaching targets in Iran and Pakistan. In addition, there is good evidence that the Israeli Air Force has been thinking seriously about reaching targets in the Arabian Sea sub-region. Some years ago, a semi-official Israeli report recommended that Israel's warplanes be made capable of operating within a combat radius of 2,000 kilometres and launching second-strike attacks in retaliation for the use of WMD. The report called for a capability to mount rapid air strikes at the Indian Ocean entrance of the Red Sea (Bab-el-Mandab), against Iranian targets in the Persian Gulf, Sudan, and, in a worst-case scenario, Pakistan. In recent years, Israel has almost certainly operationalised this requirement.

Israel's navy, similarly, has been developing plans to operate in the Indian Ocean so as to deter Iran and, quoting from a government report), if necessary, "intervene in land battles... and come out victorious through the use of advanced weapons systems". The service is to be capable of deploying 30% of Israel's strategic nuclear weapons by 2020 and of firing missiles that could reach targets at least 300 kilometres inland.[1]

According to *Jane's*, the US has helped Israel to deploy US supplied Harpoon cruise missile armed with nuclear warheads on Israel's fleet of Dolphin-class submarines. Israel acquired its three Dolphin-class submarines, which can remain at sea for a month, in the late 1990s. Reportedly, Israel's seaborne nuclear doctrine is designed to place one submarine in the Persian Gulf, another in the Mediterranean Sea, and the third on standby. Moreover, a December 2004 report claims Germany is selling Israel two additional Dolphin units.[2]

China took a step toward what will soon be a Chinese sea-based nuclear weapons capability with the recent launch of the lead hull of China's next-generation SSN, the Type 093. The boat, which is expected to enter service in the coming year, with additional units to follow, reportedly is comparable to the US Navy's first generation Los Angeles class SSN.

It is estimated that this boat will be equipped with wire- and wave-homing torpedoes, and submarine-launched anti-ship cruise missiles and mines. It may also be capable of firing anti-submarine warfare (ASW) missiles and land-attack cruise missiles (LACMs). China is also developing a new design Type 094 nuclear-powered ballistic missile submarine (SSBN). Incorporating some Russian technology, the Type 094 SSBN is expected to be a dramatic improvement over the sole Type 092 Xia class SSBN in the inventory, with improved quieting and sensor systems, and a more reliable propulsion system. Other improvements in sonar, propulsion, training, and the application of quieting techniques will contribute to a significant improvement in the capabilities of

China's submarine fleet. Each of the Type 094 SSBNs will mount 16 JL-2 submarine-launched ballistic missiles (SLBMs) with a maximum range of 8,000 km.

India's intention to add a sea-based leg to its nuclear posture is long-standing and was stated clearly in the Draft Nuclear Doctrine promulgated by India's National Security Advisory Board in 1999. The Cabinet Committee on Security also implicitly endorsed this goal in its 2003 restatement of many of the Doctrine's key points. Most recently, the new *Indian Maritime Doctrine* affirmed the importance of a sea-based leg.

To this end, and others, India continues to upgrade its existing submarine fleet while also developing or acquiring newer, more advanced submarines. Many of these submarines are being fitted with cruise missiles with land attack capabilities, reflecting the Indian Navy's (IN) emphasis on littoral warfare. Over time, some of these cruise missiles almost certainly will be armed with nuclear warheads.

The IN's principal subsurface combatants currently are four German Type 1500 and ten Russian-produced Kilo submarines. The Kilos are undergoing refits in Russia, including the addition of Club cruise missiles believed to have both anti-ship and land-attack capabilities at a range of up to 200 km. The four or five boats already refitted with these weapons constitute the IN's first submerged missile launch capability. In addition, one of the Type 1500 class submarines is also undergoing a refit.

India also likely will be building six to twelve French-designed Scorpene submarines, each of which will carry 16 Brahmos or Exocet cruise missiles. The Scorpene's design allows for the installation of a small nuclear reactor. One report claims the contract also provides for India's acquisition of critical underwater missile launch technology. Other prospective Indian submarine acquisitions include four to six Amur 1650 SSKs, and two each of the more advanced versions of the Kilo and Shishumar submarines.

India has also lately accorded higher priority to the construction of an indigenous nuclear-powered missile submarine, the Advanced Technology Vessel (ATV). With Russian assistance, fabrication of the hull and integration of the ATV's nuclear reactor is thought to be already under way. Sea trials for the ATV, which may be a derivative of the Russian Akula submarine, are expected in the next year or two. In the long run, the main armament of the ATV will likely be nuclear-armed cruise missiles.

Finally, New Delhi is negotiating with Moscow to lease two Akula II nuclear-powered submarines. While normally configured with intermediate range cruise missiles capable of mounting 200-kt nuclear weapons, it is expected that the Brahmos cruise missile, which could be armed with a nuclear warhead, will be the principal weapon for these boats.

Pakistan would seem to be far from joining the ranks of nations with sea-based strategic deterrent forces. Islamabad, however, in recent years, has increasingly regarded the Indian Ocean as central to its security. Pakistan's vulnerability from the sea was most recently exposed in 1998, when 75 to 100 Tomahawk missiles were fired at Afghan targets from US warships and submarines in the Arabian Sea, flying undetected over Pakistan's airspace.

A second impetus for Islamabad is Pakistan's endemic problem of a lack of strategic depth. Many Pakistani security specialists consider the country too small and too geographically narrow to be properly or easily defended. This failing was relieved to some degree as long as Afghanistan and its government were Pakistani clients. With that more desirable state of affairs now in the past, Islamabad will be looking to the Indian Ocean as an alternate means of addressing this problem.

One means of doing so may be a sea-based strategic deterrent. Pakistan, because it lacks a no-first-use doctrine, could worry that New Delhi, in a confrontation, would try to deny it the opportunity to launch a first strike. Under these circumstances, minimum credible deterrence for Pakistan will require both first- and second-strike capabilities.

In 1999, the Pakistani navy was in fact "assigned a nuclear role," and Pakistan's navy chief has affirmed Islamabad's intention to develop a sea-based deterrent. This could be bluster, but Pakistan's acquisition of Agosta submarines could be quite important in this connection. These boats will provide Pakistan with a significant conventional-strike capability in the Arabian Sea, and according to one Pakistani naval analyst, "the Agosta submarine. . . can be used to fire a nuclear missile. As the submarine can stay under water for 60 days. . . it is said to be the best way to protect Pakistan's nuclear weapons and also gives Pakistan the capability of a second nuclear strike".[3] A former Indian Navy chief apparently agrees: "Pakistan obviously did not spend such a huge amount of precious foreign exchange on acquiring new submarines, merely to have them launch conventional missiles and torpedoes. They had a long-term strategy in mind for the use of these subs".[4]

Scientific and technical challenges will make it difficult for Islamabad to develop the capability to launch nuclear-armed ballistic missiles from a submerged submarine. However, as in India's case, the path toward a submerged-launch cruise missile capability would be less onerous. It remains to be seen whether Pakistan can adapt the anti-ship Harpoon Block I missiles it has in its inventory for this purpose or will acquire other more suitable cruise missiles.

Aside from nuclear weapons that are directly sea-based, Asia's nuclear weapons also will increasingly take on a "maritime" character because the battlespace in which they could be employed will be in the maritime domain. This is so because many of the scenarios entailing the use of nuclear weapons involve the seas and ocean space of the Asia-Pacific. China and a future nuclear-armed Taiwan, for example, could fire nuclear weapons at one another across the Taiwan Strait. China and a nuclear-armed Japan could do likewise across the Yellow Sea and Sea of Japan. There are other possibilities. The US or India could attack China with nuclear weapons "from the sea" as could China or the US via-á-vis India at some point. Conversely, China or India, in the hazy future, could defend themselves by employing nuclear weapons against advancing US naval forces in the Pacific or Indian oceans.

While these gruesome scenarios may be far-fetched, worst-case scenarios do sometimes become reality and Asia's nuclear-armed states will plan for such contingencies. Moreover, the capacity of Asia-Pacific states to conduct such attacks is advancing. One enabler is the new availability of delivery systems, many with a maritime character, capable of carrying nuclear ordnance over long distances. Many Asia-Pacific states, of course, are continuing work on a range of ballistic missiles. Of particular note is the proliferation of advanced cruise missiles and of long-range aircraft.

The developmental Indo–Russian Brahmos supersonic cruise missile, for example, is reported to be configured with a nuclear payload and may eventually be produced in versions that can be launched from either land, air, sea, or sub-sea platforms. New Delhi is expecting to operationalise its first Brahmos missiles, presumably at the outset with conventional warheads, on a warship before the end of the year. India also hopes to export the Brahmos.

China, similarly, has been developing a range of land-attack cruise missiles that could carry nuclear warheads. A vertical-launch cruise missile, the HN-2C, reportedly is under development for use with the diesel-electric Song class submarines or with the nuclear-powered Type 093. According to Jane's, its range is believed to be 755 nautical miles. There also are versions of this missile with an extended range, 1,600 nautical miles in the case of the HN-3, as well as a ship/submarine-launched variant, the HN-3B, which is under development.

Long-range aircraft are also becoming more widely deployed in the region. For example, China and India may acquire Russian-produced Tu-22M3 long-range maritime strike aircraft. Similarly, even seemingly "tactical" fighter aircraft, once confined to missions of limited range, are now acquiring the characteristics of strategic bombers as a result of the addition of aerial refuelling capabilities and support from airborne warning and control aircraft. For example, given their range and India's capacity to refuel these aircraft en route, India's growing fleet of Su-30MKI aircraft could well take on the mission of strategic nuclear delivery in the future. Similarly, India's new interest in the US F-16 fighter may have been prompted in part by a recent visit by Indian Air Force personnel to Israel's long-range F-16I squadron.

The capacity of Asia-Pacific states to conduct such attacks is also growing due to the proliferation of forward bases, many with a maritime character. The US-leased naval and air facility at Diego Garcia, for example, is regarded by many regional observers as a bastion from which the US could conduct strategic strikes with nuclear weapons. The US air and naval complex on Guam, similarly, has been acquiring a new importance in the recent past.[5]

The Republic of Korea, reflecting Seoul's growing maritime consciousness, recently announced plans to build a strategic naval facility on Jeju Island. The base is intended to become home to a strategic fleet slated to protect Korean trading routes to the Straits of Malacca and probably beyond.[6]

India, for its part, can be expected to develop its facilities in the Andaman and Nicobar Islands over the long term, in part, so as to strengthen its ability to conduct nuclear weapons strikes, either using aircraft or submarines, against China. India was reportedly planning to station Su-30 MKI long-range fighter/bomber aircraft on Car Nicobar in the Andamans beginning in January 2005. It is likely that the effort was intended to complement a similar deployment of Su-30s, also undertaken with China in mind, to Bareilly Air Base near the China–India border. While the Car Nicobar deployment was aborted due to the December Tsunami, India's air force chief says the deployment will proceed within six months.

New Delhi will also be developing staging facilities in the Laccadives and perhaps even the Maldives, where India is building a new military reconnaissance post, at some point as well. These island groups lie directly astride the major Indian Ocean SLOCs and facilities here would have utility either to defend or attack SLOCs and for other, long-range strategic missions that could involve nuclear ordnance.

India also recently began operations at its new INS Kadamba naval and naval air base under construction at Karwar on the Malabar Coast of the Arabian Sea. This facility, which will be able to receive India's new aircraft carriers, may also serve as a base for the nuclear submarines that the Indian Navy may acquire on lease from Russia and also for those that it will build indigenously. The construction of a naval air station will begin this year.

Indian engineers are also working to upgrade and develop the Iranian port of Chabahar, which Tehran has designated as the headquarters of Iran's third naval region in 2004. This initiative presumably is intended to facilitate trade and is part of a larger Indian Ocean-to-North Sea initiative involving Russia and others, and mainly centred on the Iranian port of Bandar Abbas. Pakistani and Chinese observers, however, will worry that Tehran will eventually permit Indian naval forces to use the port and will regard developments at Chahbahar as a response to China's own development of a Pakistani port and naval base at Gwadar, some 100 miles eastward.

China is also contemplating the use of strategic outposts to enhance its capacity to conduct nuclear weapons strikes. A new Chinese naval base on Hainan Island in the South China Sea will reportedly allow the Chinese Navy to support new nuclear submarine operations, including potential deployments as far away as the Persian Gulf.

China is also building a new port and naval base for Pakistan at Gwadar, which China will presumably have access to in the future. Reportedly, when China agreed to offer financial and technical assistance for the project, it asked for "sovereign guarantees" to use the port facilities, a stipulation to which Pakistan agreed, despite US unease. Indeed, a Pakistan naval chief has been quoted to the effect that "the Chinese navy would be in Gwadar to give a fitting reply to anyone".[7] China has also allegedly begun to operate a signals intelligence facility at Gwadar. The first phase of this project is complete with three functioning berths. The second phase will feature the construction of nine more berths and terminals which will also be financed by China. Once completed, the Gwadar port will rank among the world's largest deep-sea ports.

Israel, finally, may be using an Eritrean Island near the southern entrance to the Red Sea as a staging base for submarines that can carry cruise missiles with nuclear warheads.

In sum, due to the strategic geography of the Asia-Pacific, the new availability of delivery systems, many with a maritime character and the proliferation of forward bases, the nuclear weapons of this region will be increasingly "maritime" in the future. This is a reality, of course, well recognised by those planning missile defences systems and it is why some of these systems are, or will be, sea-based. Among such systems are the Aegis Ballistic Missile Defence program and a sea-based version of the Kinetic Energy Interceptor. The US, Japan, and probably Australia are all likely to have at least a rudimentary sea-based missile defence capability before very long.

The foregoing developments will have a significant effect on the maritime balance of power in the Asia-Pacific. This maritime balance will be altered as some of the more major Asia-Pacific nations deploy nuclear weapons at sea or prepare for nuclear weapons contingencies involving the maritime battlespace.

In this way, the growing maritime character of many of the nuclear armaments of the region will be one of a concert of factors that will increase the relative power within the region of China and India and perhaps of one or more other Asia-Pacific nations. This will be so even though nuclear weapons have not been used anywhere in the world since 1945 and notwithstanding the continued questions about the usability of such weapons.

The maritime balance will also be altered as select Asia-Pacific nations, almost certainly including China and India, pursue the nuclearisation of their maritime forces and in the process boost their relative maritime power with respect to the major "external" actor in the region, the US. This eventuality, when it happens, will make it more difficult for the US to pursue the traditional strategic course of major powers external to the region, namely the use of the region's peripheral seas and oceans to intervene in the affairs of regional powers and bring power to bear on the continent itself, to include the interior of Eurasia.

Due to the possibility of a shift in the maritime balance of power arising from the nuclearisation of China and India's maritime forces, the US and various other Asia-Pacific nations are attempting to put in place missile defence systems to ensure against a significant alteration in the maritime power configuration in the Asia-Pacific. However, much will depend on the degree to which there is real progress toward a situation where missile defences are effective.

The US is structuring its missile defence program in a manner that encourages industrial and technological participation by friends and allies. For example, Japan formally agreed to collaborate with the US in creating a two-tiered missile defence system in 2004, comprising the Aegis/Standard SM-3 missile for ship-based, theatre-wide missile defence, and the Patriot PAC-3 missile for point defence. Also in 2004, Tokyo agreed to exempt joint missile defence development from its longstanding arms export ban. The exemption will permit Japan to jointly develop and produce missile defence systems with the US and to export Japanese missile defence components.

Australia also formally joined the US missile defence program in July 2004. Canberra plans to spend $45 million to upgrade its Jindalee over-the-horizon radar network (JORN) in order to give it greater range and sensitivity to detect incoming missiles during their early boost phase. Despite this development, Australia yet to acquire missile defences.

India–US missile defence cooperation continues to make cautious progress. Most recently, a US team from the Defence Security Cooperation Agency visited India and presented a briefing on the Patriot system. India is also pursuing various indigenous approaches toward missile defence.[8]

Over the long run, there is hope in some quarters that missile defence will render obsolete the nuclear weapons capabilities of most, if not all, nations and that the global threat posed by nuclear weapons will be largely eliminated. However, it is far more likely that missile defence will simply constitute just another factor in the assessment of relative military power, which includes both offensive and defensive components, of the various Asia-Pacific nations.

The US, Japan, Australia and probably India are hoping that missile defence will enhance the self-defence and military capabilities of their nations relative to China and North Korea. India is also hoping that missile defence will achieve the same end with respect to Pakistan.

China, Pakistan and North Korea, on the other hand, appear to calculate that missile defence will probably will strengthen the capabilities of their foes and worry that they will suffer a relative loss of power as missile defences are developed and improved. While these apparent calculations may prove on the mark, it is far too early to have any clear sense of the implications of missile defences for the Asia-Pacific balance of power, including the balance at sea.

Notes

1. " 'Secret' Report Advises: Navy to Operate Far from Israel's Beaches", *Voice of Israel (Jerusalem)*, 13 February 2002.
2. Donald L. Berlin, "The Indian Ocean and the Second Nuclear Age", *Orbis (Winter 2004)*, pp. 64–67. It is noteworthy that Israel and NATO conducted their first ever combined naval exercise in the Red Sea in late March 2005.
3. Major General Dipankar Banerjee, "Trends in Force Modernisation in South Asia", *Paper Presented at the Conference on Conventional Arms Rivalry in the Asia-Pacific*, 23–25 October 2001, Asia-Pacific Center for Security Studies, Honolulu, Hawaii. Quote from Hafiz Tareq Manzoor, "Importance of the Indian Ocean", *Jamaat-ud-Daawa Pakistan*, 29 September 2002. Translated from Urdu by the Foreign Broadcast Information Service (FBIS).
4. Admiral (Ret.) J. G. Nadkarni, "Raising the Nuclear Threshold", *Rediff India Abroad*, 17 June 1999. Available at http://www.rediff.com.
5. Andrew Koch, "US basing plans shape up for speed and flexibility", *Jane's Defence Weekly*, 16 June 2004.
6. "Navy planning major base on south Jeju", *JoongAng Daily*, 1 April 2005.
7. Quoted in G. Parthasarathy, "The Indian Ocean — Interests of Extra-Regional Powers and Interplay of Global Forces", *Paper Presented at the Defence Services Staff College*, Wellington (Tamil Nadu), India, 25 February 2003.
8. Many observers in India and elsewhere continue to question the efficacy of missile defence. See Kartik Bommarkanti, "A theatre of mistaken missiles", *The Indian Express*, 11 March 2005. The article was carried by the Foreign Broadcast Information Service.

V. Conclusion

Chapter 12

The Emergent Maritime Future of the Asia-Pacific Region

Sam Bateman

Introduction

The maritime scene in the Asia-Pacific region is extremely volatile at present. Sea-borne trade is booming, exploration for offshore oil and gas is running at levels unprecedented in the past, levels of naval activity are high, and naval budgets are continuing to grow at a fast rate. However, an atmosphere of maritime insecurity and uncertainty prevails in the region rather than one of security and certainty. Lingering bilateral tensions are re-surfacing more frequently, especially in the context of disputed claims to sovereignty over islands or offshore areas. The first few months of 2005, for example, have seen tension between South Korea and Japan over their claims to sovereignty over the Takeshima/Dokdo islands, China's protests over the allocation by Japan of oil and gas exploration rights in an area of the East China Sea claimed by China, and a dispute between Indonesia and Malaysia over hydrocarbon rights in the Sulawesi Sea.

Energy and the need to secure sources of supply are increasingly important factors driving maritime developments in the region. This is evident in the strong interests of Northeast Asian countries in the security of sea lines of communication (SLOCs) across the Indian Ocean and through the "choke points" of Southeast Asia, and in the competition for offshore oil and gas resources. Managing this volatile maritime scene will be rather like "keeping the lid on the pressure cooker", and is a major challenge for the region. The emergent maritime future of the region vitally depends on how well this challenge is met.

By 2009, Asia-Pacific countries may be spending a combined US$14 billion on new naval ships or almost double the figure for 2003.[1] Defence manufacturers in Europe and North America are clearly excited about the naval market in the region. Naval "shopping lists" include "state of the art" submarines, larger surface warships and even aircraft carriers although some other name might be used to describe them. The three nuclear powers of the region, China, India and Russia, are continuing to attach importance to sea-based nuclear weapons in their operational and force development planning.

While these developments on the regional maritime scene are largely in response to perceptions of increased maritime insecurity, the developments themselves have potential to add to insecurity in the region. They beg questions such as "does the current maritime security outlook really justify these acquisitions?", "can we continue in the way we are going at present?", and "where will it all end?" In discussing the emergent maritime future of the Asia-Pacific region, this paper seeks answers to questions such as these.

Shifts in Global Maritime Power

A basic feature of the emergent maritime future of the region is the ongoing shift in the balance of global maritime power away from its traditional power centres in Europe and North America and towards the Asian region.[2] This shift has been discussed by Joshua Ho in terms of trends in the four areas of inter- and intra-regional trade flows, regional energy demand, strength of regional merchant fleets and strength of regional navies.[3] Strong growth is evident in all four areas, and provided economic growth continues, these trends should continue into the future. The combined gross domestic products of China, India and Japan may surpass those of the US and the European Union within the next 15 years. It is not improbable to assume that these growth figures might also translate directly into growth in maritime power, including more potent naval capabilities.

By global standards, most regional countries might now be regarded as *medium maritime powers*.[4] Indonesia, Malaysia, Russia, Singapore, Thailand, South Korea and Taiwan all have some claim to fall within this category each with extensive maritime interests, a significant dependence on the sea, both strategically and economically, and capable maritime forces. All are major maritime trading nations. Japan, China and India are already beyond the medium power category and worthy, with their large navies, of being termed *major maritime powers*, while the US maintains a significant presence in the region as the sole *super maritime power* with global deployment capabilities.

Regional Developments

Northeast Asia

Northeast Asia remains an unstable part of the region, and is likely to remain so in the foreseeable future. This is not just a matter of Taiwan and the rogue behaviour of North Korea, but reflects lingering bilateral tensions between pairs of regional countries: Japan and Russia, South Korea and Japan, and China and Japan. Japan is increasingly concerned about the strategic ambitions of China. The bitter enmity between these two major powers has flared up again during 2005, and will be a powerful influence on the emergent maritime future of the region for many years to come. There are longer-term strategic implications of strengthened military cooperation between China and Russia that includes sales of high technology naval weapon systems. Unresolved disputes over the sovereignty of the Kurile Islands, Takeshima/Dokdo and the Diaoyu/Senkaku Islands do not help bilateral relations in the region. With this ongoing instability, it is not surprising that all Northeast Asian navies are pursuing ambitious force development and operational plans.

By virtue of its large navy and extensive shipping and fishing interests, Japan is a major regional maritime power although until recently, it has been hesitant to use this power to extend its regional influence. However, that has now changed with Japan using the threats of terrorism and piracy to establish a strategic presence in Southeast Asia and the Indian Ocean. The security of SLOCs in these waters is a vital element of Japan's comprehensive approach to security, particularly its energy security. After initial unfavourable reactions from regional countries, Japan is now regularly deploying ships and aircraft of the Japan Coast Guard (JCG) to Southeast Asia to assist in dealing with piracy and terrorism. The use of the Japanese Maritime Self-Defense Force (JMSDF) would have been unacceptable for this activity for Japan constitutionally, as well as being politically sensitive to regional countries. Nevertheless, JMSDF ships, including Aegis destroyers, have been deployed to the Indian Ocean in support of US forces under the scope of new anti-terrorism legislation that circumvents the limitations of the Japanese constitution.

Recent decreases in the size of Japan's defence budget are mainly a reflection of the assessment that Japan now has less need for large Air and Ground Self-Defense Forces to defend against a large-scale invasion of the Japanese homeland. Current priority security concerns for Japan are the threat of missile attack from North Korea, the rise of China, terrorism, and the risk of disrupted energy supplies. Increasing importance is attached to naval capabilities, including helicopter carriers to enter service in 2010, upgrades of the *Kongo*-class Aegis destroyers to give them a ballistic missile capability, an enlarged version of these vessels, and a new class of submarine with air-independent propulsion.

South Korea is another regional country that has significantly increased its maritime power in recent times, and continues to do so. It has significant fishing, shipping and shipbuilding interests and plays a very active role in regional maritime forums, including those on oceans management and marine environmental protection, as well as in regional security forums, such as the Council for Security Cooperation in the Asia-Pacific (CSCAP). The Republic of Korea Navy (ROKN) is growing strongly, reflecting a desire for capabilities for the independent protection of SLOCs, as well as a concern about longer term strategic outcomes. Korea could well find itself the proverbial "meat in the sandwich" should the relationship between Japan and China deteriorate further.

The ROKN has ambitious force development plans including the acquisition of two large amphibious assault ships probably of about 13,000 tonnes and capable of carrying up to 10 helicopters.[5] The third KDX-II stealth destroyer is fitting out and there are now plans to build three 7,000 tonne Aegis-equipped destroyers by 2012 under the KDX-III program. The KDX-II ships are equipped with SM-II and Harpoon missiles, a Rolling Airframe Missile (RAM) defence system to defend against supersonic anti-ship missiles, and other guns, as well as Super Lynx helicopters. The ROKN's current submarine force is based on the German Type 209-class but three Type-14 class with air independent propulsion (AIP) will enter service from 2007 and larger submarines may follow.

China is the ascending regional sea power. In a classical Mahanian approach, China seeks to use sea power in all its dimensions to spread its influence regionally. China is moving towards being the complete sea power with a blue-water navy, one of the world's largest merchant fleets, distant water fishing capabilities, and a rapidly expanding ship building industry. "Out of area" deployments by Chinese naval vessels are becoming common.

China continues to expand its submarine fleet with additional *Kilo*-Class boats and new nuclear-attack submarines probably derivatives of the

Russian *Victor*-class. It will acquire a second pair of *Sovremenny*-class destroyers possibly fitted with vertical launch missile systems, as well as building locally designed air defence destroyers. In relative terms, the PLA-Navy has been the main beneficiary of recent increased defence budget allocations in China. There continue to be rumours of plans to acquire an aircraft carrier capability and it was reported in 2004 that China is to ask an un-named European country to build several helicopter carriers.[6] These developments accord with China's aspirations to become a major regional, blue-water sea power. The naval planners in Beijing justify these developments on the basis of China's extensive and growing maritime interests, including sovereignty claims in the South China Sea, as well as increasing dependence on energy imports.

China has begun to "kick" some diplomatic goals of late. These are in response to new Chinese fears of encirclement and containment suggested by statements from US Secretary of State Condoleezza Rice during her recent visits around the region.[7] There is new Chinese preparedness to enter into maritime cooperative activities (a policy of "sincere cooperation"), including in disputed areas of the South China Sea. In March 2005 oil corporations from China, the Philippines and Vietnam signed a tripartite agreement for joint marine seismic research in the South China Sea. In April 2005 China committed to a string of partnership agreements with Indonesia, including on maritime cooperation and the transfer of defence technology. Along with China's apparent preparedness to contribute to the safety and security of the Malacca and Singapore Straits, these developments demonstrate China's intentions to build maritime influence in Southeast Asia and secure its oil imports from the Middle East.

Budgetary problems hamper the modernisation plans of Taiwan's navy. Due to escalating costs, it has been forced to cut the numbers of surface-to-air missiles and anti-ship missiles that it is buying with the four *Kidd*-class destroyers from the US and delay the purchase of submarines. Problems have also been experienced with plans to acquire P3 maritime surveillance aircraft and modern conventional submarines. Due to concerns about technology "leaking" from Taiwan to the mainland, support from the US for the armed forces of Taiwan does not involve "cutting edge" military technology. These developments mean that the naval capabilities of Taiwan are falling behind those of the mainland.

Since the collapse of the Soviet Union, the Russian Pacific Fleet has been as much affected by depressed budgets as other elements of the Russian military. It has been through a period of sharp decline in its order of battle with its submarine fleet, for example, declining from 54 units in 1995 to about 17 at present. However, in pursuance of new naval doctrine based on realistic budget expectations, the Pacific Fleet is seeking to regain some of its former influence through out-of-area deployments and ambitious exercise activities.

International naval analysts remain sceptical about whether it will be possible to transform the Russian Pacific Fleet back into a significant strategic force. The problems of under-funding and morale may be simply too large. Nevertheless, the "trump cards" still available to Russia are its nuclear weapons capability and high-tech weapon systems. The Russian Pacific Fleet has increased the frequency of its nuclear exercises in recent years, and this has led to speculation that nuclear weapons are still considered the main means of curbing the US in any possible conflict in East Asia.

Southeast Asia

Southeast Asian countries recognise the potential for maritime threats, not least of all the risks of conflict in the South China Sea, and the strategic implications of their location near major shipping "choke points". They seek to develop maritime forces (ships, aircraft, and submarines) with a potentially powerful capability for sea denial. The new platforms and weapons are capable of operations over wider areas and longer ranges than was the case with previous generations of systems. Even small Brunei now has 1,900 tonne missile corvettes in service with vertical launch anti-air warfare (AAW) and surface-to-surface anti-ship missiles.

Southeast Asian countries, particularly the states adjacent to the Malacca and Singapore Straits, are presently disconcerted by the level of attention being given to the security of the Straits by countries from outside Southeast Asia. Singapore supports the concerns of these user states, but Malaysia and Indonesia have been offended by suggestions they are not capable of providing security in what after all are largely their own territorial waters. There are also suspicions that the user states are only using the threats of piracy and terrorism to justify their longer-term naval presence in the region. It was not surprising therefore to hear a recent call by influential Indonesian academics for Thailand and Indonesia to work closer together to establish a maritime bloc to balance the maritime power of countries like China and India.[8] Other Southeast Asian countries might also be sympathetic to such an arrangement.

Thailand and Indonesia have aspired in the past to be the "heavy weights" of Southeast Asia but both suffered grievously from the economic crisis of the late 1990s. Their leadership of a Southeast Asian maritime bloc would be an interesting development, particularly as they represent the different perspectives of "continental" Southeast Asia on the one hand and "maritime" Southeast Asia on the other. Membership of the former group includes Vietnam, Laos and Cambodia, as well as Thailand, while the latter comprises Malaysia, the Philippines, Brunei and Singapore, as well as Indonesia.

The Republic of Singapore Navy (RSN) is the technological trendsetter among Southeast Asian navies. While Indonesia has operated a small submarine fleet for many years, the RSN "upped the ante" in the late 1990s with the acquisition of four Swedish *Sjormen*-class submarines, all of which have now entered service. The first of the RSN's new blue-water frigates, RSS *Formidable*, was launched in France in January 2004. The other five vessels of this class will be built in Singapore. These ships are highly capable, designed to be stealthy and equipped with advanced combat systems, including Harpoon missiles, the Aster Anti-Missile Missile (AMM) system and an advanced ASW suite. Along with the submarines, these vessels demonstrate the preparedness of the RSN to operate well beyond the immediate confines of the Singapore Strait and its approaches.

In Malaysia, the *Meko A 100*-class offshore patrol vessel (OPV) building program continues on track with the first vessels entering service this year although reports suggest that not all 27 vessels originally in this program will be acquired and maybe only two will be acquired eventually. Malaysia is also buying two *Scorpene*-class submarines, which are based on a proven French design. The 1,500 tonne *Scorpene* is a new-generation medium-sized conventional attack submarine with capabilities for missions ranging from anti-submarine and anti-surface warfare to special operations and intelligence collection. To be based near Kota Kinabalu in Sabah, the first *Scorpene* will be delivered in 2007 and the second a year later.

A roughly 15% increase in Thailand's defence budget was announced in September 2003. However, the Thai Army and Air Force appear likely to have the major share of this increase rather than the Royal Thai Navy (RTN). Nevertheless, the new Chief of the RTN has announced plans in March 2004 to purchase two frigates from Britain, additional patrol vessels and new weapons and sensor systems for the aircraft carrier, *Chakri Naruebet*.[9] The RTN also remains interested in acquiring submarines.

With the Indonesian economy still struggling after the economic collapse of the late 1990s, Indonesia's navy remains hard-pressed to meet the security requirements of a far-flung archipelago. However, it hopes to reverse the downward capability trend as soon as possible although the tsunami disaster of December 2004 has been a set back for these plans. New submarines might be acquired possibly from South Korea. Indonesia's major surface combatants at present are six ageing frigates transferred from the Netherlands in the late 1980s and three smaller Dutch-built *Fatihillah* class frigates of more recent origin. However, reports have suggested that two new corvettes might be ordered from the Netherlands. Indonesia could now be regarded as potentially a good market for foreign shipbuilders as China, South Korea and Italy are also believed to have offered surface warships to the Indonesian navy. The JCG is assisting Indonesia with the development of a Coast Guard force.

Despite being an archipelagic country with extensive maritime interests and conflicting claims to sovereignty in the South China Sea, the Philippine Navy remains the weakest navy in Southeast Asia. Its major units are an obsolete former US Navy (USN) frigate and three ex-British *Peacock*-Class patrol boats. The US is to transfer a *Cyclone*-class patrol vessel to the Navy and Tenix in Australia has built several patrol boats of various sizes for the Philippine Coast Guard.

The Vietnamese Navy is also relatively weak. However, it does have two coastal submarines transferred from North Korea and is reported to be seeking a new frigate/corvette type vessel to provide a credible offshore capability. At present the Vietnamese Coast Guard undertakes most offshore patrolling.

South Asia

The security outlook in South Asia appears more optimistic than it was just a year or so ago. There have been some positive confidence building developments between India and Pakistan, as well as between China and India, and the internal security situation in Sri Lanka appears contained for the time being. However, the Andaman Sea has been the scene of a fairly high level of illegal activity, including illegal fishing and drug smuggling. It begs an increased level of cooperation between littoral navies and coast guards to provide law and order at sea.

India is actively pursuing ambitious programmes for naval force expansion and the establishment of new naval bases. The easing of tensions between India and Pakistan is allowing India to shift a greater proportion of its defence budget towards a "more assertive maritime strategy".[10] India's new maritime doctrine released in May 2004 aims to build a major ocean-going fleet to dominate the Indian Ocean.

India has long had the most powerful regional navy in the Indian Ocean. However, it is now proceeding to extend its maritime influence eastwards, and is seeking a greater role in regional political and security affairs through the application of its sea power. This is largely to counter any moves by China into the Indian Ocean. India's "Look East" policy includes naval deployments East of Singapore. India's role in the region has been boosted by the developing strategic relationship with the US that includes a strong naval dimension. Regular exercises are taking place between the USN and the Indian Navy, including ones involving American nuclear submarines. The Indian Navy has also cooperated with the USN in escorting high value shipping through the Malacca Straits.

Maritime capabilities are receiving prominence in the development of India's armed forces. India is to re-establish a credible aircraft carrier capability with the acquisition of the Russian carrier *Admiral Gorshkov*, and by building a new class of locally built carrier. The latter vessels will be about 37,500 tonnes, and represent India's most ambitious military programme to date. The Indian Navy will further develop its large fleet of powerful surface combatants with *Talwar*-class frigates built in Russia and other vessels built locally; and modernise its submarine fleet with the likely purchase of six *Scorpene* submarines from France and the lease of *Akula*-class nuclear attack submarines from Russia.

With the exception of its submarine fleet, which includes three *Agosta*-class 90-B conventional submarines equipped with Exocet anti-ship missiles, Pakistan's navy operates mainly obsolete vessels. There have been reports of Pakistan negotiating to buy an unspecified number of F-22 frigates from China to replace the two old gun-armed *Leander*-class frigates. Prior to the present détente with India, Pakistan's navy announced plans to acquire nuclear weapons but it was not clear how it would deploy such missiles.

Maritime Strategy

This review of regional naval developments suggests two major trends with maritime strategy that could be features of the emergent maritime future of the region. The first is economic and political, and the second military and operational. The first involves a classical Mahanian approach with naval forces being used to extend regional strategic influence. The major powers of Russia, India, China and Japan, as well as the US, demonstrate this approach. It includes perceptions of an increased need to secure SLOCs, possibly in waters well away from home, and is most apparent in the waters of Southeast Asia. Unless managed carefully, there are serious long-term implications of India's apparent desire to demonstrate a capability to operate East of Singapore, and China's similar intentions to operate into the Indian Ocean.

The second trend relates to the increased operational significance of littoral areas. Major Western navies are focussing on littoral operations and expeditionary forces while coastal States, especially some in the region, perceive a growing need to protect their sovereignty and defend their own littoral. The littoral focus of major navies requires capabilities for what is variously known as sea assertion, sea use or power projection, while that of the coastal States involves sea denial with submarines, anti-ship missiles and small attack craft.

Expeditionary forces and naval power projection capabilities, including large amphibious ships, land attack cruise missiles and versatile surface combatants to exercise control in littoral areas are not just the monopoly of the USN. Germany, Italy and Spain are following this approach, as well as the main European navies of Britain and France. France already maintains a significant naval presence in the Pacific and plays an active supportive role in regional arrangements for maritime surveillance and enforcement.

This apparent contrast in maritime strategic approaches has other consequences. It is evident, for example, in an apparently increased interest in the region in military oceanographic research and intelligence collection. The extent, variety and sophistication of signals intelligence (SIGINT) operations in East Asia have increased significantly over the last decade.[11] Aircraft, surface ships and submarines conduct these operations. Good oceanographic knowledge is an important "force multiplier" in maritime operations, but particularly for submarine operations, anti-submarine warfare and mine warfare. While oceanographic surveying in an exclusive economic zone (EEZ) is subject to the jurisdiction of the coastal State, the US and other maritime powers argue that hydrographic surveying and research activities conducted for military purposes are not.[12]

Military surveying and intelligence collection activities in the region are going to become both more controversial and more dangerous in the future. Most of these activities in the region are conducted in the EEZ of one coastal State or another. Some regional countries have declared security zones that extend into the EEZ, or have specifically claimed that other States are not authorised to conduct military exercises or manoeuvres in the EEZ without their consent. As a result of concern over the US "spy plane" incident off Hainan in 2001 and more recent incidents involving US "military survey" ships operating in its EEZ, China enacted new legislation in 2002 restricting surveying and intelligence collection activities in its EEZ.[13]

The growth of regional coast guards is another important maritime strategic development for the emergent maritime future of the region. Coast guards are now more significant in the region and make a major contribution to maritime security cooperation. Existing coast guards are being expanded and some countries (such as Vietnam, Indonesia and Malaysia) that had not previously had coast guards have either established, or are in the process of establishing them. Coast guard units are more suitable than warships for employment in sensitive areas where there are conflicting claims to maritime jurisdiction and/or political tensions between parties. In such situations, the arrest of a foreign vessel by a warship may be highly provocative whereas arrest by a coast guard vessel may be accepted as legitimate law enforcement. Coast guard vessels and aircraft are also generally less expensive than naval units.

Comprehensive Maritime Security

The disastrous tsunami on 26 December 2004 demonstrated the importance of a comprehensive approach to regional security. The emergent maritime future of the region must comprehend trends with resource security, food security and environmental security as major non-military dimensions of regional security. Serious environmental issues loom on the horizon but with the attention being given to the terrorist threat, they have tended to drop off regional agendas. With an ever-increasing world population and continued economic growth and industrialisation, albeit unequally distributed across the globe, the scarcity of non-renewable resources will increase, global warming will continue, and environmental pressures intensify. The pressures at sea will be particularly acute with increased levels of shipping traffic posing greater risks to the marine environment; the marked degradation of marine habitats and the loss of fish stocks; and increased pressure to exploit offshore hydrocarbon resources with consequent risks of potential conflict and disagreement between competing claimants.

Impact of Globalisation

The international system is going through a period of significant change. It has become trite to observe that the world changed forever on 9/11. However, the changes are not only in response to the threat of terrorism but also include other consequences of globalisation and interdependence. These changes underpin the emergent maritime future of the region, including a more evident concern for the security of shipping and seaborne trade. The moves by China, Japan, India and Russia to use their navies and coast guards to extend their regional influence, and the no longer remote possibility of

European navies becoming involved in the region are also consequences of increased globalisation and interdependence.

Globalisation is much more than just an economic phenomenon. It also has significant security implications. Regional naval developments can no longer be assessed purely in the context of the region itself. This is not just a matter of terrorism being a global threat but also flows from the nature of world trade and the international arms industry with European and North American companies competing aggressively for the Asian naval market. Then there is the contrast already mentioned between on the one hand, the focus of Western navies on littoral operations and expeditionary forces and on the other, regional navies developing more powerful sea denial capabilities to defend their littoral. While current naval developments proceed, the possibility that these strategic cultures could clash at some time in the future is not entirely fanciful.

Issues for the Future

Maritime power, especially the way countries apply it, holds the key to future regional security. Regional countries are spending more and more on their navies. The major maritime powers of the US, China, India and Japan, as well as Russia, all seek to extend their strategic influence in the region using sea power while many coastal states are developing powerful sea denial forces. Problems might arise because these developments are all focussed in the relatively narrow seas of East Asia that are distinguished by high levels of maritime activity, dense and increasing shipping traffic, conflicting claims to maritime jurisdiction, increased exploration for offshore oil and gas, and unresolved maritime boundaries. A higher level of cooperation in managing these pressures at sea is an essential requirement of the emergent maritime future of the region.

The proliferation of submarines in the region, including their use as launching platforms for nuclear weapons, is of particular concern. With regional navies, the USN, the Australian Navy and possibly the Indian Navy, all operating submarines into the East Asian seas, these waters will become "crowded" underwater in the future. It is timely to consider the implications of these developments, including what might be done to reduce the risk of incidents with "intruder" submarines such as those periodically experienced in European waters during the Cold War. However, surveillance and intelligence collection are major roles for submarines and submarine issues are extremely sensitive. This is contrary to the desirable confidence building measure of transparency.

Something has to give and some concept of an end-game is required for current naval developments. The region faces major challenges in managing these developments and keeping "the lid on the pressure cooker". There is a pressing need to build a regional security environment in which countries are more prepared to cooperate and reduce their naval spending and levels of naval activity. However, this objective is unattractive in the region at present.

The strategic affairs of the Asian region, and its emergent maritime future, will be largely determined by the region itself. Much will depend on the three major Asian powers — Japan, China and India — their relationships with each other, and with the US, and the strategic role they choose to play. The region has never before seen such competition between major players for influence, and to forge friendships with other regional countries. China feels that the US, India and Japan are working towards its maritime strategic containment; India believes China is trying to encircle it and establish a maritime strategic presence in the Indian Ocean; and Japan fears the strategic rise of China. All of this competition has a very significant maritime dimension that gives little prospect of maritime stability in the foreseeable future.

Nearly 10 years ago, Kent Calder described the increasing energy dependence of Northeast Asia as part of "the deadly triangle of growth, energy shortage, and armament".[14] This "deadly triangle" is still a large part of the emergent maritime future of the region with continued economic growth leading to increased demand for energy while concurrently providing the resources for greater defence spending. It is an unfortunate reality of the modern world that real growth in defence spending tends to move upwards at about the same rate as real economic growth.

Issues of comprehensive security and maritime confidence and security building measures (MCSBMs) have been off the agenda in recent years. In the best interests of a stable maritime future for the Asia-Pacific region, they should be put back on the agendas of regional forums, both Track 1 and Track 2. The challenge now is to build a regional security environment in which countries are more prepared to cooperate and reduce their naval spending and levels of naval activity. This might be a challenge that will be picked up by the new East Asian summit should it become an established forum for regional security cooperation and dialogue.

Notes

1. "Naval ship spending to increase in Asia Pacific, defense experts say", *The China Post online*, 11 November 2003. Available at http://www.chinapost.com.

tw/p_detail.asp?id=43042&GRP=A&onNews= <Accessed on 15 November 2003>.

2. Maritime power in this context includes commercial maritime interests: merchant shipping fleet, seaborne trade, fishing interests, size of resources zones, and shipbuilding capacity, as well as naval and coast guard capabilities. In military terms, maritime power is no longer the sole prerogative of navies. Many regional countries also have coast guards or are in the process of establishing one. Maritime aircraft for both strike and surveillance must also be included as essential and integral elements of a nation's maritime power. Marine infantry should also be included.

3. Joshua Ho, "The Shifting of Maritime Power and the Implications for Maritime Security in East Asia", *Working Paper No. 68*, Institute of Defence and Strategic Studies, Singapore, June 2004.

4. Richard Hill originally used the expression *medium maritime power* to describe a country that has the capability to exercise some autonomy in its use of the sea. Rear Admiral J. R. Hill RN, *Maritime Strategy for Medium Powers* (Annapolis: Naval Institute Press, 1986), pp. 46–48.

5. Commodore Stephen Saunders RN, "Executive Summary" in *Jane's Fighting Ships 2003–2004* (Coulsdon, Surrey: Jane's Information Group, 2004), p. 7.

6. "China looks for helicopter carriers", *The Navy*, Vol. 66, No. 2, April–June 2004, p. 14.

7. Willy Lam, "Beijing's Alarm over New "U.S. Encirclement Conspiracy", *Jamestown Foundation China Brief: A Journal of News and Analysis*, Vol. V, Issue 8, April 12, 2005.

8. Achara Ashayagachat, "Jakarta floats proposal for maritime bloc", *Bangkok Post*, Wed 6 April 2005.

9. "Thailand plans for the future", *The Navy*, Vol. 66, No. 1, March 2004, p. 20.

10. Jim Bencivenga, "Footsteps Heard at Sea", *Christian Science Monitor Online*, 8 April 2005.

11. Desmond Ball, "Intelligence Collection Operations and EEZs: The Implications of New Technology", *Paper Prepared for the Tokyo Meeting, The Regime of the Exclusive Economic Zone: Issues and Responses*, co-organised by the East-West Center and the Institute for Ocean Policy, Tokyo, 19–20 February 2003.

12. Sam Bateman, "Hydrographic surveying in the EEZ: differences and overlaps with marine scientific research", *Marine Policy* 29, 2005, pp. 163–174.

13. Bill Gertz, "China Enacts Law Extending Its Control", *The Washington Times*, 27 January 2003.

14. Kent E. Calder, *Asia's Deadly Triangle — How Arms, Energy and Growth threaten to destabilize Asia Pacific* (London: Nicholas Brealey Publishing, 1996).

Chapter 13

The Evolving Maritime Balance of Power in the Asia-Pacific: Maritime Doctrines and Nuclear Weapons at Sea

W. Lawrence S. Prabhakar

Introduction

The emergent Maritime Order in the Asia-Pacific reflects the evolution of a new balance of power dynamic that posits rising powers and status quo powers. The maritime geo-strategic trends in the Asia-Pacific are driven by robust energies of economic globalisation predicated on maritime trade and impressive regional economic growth and integration. Even as economic globalisation and trade had grown impressively, even as the accents of regional integration and cooperative security had grown in formidable strengths, the premises of a *competitive-cooperative* balance of power have been emergent at the beginning of the 21st century.

The IDSS Conference on *The Maritime Balance of Power in the Asia-Pacific* was an exploratory project that was intended to assess and analyse the quintessence of the emergent maritime doctrines and the evolving maritime geo-economic and geo-strategic milieu in the ambient Asia-Pacific region. The geo-political, geo-economic and geo-strategic order of the Asia-Pacific is predicated on the maritime realm necessitating the focus of the analysis on issues of maritime order, maritime doctrines and the maritime-naval issues of transformation.

The contributors to the conference on *The Maritime Balance of Power in the Asia-Pacific* were asked to ponder the following issues and questions even as they wrote their conference papers and edited the same to its present version:

(1) What are the evolving paradigms of maritime/naval transformation that had induced the emergence of the new maritime doctrines and the resultant dichotomy of *competitive-cooperative* maritime orders in the Asia-Pacific?

(2) What are the consequences of Rising Powers specifically Rising China and Rising India in the context of the maritime balance of power in the Asia-Pacific?

(3) To what extent globalisation and maritime trade have enhanced the cooperative-convergent premises of maritime security in the region?

(4) What are the emergent naval force postures of the US, Japan, China and India as the pivotal maritime powers of the Asia-Pacific — reflected in their new naval/maritime doctrines that have unequivocally emphasised for an enhanced naval profile, presence, role and operations in the region?

(5) What are the implications and impact of the "*Second Nuclear Age*" in the Asia-Pacific with the dominant navies of China and India, preferring the deployment of nuclear weapons at sea and the consequent transformation in doctrines and operations of the super power nuclear navy of the US;

(6) How far has the issue of ballistic missile defences at sea been viewed as a strategic, political-diplomatic and a viable security architecture that has facilitated the strengthening of the regional bilateral alliances?

(7) What would be the viable matrices to balance the competitive drives of naval force modernisation, defense transformation and the increased preference of nuclear weapons and missile defences by viable means of cooperative maritime security that has increased salience in the context of the challenging maritime transnational-asymmetric issues and the positive prospects of globalisation and maritime trade?

The second objective of focus in this volume has been the significance and gravity of maritime asymmetric threats and weapons of mass destruction as significant levers of destabilisation with their colossal disruptive impact on the maritime trade in the region. The focus of the analysis was on the regional medium powers in South East Asia with their energies focused on the process of globalisation along with their deft contention with the maritime asymmetric threats and the menace of clandestine transport of weapons of mass destruction in the littoral waters. Regional naval build-ups have been rationalised with these threat matrices and have focused on conventional naval modernisations that have been platform-centric with transformational effectiveness. The issues of contested Sea Lanes of Communication (SLOCs) with the imperatives of energy and trade sea-lanes have been prominent.

The third objective of focus in this volume is the analysis of the various naval force postures that have evolved in the context of the milieu of strategy, doctrines and technology that have been galvanised by naval transformation. The analysis of the issues of naval transformation evident in the maritime doctrines and force postures of the US, Japan, China and India reflects how traditional matrices of threats and challenges and the non-traditional asymmetric and transnational sources of threats and challenges have seriously influenced the process.

In the context of assessing the competitive naval arms build-up by the extra-regional powers, viz., the US, Japan, China and India, it is evident that there is a quest to balance rising powers with the imperatives of doctrinal adaptation and technological transformation.

Significantly the maritime dynamics of the Asia-Pacific correlates with the matrices of maritime power evident in the inter-regional maritime orders in South East and North East Asia. The two regions have featured intensive naval and air modernisation that have been platform-centric into a transformation centric process.

Globalisation and maritime trade on the other hand had also fostered the accents of maritime cooperation premised on the issues of cooperative maritime security with the convergence of maritime interests between South East Asia and the naval quartet of the US, Japan, China and India. The resultant has been the emergence of a several initiatives built on: (1) Regional maritime security cooperation in response to non-traditional asymmetric transnational challenges, viz., the Proliferation Security Initiative/Container Security Initiative, (2) Building the potential for maritime coalition for regional maritime security issues, and (3) Maritime regime building that is focused on the Law of the Sea and the issues of SLOCs.

Is there a Maritime Balance of Power in the Asia-Pacific?

The issue of debate — Is there a maritime balance of power in the Asia-Pacific?

The Asia-Pacific represents a region of great powers whose power profiles and capabilities have been at varying levels. The US continues as the *super maritime power* given its formidable naval order of battle of assortment of robust surface strike capabilities, varied submerged nuclear capabilities of cruise and ballistic missile inventories, superior naval–air capabilities and massed firepower from its nuclear powered aircraft carriers and its resilient and muscular expeditionary amphibious capabilities in the Euro-Atlantic and the Indo-Pacific Oceans that provides it the mainstay of superior sea-based power projection of unparalleled significance.

Russia continues to maintain its maritime power capabilities at a much diminished level; but certainly above that of the medium maritime powers. Russia is a *great maritime power* given its naval order of battle of an assortment of surface-strike capabilities, varied submerged nuclear and conventional capabilities, significant naval–air capabilities and its modest expeditionary amphibious capabilities into the Pacific and the Indian Oceans.

China, Japan and India are *medium maritime powers* measured in terms of an assessment of relative profiles of naval orders of battle, diversified platforms, operational capabilities in terms of naval–air, amphibious expeditionary forces, surge capabilities, nuclear weapon deployments at sea and sea-based missile defences.

Australia and South Korea are maritime powers of significant consequence that have compatible platforms and operational capabilities with increasing effectiveness in limited power projection. In synergies with the US naval power, Japan, Australia and South Korea would be able to enhance their effectiveness in endurance for longer range deployments and support roles in *out of area deployments* like the Indian Ocean deployments.

The littoral countries of South East Asia Malaysia, Indonesia, Singapore, Thailand, Vietnam, and Philippines are small maritime powers in view of their platform profiles and operational capabilities; North East Asia features the Koreas, Taiwan which are growing navies in the region that have enhanced operational capabilities thanks to the naval transformational process.

Given the four-tier structure of naval order of battle, it is difficult to ascertain the level and scope of balance of power in the region. The question — *Is there a traditional hard power balancing against the US by the other powers* or *are there increasing concerns about a rising China and its naval capabilities that has alarmed the regional powers?* While the former is ruled out, the latter is viewed with increasing significant attention.

The US naval presence is being viewed with mixed perceptions. The prevalent anti-access political and military perceptions view the US naval presence in the region as hostile and aggressive and in fact have worked attempting to erode the effectiveness of US presence in the region. On the other hand there have been the coalition of willing states in the Indo-Pacific region that have viewed US naval presence as benign and stabilising in an environment that has been highly competitive and destabilising owing to growing anti-access forces.

In the context of the contemporary analysis of Balance of Power in a thematic perspective, three perceptions are relevant in the post-Cold War era, viz., Hard Balancing, Soft Balancing and Asymmetric Balancing.[1]

Hard Balancing refers to the traditional realist — the classical and neoclassical approach of forming and maintaining open military alliances to balance a strong state or forestall the rise of a power or a threatening state. Arms build-up, rearmament with internal and external sources of modernisation and transformation could be means to achieve the balance of power. In the post-Cold war era, this is limited to regional theatres like the Middle East, South Asia and East Asia. It is quite contextual to the Chinese–Japanese arms build-up dynamic as the mutual balancing dynamic is now in its robust form.

Soft Balancing is the subtle means of building coalitions with manifest non-offensive multilateral measures aimed to neutralise the rising or potentially threatening power. Soft Balancing has a prospective dimension to forestall the future offensive potential of the rising power or the dominant power's threatening posture.

What kind of responses would hard balancing and soft balancing elicit from the hegemonic state or the rising power would be difficult to assess as it has a time-spatial context. Quite often the polarity of power to counterbalance the rising power or the hegemonic power could elicit immediate formidable political, economic and military countermeasures that would have high economic stakes.

A Rising China has its concerns and implications for Japan, India and the regional powers of the Asia-Pacific. This has resulted in reinforcing of alliance relationships of Japan with the US. On the other hand, apprehensions of US hegemonic power in the region by China has been evocative even as China engages the region in terms of its East Asia Initiative and its bids to woo the ASEAN countries like Malaysia, Indonesia vis-à-vis the US. These responses have provoked the debate on the possibilities of soft balancing the US in the near- and medium-term in the region.

Asymmetric Balancing emerges in the interstate dynamics and the state and non-state actor dynamic responses. Asymmetric balancing strategies involve terrorism, insurgency and state support to non-state actors in engaging a dominant hegemonic power. Anti-access strategies are viewed as viable means of asymmetric balancing against the hegemonic power by the rising power or the role of brinkmanship states like North Korea and Iran to asymmetrically balance the hegemonic power.

The Maritime Balance of Power in the Asia-Pacific has its assorted features of all the above three dimensions of the contemporary axioms of Balance of Power. At the interstate level of the competitive maritime dynamic, the rise of China and the regional power responses to its strategic modernisation are strongly evident. It is evident in the naval modernisation of Japan and the global forces realignment of the US in the Asia-Pacific. There is also the ambient Indian maritime engagement of the Asia-Pacific and its naval exercises with the South East Asian and North East Asian navies in as much as China has been engaging in South Asia with Pakistan and Myanmar in "India's backyard".

Japan has been in the process of "normalising"[2] its role as a responsible regional power and has expanded its maritime deployments with "out of area" roles in the Indian Ocean in synergies with the US roles in Afghanistan and Iraq.

The small maritime powers of the region have been bandwagoning with the US as a convergence in terms to counter the asymmetric threats in the region, viz., counterterrorism. In other cases, states like Malaysia and Indonesia have been initially alarmed at the US proaction in terms of the Regional Maritime Security Initiative, but have now quietly accepted US assistance and facilitation of intelligence and capabilities in counter-asymmetric missions.

Thus an evolving balance of power dynamic is in momentum in the Asia-Pacific with a mix of balance of power strategies at work.

The Salience of Maritime Doctrines and Naval Force Build-ups

The emergent maritime balance of power dynamic in the Asia-Pacific is evident in the salience and role of new maritime doctrines and naval force build-ups. The salience of the new maritime doctrines of the US, Japan, China and India is evident by their ambient and proactive engagement of their resources and capabilities for the stakes of influence and dominion in the region. Three distinctive trends have been evident:

(1) Globalisation and economic trade in the region has significantly enhanced maritime power and has fostered the evolution of maritime power and strategy in the non-offensive domains of benign and constabulary naval roles and missions. While the traditional coercive and compellence missions remain relevant, there has been definitive reorientation of these roles

in the new geo-maritime milieu — the redefinition of maritime strategy has been to address issues of non-traditional concerns.

The new maritime doctrines have been able to articulate issues of naval transformation in the *competitive-cooperative* dichotomy. The new naval roles of Benign and Constabulary missions have served to enhance the maritime interoperable roles between navies of varying power and profiles — from the *super maritime power* to the *small maritime powers.* The emergence of transnational natural disasters like the Asian Tsunami in December 2004 had activated the dimension of humanitarian maritime missions and synergies to the disaster affected areas. Thus the new maritime doctrines in the Asia-Pacific fully capture the essence of the Benign, Constabulary and the evident Humanitarian maritime missions in the national maritime doctrines of the powers. While at the same time, the doctrinal focus and operational loci has also been to generate viable counter responses to maritime asymmetric threats.

Maritime interoperability has been the theme of the US and its allies in developing viable operational strategies to a broad spectrum of traditional and non-traditional maritime challenges and threats.

(2) Defence and Naval transformation has been the second distinctive catalyst that had integrated the national maritime/naval capabilities, platforms and operational roles into new doctrinal visions and synergies. Defence transformation in the Asia-Pacific has indeed integrated the diverse platforms to a viable battlespace domain by the integration of the sensors and shooters. Technological drivers had induced the operational integration process and that in turn has influenced doctrines. Naval transformation has induced new concepts of the autonomous use of the sea of projecting power into the littoral *From the Sea to the Littoral* and the possible neutralising of the consequent anti-access littoral security countermeasures.

Maritime Doctrines have been configured on the planks of the debate in the trends in technological transformation, operational milieu and the national capabilities and resources for innovation.

(3) The *competitive-cooperative* dichotomy in the Maritime Order of the Asia-Pacific is the third distinctive catalyst that has induced doctrinal transformation. With the end of the Cold War; the disappearance of the bipolar strategic rivalry and the consequent rise of low intensity conflicts in the continental and the maritime domains have infused a new vision for reorienting maritime doctrines.

The US, Japan, China and India have been engaged in the articulation of ambient national maritime doctrines in tune with their globalisation driven economic and trade objectives; the securing the Exclusive Economic Zones; the security of the SLOCs; the quest for maritime access and basing; the significant quest for energy resources, trade and more so for the accents of maritime cooperation.

In a dynamic balancing process that is evolving in the Asia-Pacific, the roles of the US, Japan, China and India are pivotal along with Russia, Australia and South Korea that would have new roles and engagement of their capabilities in varied maritime operations.

The Significance of Nuclear Weapons and Missile Defences — At Sea

The Maritime Balance of Power in the Asia-Pacific is in witness of the evolution of the *Second Nuclear Age* and the increasing significance of nuclear weapons.[3] The maritime basis of nuclear weapons arises with the developments in technological templates and the gradual evolution of the advanced Command, Control, Communications, Computers Intelligence, Information, Surveillance and Reconnaissance (C4I2SR) assets. The US, Russia, China in the Asia-Pacific are the known nuclear weapon states (NWS) who have deployed considerable nuclear assets at sea in the form of nuclear-tipped cruise missiles and nuclear-tipped ballistic missiles based on nuclear attack and fleet ballistic missile submarines. Israel is yet another power that has attained operational capability to possibly launch nuclear tipped Land Attack Cruise Missiles (LACMs) from its *Dolphin* class conventional submarines.

India and Pakistan have conventional submarines and are acquiring Air Independent Propulsion (AIP) submarines that could feature possible cruise missiles with nuclear warheads. India has been actively pursuing its indigenous Advanced Technology Vessel program with possible nuclear-tipped cruise missiles and has been attempting to lease/acquire the Russian nuclear attack submarines of the *Akula* class.

The evolution of the nuclear triad has been a substantial technological development with operational robustness during the Cold War and the templates of the same have continued since then.

The strategic environment of the Asia-Pacific would be a high intensity engagement of the nuclear naval order of battle — in terms of the deployed surface and sub-surface nuclear platforms equipped with long-range land attack cruise missiles with nuclear and conventional warheads. The nuclear navies of the US Fifth Fleet, Russia, France, UK and China would be the dominant extra-regional navies deploying substantial nuclear assets in the surface and sub-surface platforms. Besides the regional navies of India, Israel, Pakistan and possibly Iran are likely nuclear naval powers in the coming years. Pakistan and Iran could perhaps in the longer run, possess nuclear-tipped land attack cruise missiles on board conventional submarines.

Sea-based deterrence would thus emerge as the dominant technological and deployment option given the versatility of operations. Sea-based nuclear deterrence in submerged deployments offers the operational capabilities of survivability, endurance, deception, manoeuvre; dispersal, precision strike and connectivity with a host of Very Low Frequency (VLF) stations enabling flexible deployment.

The quantum of dedicated anti-submarine forces to track the nuclear-propelled submarines would have to be quite high and the reliability to track them in the waters of the Asia-Pacific and in the warm waters of the Indian Ocean regions would be quite formidable given the isothermal complexities of the warm layers and high salinity.

Nuclear weapons at sea offer the regional powers distinct advantages vis-à-vis the extra-regional nuclear naval powers in any crisis escalation situation.

(1) Sea-based deterrence would enhance the *credibility* of *assured retaliatory capability* in the event of a pre-emptive first strike that would be precision attack with decapitating effects on land assets;
(2) Sea-based deterrence offers the advantages of *dispersal and stealth* in the face of vulnerability of nuclear land-based assets;
(3) Given the advantages of dispersal and stealth, the key to assured retaliatory capabilities would be *survivability* that enhances credible deterrence.

Nuclear weapons at sea would be the evolving technological and operational template of the nuclear weapon states and the new nuclear powers. True to the benchmarks of the Second Nuclear Age, the proliferation of nuclear weapon states and the varieties of nuclear weapon platforms and operational deployments are likely to increase the complexity and intensity of the arms race — resulting in a cascade of nuclear and missile proliferation in the Asia-Pacific.[4]

Sea-based missile defence known as Navy Theatre wide systems would be emergent technological templates that would provide for mobility and flexibility of targeting against hostile regional ballistic missiles. Shipboard missile defence systems would provide the "shield" in an offence–defence technology template. Sea-based missile defence systems offer the advantage of mobility in that it makes the missile defence missile system less vulnerable to a pre-emptive strike and allows for adaptation on a flexible scale.

US sea-based missile defence systems provide for offshore basing without having to deploy in land territory that either would be vulnerable to pre-emptive adversarial ballistic missile strikes and /or the political consequences of deploying missile defences in allied territory. The Asia-Pacific Region would emerge as a significant region for the deployment of missile defence systems by the US, Japan and perhaps Australia — specifically sea-based missile defence systems in view of the hostile regional nuclear missile arsenals.

The obvious implication of the substantial sea-based Theatre Missile Defence (TMD) deployments would be to target and neutralise the hostile regional nuclear arsenals with ballistic missile inventories of Iran in the Indian Ocean Region and North Korea in the Sea of Japan. The sea-based Navy Theatre wide systems would be primarily oriented to intercept missiles in early boost phase and limited capabilities of intercept during in flight before countermeasures are dispersed.

The Future Pathways

The evolving Maritime Balance of Power in the Asia-Pacific presents a chequered setting that is intrinsic of the competitive and cooperative dimensions of maritime strategy. The multi-tiered power structure the Asia-Pacific of maritime super power, Great maritime powers, medium maritime powers and the small maritime powers presents the canvas of competing maritime interests and complex interdependence that offers the region a challenging future.

The future pathways of the Asia-Pacific region is intertwined with the prospects of the enhanced impact of globalisation and interdependence and the diminishing prospects of a major war in the region. However, the intensity of the acrimonious power rivalries of the region, the intense territorial contestations does not completely rule out the break out of limited hostilities in the region that would indeed be perilous to the peace and stability of the region.

Three factors would determine the future pathways of the maritime balance of power in the Asia-Pacific region that would have its decisive influence either in enhancing the stability of the region or could perhaps trigger the descent of the region into a spiral of crisis.

The evolving future pathways of maritime Asia-Pacific would lie in the process of the balancing dynamic in the region. The Balance of Power dynamics would be determined by the nature and scope of alliances in the region. A Rising China and a hegemonic America would be the primary stakeholders in the ensuing balance of the region. While the stakes of the balance are being determined, regional powers would either bandwagon or would be buffering vis-à-vis the two powers for economic advantage and security gains.

The Asia-Pacific region is thus a pivotal region for the traditional structure of power rivalries even as historical memories and prevalent unresolved territorial and maritime boundary issues persist with the possible prospects of crisis escalation in the future.

The role of the US would be crucial even as it nurtures and builds new synergies in its bilateral alliances with Japan, South Korea and Australia and reinvigorating its bilateral strategic relationships with Singapore. It has been endeavouring for better relations with Malaysia and Indonesia. The new bilateral agreements and arrangements with Thailand, Pakistan and Philippines as non-NATO allies; the emergent strategic partnership with India provides the menu for the evolving alliance system in the region. There are also similar patterns of alliances that China and Russia have been building to deter the growing American power in the region.

The Russian–Chinese strategic relationship since July 2001 has been growing in its military-technical collaboration scope and the determined attempts to deter the hegemonic influence of the US. Joint military exercises and strategic coordination have been the substance of the Russian–Chinese collaboration. Iran, North Korea would be important constituents of this axis of strategic influence in the future.

Secondly, the future pathways of the Asia-Pacific region would be evident in the evolving technological templates. The process of defence transformation and specifically maritime and naval transformation has been a crucial factor. Maritime/naval transformation would determine the pace of the transformation of navies of their order of battle that in turn would drive the evolution of maritime doctrines and the operational milieu. Maritime/naval transformation would address a host of issues that would determine the nature of access and basing, the scope of expeditionary operations, the robustness of littoral power projection overcoming anti-access measures, the efficacy of unmanned surface and underwater platforms and operations, the range and lethal strike capabilities of carrier-based naval aviation, the integration of net-centric platforms and operations, and the evolution of the dominant battlespace in the maritime-aerospace realms and nuclear weapons and missile defences at sea.

The third future pathway of the maritime Asia-Pacific would be determined by how the region would respond to the asymmetric and transnational issues and challenges. The persistence of asymmetric and transnational issues and challenges would be the basis of convergent and cooperative security of the regional powers. Maritime asymmetric threats like maritime terrorism, piracy, light and small arms trafficking had evoked considerable consensus in cooperative security and new initiatives of synergies in action that emerges as a Comprehensive Maritime Security that would be the appropriate response to the plethora of challenges and threats.

The evolving benign, constabulary and the humanitarian missions of the navies of the region along with the proactive roles of the Coast Guards in redundant roles and operations with the navies would serve as appropriate responses in the area. The relevance and the imperative of maritime security and confidence measures and nuclear risk reduction measures would be significant for the Asia-Pacific region as the high intensity competitive dynamics prevail. Maritime regime building and maritime safety measures would be the initiatives that would address the issues of cooperative maritime security in the region.

Notes

1. T. V. Paul, "The Enduring Axioms of Balance of Power Theory and Their Contemporary Relevance", in T. V. Paul, James Wirtz and Michael Fortmann, *Balance of Power: Theory and Practice in the 21st Century* (Stanford: Stanford University Press, 2004).

2. Christopher Hughes, "Japan's Re-emergence as a 'Normal' Military Power", *Adelphi Paper 368–9*, 2004.

3. See Colin S. Gray, *The Second Nuclear Age* (Boulder, Colorado: Lynne Rienner, 1999) and Paul Bracken, *Fire in the East: The Rise of Asian Military Power and the Second Nuclear Age* (New York: Harper Collins, 1999); Victor D. Cha, "Nuclear Weapons, Missile Defense, and Stability: A Case for 'Sober Optimism' " in Muthiah Alagappa (ed.), *Asian Security Practice: Instrumental and Normative Features* (Stanford: Stanford University Press, 2003).

4. Michael Krepon, "Missile Defense and the Asian Cascade", in Michael Krepon, *Nuclear Risk Reduction in South Asia* (New York: Palgrave Macmillan, 2004).

Index